Derek Wilson spent most of his early life
in Harrow and went up to Peterhouse,
Cambridge, in 1956. He studied History
and Theology and developed a deep
interest in the Reformation, which he was
able to view from the standpoint of two
different but related academic disciplines.
In 1964 he was awarded the University's
Archbishop Cranmer Prize for post-
graduate research in Reformation studies.
The present work is based, in part, upon
the paper he submitted for that
competition. He became a schoolmaster
and has just returned to Britain after
seven years in Kenya, where he was senior
history master and housemaster in a
multi-racial boys' school. He has written
several history text books on widely
differing themes. A *Tudor Tapestry* is the
result of a long period of research which
began in his Cambridge days. As he puts
it, 'I have lived with Anne Ayscough for
over ten years.' He has now re-settled in
Britain to take up a full-time writing
career.

# *A Tudor Tapestry*

## Men, Women and Society
## in Reformation England

# A Tudor Tapestry

## Men, Women and Society
## in Reformation England

Derek Wilson

UNIVERSITY OF PITTSBURGH PRESS

First published in England 1972 by William Heinemann Ltd. Publishers

Library of Congress Catalog Card Number 71–158187
ISBN 0–8229–3242–3
© Derek Wilson 1972
Foreword © A. G. Dickens 1972
Maps drawn by G. Hortfield Ltd
All rights reserved
Manufactured in Great Britain

*To my parents*

# Contents

|  |  | Page |
|---|---|---|
| List of Illustrations |  | vii |
| Foreword by A. G. Dickens |  | I |
| Preface |  | 3 |

*Chapter*

| 1. | A Knight's Progress | 7 |
| 2. | King's Bishop | 37 |
| 3. | Knights Defensive | 55 |
| 4. | Pawns in the Game | 85 |
| 5. | Check, Countercheck | 123 |
| 6. | Rival Knights | 151 |
| 7. | A Perilous Move | 168 |
| 8. | The Final Assault | 198 |
| 9. | 'One by One Back in the Closet Lays' | 225 |
|  | Notes | 243 |
|  | Bibliography | 273 |
|  | Index | 279 |

48532

# List of Illustrations

*facing page*

Henry VIII arriving at the Field of Cloth of Gold (*reproduced by gracious permission of H.M. the Queen*) — 8

Europe, the Diplomatic Triangle: Henry of England (*National Portrait Gallery*), Charles of Spain and the Holy Roman Empire (*Mansell Collection*) and Francis of France (*Mansell Collection*) — 9

Memorial brass of Sir William Ayscough and his wife in St Peter's Church, Stallingborough (photo: L. C. Holton), and Sir William Ayscough's Will, 1540 (*Public Record Office*) — 24

Lincolnshire's once great abbeys, Thornton (*Country Life*), and Crowland (*Radio Times Hulton Picture Library*) — 25

Lincoln Cathedral and the events of October 1536. The Chapter House (photo: Leslie H. Hare); the Cloisters (*Radio Times Hulton Picture Library*); and the West Door (*Radio Times Hulton Picture Library*) — 72

Centres of the Lincolnshire Rising. St James's Church, Louth (photos: David Dunn), and St Mary's Church, Horncastle (*Radio Times Hulton Picture Library*) — 73

Thomas Cromwell (*National Portrait Gallery*), and the Evangelists Stoning the Pope, a contemporary painting (*reproduced by gracious permission of H.M. the Queen*) — 88

Title page from the Great Bible, 1539 (*British Museum*) — 89

Henry VIII in triumph. A woodcut from John Foxe's *Acts and Monuments.* — 120 *facing page*

The Windsor Persecution. A woodcut from John Foxe's
*Acts and Monuments*                                                   121

Members of the Conservative Faction: Stephen Gardiner,
Bishop of Winchester (*Mansell Collection*), Thomas
Howard, Duke of Norfolk (*reproduced by gracious permission of H.M. the Queen*) and Sir Richard Rich (*reproduced by gracious permission of H.M. the Queen*)                        136

Members of the Reforming Faction: Thomas Cranmer,
Archbishop of Canterbury (*National Portrait Gallery*),
Edward Seymour, Earl of Hertford (*reproduced by per-
mission of the Duke of Buccleuch*) and John Dudley, Lord
Lisle (*reproduced by permission of Viscount De L'Isle, V.C.,
K.G., from his collection at Penshurst Place*)                          137

Two of the King's closest friends: Sir William Butts,
Royal Physician, and Charles Brandon, Duke of Suffolk
(*National Portrait Gallery*)                                          216

Catherine Parr (*National Portrait Gallery*). And Wriothesley Foiled, a Victorian artist's impression of the failure
of the attack on Catherine Parr. Painting by William
Fisk, 1838 (*by courtesy of Mr and Mrs Ed Robinson,
Birmingham, Alabama*)                                                 217

The burning of Anne Ayscough, John Lascelles, John
Hadlam and John Hemsley. A woodcut from John Foxe's
*Acts and Monuments*                                                   232

The monument of Sir Francis Ayscough in St Peter's
Church, Stallingborough (photo: L. C. Holton), and
Sir Francis Ayscough's Will, 1564 (*Public Record Office*)             233

---

*page*

Family trees of the Ayscough, Markham, Babington, Hercy
and Lascelles families                                                10–14
Map of the Lincolnshire Rising, October 1536                           57
Map showing the leading men of the East Midlands                      92–93

# Foreword

W E already possess a vast literature on the reign of Henry VIII and on the earlier stages of English Protestantism, yet Derek Wilson's book forms a wholly justifiable addition. Vividly and warmly written, it never forgets that history concerns the human individual and creates a brotherhood linking past and present generations. Moreover it sees this revolutionary period from several angles, some of them still too often neglected. Its approaches are both central and regional, but it has its feet where most Tudor men and women had theirs – on the soil. Into the central story of court and capital, it fits the slow-moving provincial society of Lincolnshire. And in the end the two themes fuse together in the high drama of Anne Ayscough's suffering and death.

In a lucid preface Mr Wilson explains the plan which several years ago he proposed to himself, one which he has now duly executed. While he compares his book with a narrative-series of tapestries, one might equally compare it with a landscape, the deepest recessions of which are from time to time pulled into focus by the telescope of research. During recent decades an increasing number of Reformation scholars have striven to explore their subject in social depth, instead of resting content with the superficial narrative of princely, parliamentary and ecclesiastical action. Why, and by what stages, did the townsmen of Zürich or Strassburg lend their adherence to Protestantism? What social structures and conditions reigned among the Tyrolean Anabaptists, or among the early Huguenots of Paris or Lyons? By what channels did Bible-reading habits permeate the provincial English gentry? The failings of Weber's and Tawney's social analyses having been exposed, can we now construct more viable alternatives based upon massive evidence rather than upon dogmatic and question-begging ideologies? Our chances depend upon contributions like this present book, which shows how, despite their baffling silences, the records can in fact be made to reveal some fresh prospects. Even within the more familiar corners of the Henrician court Mr Wilson finds opportunities to correct the tenacious Victorian sagas still current in that last lair of tradition: the visual entertainment-media.

The day may indeed come when the entertainers make more of Anne Ayscough, with her sharp tongue and her indomitable convictions. Like Margaret Clitherow of York, her Catholic counterpart, and like a host of other heroic lay-women throughout Europe, she reminds us that the great religious struggles liberated many of her sex from the intellectual servitude hitherto assigned them by Church and State. The Reformation could in fact transcend both sex and social class, and though after the decades of crisis traditional patterns tended to reappear, the faces of authority and hierarchy never looked so confident again. As a transforming force, economic motivation mattered less than ideas, and amongst the latter religious ideas still bulked large.

In England historians have persistently, and absurdly, centred the Reformation upon the marital adventures of Henry VIII and the dissolution of the monasteries, affairs which had little to do with the growth of Protestantism. On the other hand, Mr Wilson's story is one of those which bid us take Protestantism seriously. After all, two facts cannot be explained away: that in 1520 the English were predominantly Catholic, and that less than fifty years later they had become predominantly Protestant. For this transformation Anne Ayscough and a very few hundred other martyrs bore a large share of the responsibility. From among the semi-literate but tough and argumentative artisans, even in rarer instances from among the acquisitive country squires, there could arise unconquerable minds to defy the horrifying weapons of authority and to lead England into a new phase of her destiny. In short, this is an approachable and scholarly book upon a great theme. It can be read at various depths, but it will serve the ends of any reader who wants to explore the mid-Tudor age and with it the social and psychological roots of modern England.

A. G. DICKENS

# Preface

B ETWEEN the years 1520 and 1546 England experienced
one of the greatest social, political and religious upheavals in
its entire history. In 1520 Henry VIII was a pious Catholic
King married to an even more pious Catholic Queen. Dotted about
the shires were cathedrals and great abbey churches – Fountains, Tintern, Bury St Edmunds, Canterbury, Crowland – monuments to the power of the international Church. That power was
a reality to every Englishman, high or low. Through the sacraments his priest controlled his soul's health. Through the mass his
priest influenced the eternal destiny of his departed loved ones.
The Church was a potent political force in the land. The upper
house of Parliament was dominated by the spiritualty. The King
was expected to seek his chief ministers from the ranks of the
higher clergy. The Church was the biggest landowner in the realm
and in many corners of the country the writ of the local abbot or
prior held more sway than the King's. If the Church's wealth was
mostly in land, more impressive evidence of its affluence was to
be seen in the plate and jewel-bedecked altars and shrines of
the great churches. For all the ordinary Tudor Age citizen knew,
life had been thus since the beginning of time and there was
little reason to suppose that it would ever change. Men had tried
to change it. There were still those who murmured against the
power of the clergy or made attacks on the very doctrines which
underlay that power. Such men were either circumspect or they
were crushed by the ecclesiastical machine.

By the end of 1546, when an invalid Henry VIII had but days to
live, five royal consorts had come and gone bequeathing a sickly

son and two insecure daughters to the Tudor dynasty. The great monasteries were derelict or turned into private dwellings. Cowled abbots no longer sat in Parliament. Monks and nuns had found other vocations. The great shrines were denuded and had ceased to be centres of pilgrimage. A breed of newly enriched country gentlemen lorded it over the manors where once monastic bailiffs had held sway.

But more fundamental than all these changes was the emergence of a new individualism. Paradoxically the enactments of a totalitarian regime unleashed the independent spirits and enquiring minds of Englishmen. No longer under the thrall of the Pope; no longer under the spiritual dominion of a priesthood which alone could perform the miracle of the mass; the English layman could read the Bible for himself and reach his own conclusions about life and death, personal and institutional religion, social obligations and relationships. This individualism injected a new vitality into the growing capitalism and non-conformity of the age.

The old social order had disappeared and a new one was in the process of being designed. The ranks of the middle class were swelled by the many gentlemen who gained grants of monastic land. These small landowners became the new ruling class. They were vitally important to the Tudors as local administrators and as a barrier between the crown and the nobility. It would be impossible to overestimate the importance of this squirarchy in the history of England between the Reformation and the Welfare State. It produced most of our leading politicians, admirals, explorers, colonial administrators and generals.

The years when these great changes were taking place were, for most Englishmen, years of confusion and ferment. It could not be otherwise when authority, power and land were changing hands so rapidly and when today's heresy might be tomorrow's orthodoxy.

I have tried in these pages to give some sort of answer to the question 'what was it like to live through the English Reformation'. There are many studies of the Reformation from the point of view of its instigators – the King, his bishops and ministers of state. But how did it strike ordinary men and women – men and women who were the agents (sometimes the unwitting agents) or just the sufferers of change?

The large tapestries beloved by wealthy householders of the sixteenth century often comprised numerous panels, each depicting a scene or event in some historical or allegorical story. As the beholder looked from one panel to the next he saw that they were in a sequence and that a tragedy was unfolding before his eyes. Of course, the drama was incomplete. Each event depicted could only be loosely connected to the next. Yet the whole story was unmistakably there and the weaver's craft, displayed in the choice of colours and the overall unity of the design, had imparted an atmosphere which made the tapestry a delight to behold. By his selection of scenes and his disposition of figures the craftsman had also *expounded* his story, so that his characters were not merely immobile, two-dimensional figures created from cloth and thread; his work said something about the men and women it portrayed.

Each chapter in this book may be thought of as a panel in such a tapestry. Each one concerns different people and events. All sorts and conditions of men are depicted in this tapestry. An ageing king, six insecure queens, fawning courtiers and harassed ministers of state will be seen. Proud prelates will strut across the larger spaces and frowning scholars be observed in the cramped corners. But always more prominent are men and women whose names have not before reached the history books. Their stories have been unravelled from documents in family and county archives and interwoven here with the chronicles of the great in order to present as full a picture as possible of the crisis years between 1520 and 1546.

The research and writing of this book have occupied my leisure hours for ten years. Inevitably in that time I have picked the brains and tapped the enthusiasms of many people – more than I can possibly acknowledge by name. For inspiration and encouragement at many stages and for reading the manuscript and writing the Foreword, I am heavily indebted to Professor A. G. Dickens. Dr John Fines generously assisted me in the early stages by allowing me to read a thesis that he was working on. Mrs Joan Varley and her staff at the Lincolnshire Archives Office showed great patience and courtesy in guiding me to documentary material and answering innumerable queries by post. Similar assistance came also from the Nottingham County Archives Office, the Public Record Office and the Principal Probate Registry. Mr George Dixon introduced me to the Cathedral Library at Lincoln and was tireless in drawing my attention to little-known works on local history. I am very grateful to the Cambridge University History Faculty Board for permission to reproduce material used in my prizewinning Archbishop Cranmer Award Essay (1964). My wife typed not only the final manuscript but all the previous efforts which ended up in the waste-paper basket. To all of these, together with library staff in Cambridge and Oxford, the John Rylands Library, Manchester, and the British Museum Reading Room *and* scholars (acknowledged in notes) who have allowed me to read their unpublished theses *and* friends who have not been (openly at least) bored with the Ayscoughs, the Lascelles and their contemporaries – my heartfelt thanks.

*Note*
In all quotations from sources I have modernized spellings and punctuation and substituted words where the originals are archaic. Otherwise I have tried to interfere with the language as little as possible in order to preserve its sixteenth-century flavour.

# I

# A Knight's Progress

―――――――――――◆――――――――――――

IN 1520 the Tudor Age was still in its springtime and in the springtime of that year many nobles and gentlemen throughout the length and breadth of England were preparing for a journey. Everywhere new clothes were being ordered, tournament armour oiled and polished, horses and baggage prepared; no cost was being spared as the leading men of the realm made ready to accompany their King on a state visit to France. One of those who made eager and anxious preparations to join the royal pilgrimage – a relatively unimportant star in the galaxy of English manhood chosen for the honour of attending the King – was Sir William Ayscough Knight,[1] of Stallingborough[2] in Lincolnshire, and Basford and Nuthall in the County of Nottingham. At thirty-three he was only four years older than his King and a courtier and royal servant of long standing.

The Ayscoughs' connection with the royal court stretched back over many troubled generations. It was a William Ayscough who, as Bishop of Salisbury and royal confessor, joined in hapless matrimony King Henry VI and Margaret of Anjou. That was in 1445 and thereafter the Bishop was a regular member of the royal council. Indeed, close connection with the incompetent and divided government of Henry and Margaret was William Ayscough's undoing. In the summer of 1450 he was with the court as it hurried to Blackheath to face the challenge of Jack Cade and his rebels. On the feast of Ss Peter and Paul (29 June) the party stopped at the Bishop's manor of Edington, Wiltshire, where mass was said before the King. The excitement of the times, the absenteeism of their Bishop, the ill-repute of the government and no doubt, many local grievances combined to make a heady draught for the Bishop's simple people and so

> Many of his tenants intending to join with Jack Cade, came to Edington, took him from mass, and drew him to the top of a hill, where they cleft his head as he kneeled and prayed – not far from Edington – and spoiled him to the skin, June 29, 1450.[3]

Contemporary with the Bishop of Salisbury was Sir William Ayscough, Chief Justice of the Common Pleas. He was the head of the main branch of the family, whose principal estates lay at Bedale in Yorkshire. Sir William, the Judge, died in 1456, by which time the long-gathering storm of civil war had burst over England. The allegiance of the Ayscoughs throughout the Wars of the Roses was never in doubt. They supported the Lancastrian cause and fought under the banner of Margaret of Anjou and the Prince of Wales.

When the head of the family sought an alliance for his eldest son he married him into a family which was staunchly Lancastrian, powerful – and rich. The Tailboys were an ancient family whose estates in Lincolnshire had been first granted to them by William the Conqueror. William Tailboys, the head of the family, fought for Queen Margaret at the Battle of St Albans in 1461 and was knighted for his services. Later in the year the triumphant Yorkist government of Edward IV seized his lands and attainted him. He continued to fight on until his capture and death after the battle of Hexham in 1464. It was to Margaret Tailboys, a cousin of this Sir William, that John Ayscough was married about 1450.

A family chronicler has remarked, 'The Ayscough pedigree shows an aptitude for marrying money or at all events for going where money was.'[4] This was certainly true of the Tailboys alliance. Margaret was the heiress of John Tailboys who, though not belonging to the main branch of the family, was yet possessed of extensive and fair estates in Lincolnshire and Nottinghamshire. The principal lands which Margaret brought to her husband were at Stallingborough, a bustling coastal port situated on an inlet four miles north-west of Grimsby. Here John Ayscough made his home in the gaunt, square, moated, medieval hall of the Tailboys.[5] The estates in Yorkshire were now left for junior branches of the family as John Ayscough settled down to the life of a Lincolnshire gentleman. This he did with considerable success, despite the hold the

Henry VIII arriving at the Field of Cloth of Gold. Artist unknown.

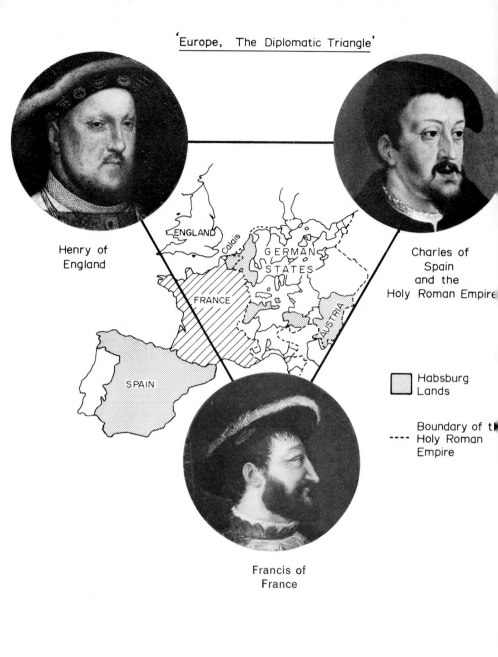

'Europe, The Diplomatic Triangle'

Henry of
England

Charles of
Spain
and the
Holy Roman Empire

Francis of
France

ENGLAND

Calais

GERMAN
STATES

FRANCE

AUSTRIA

SPAIN

Habsburg
Lands

---- Boundary of the
Holy Roman
Empire

House of York had gained on the crown of England. John never accepted the Lancastrian reversal and it is highly significant that he was only once appointed to public office. That was in 1470 when he was 'pricked' High Sheriff of Lincolnshire.[6] And 1470 was the year when Margaret of Anjou, supported by Warwick the King-Maker, had staged a brief Lancastrian come-back, successfully placing her idiot husband, Henry VI, back on the throne.

The triumph of the red rose was shortlived. By the end of May 1470 Warwick had been slain on Barnet field, Prince Edward, the Lancastrian heir to the throne, had been killed at the battle of Tewkesbury, Margaret of Anjou was a captive of Edward IV and the dotard Henry VI had conveniently 'died'. At about this time John Ayscough married a second time. His choice? Eleanor, daughter of Sir Richard Tunstall, attainted in 1460 for his Lancastrian sympathies.

Yet this staunch supporter of the red rose lived to see the final overthrow of the House of York in 1485, when Henry Tudor, Earl of Richmond, returned to pluck the crown of England from a dead Richard III at Bosworth field and to establish a dynasty. John Ayscough died in 1491 full of years and satisfaction that his family enjoyed the favour of the new ruler, Henry VII.

The new head of the family, William, was already well placed at court. He had hastened to the King's support at the battle of Stoke in 1487, when the last serious Yorkist threat in the person of John de la Pole, Earl of Lincoln, had been disposed of. In 1499 he was Sheriff of Lincolnshire. Two years later he was picked out for a signal honour.

> This year was sent into England the King of Spain's third daughter, named Catherine, to be married to the Prince Arthur, and she landed at Plymouth the eighth day of October, and was received into London in the most royal wise the twelfth day of November, then Friday. And the Sunday following she was married at St Paul's Church ... And the feast was held in the Bishop of London's palace. And the day of her receiving into London were made many rich pageants; first at the bridge, at the conduit in Gracechurch Street, the conduit in Cornhill, the standard in Cheapside (the cross newly gilded), at the little conduit; and at St Paul's west door there was running wine – red claret and white – all the day of the marriage. And at the same marriage the king made fifty-seven knights.[7]

Among the fifty-seven gentlemen to be thus honoured in the midst

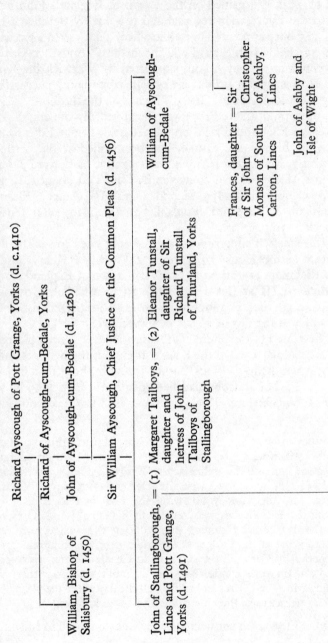

ANCESTRY OF SIR WILLIAM AYSCOUGH (c.1490–1540)

Richard Ayscough of Pott Grange, Yorks (d. c.1410)

Richard of Ayscough-cum-Bedale, Yorks

John of Ayscough-cum-Bedale (d. 1426)

Sir William Ayscough, Chief Justice of the Common Pleas (d. 1456)

William, Bishop of Salisbury (d. 1450)

John of Stallingborough, = (1) Margaret Tailboys,   = (2) Eleanor Tunstall,
Lincs and Pott Grange,        daughter and                    daughter of Sir
Yorks (d. 1491)                    heiress of John                 Richard Tunstall
                                          Tailboys of                     of Thurland, Yorks
                                          Stallingborough

William of Ayscough-cum-Bedale

Frances, daughter = Sir
of Sir John            Christopher
Monson of South    of Ashby,
Carlton, Lincs        Lincs

John of Ashby and
Isle of Wight

Sir William of Stallingborough, = (1) Margery Hildyard = (2) Alice Copingdale
Courtier (d. 1509)  of Winestead,  of County York
  Yorks

  Edward

  Anne = (1) Thomas Partington
   of Roxby, Lincs

   = (2) William Burgh of
   Kirton-in-Lindsay,
   Lincs

Robert of Bromby and
Wragby, Lincs (A minor
branch of the family lived
here for many generations)

*Sir William of Stallingborough* = (1) Elizabeth Wrottesley of Reading, = (2) Elizabeth, widow
*and S. Kelsey, Lincs and*  Berks (grand-daughter of  of Sir William
*Nuthal and Basford, Notts,*  Sir Walter Wrottesley of Staffs,  Hansard of S. Kelsey,
*Courtier (d. 1541)*  Captain of Calais)  Lincs Courtier

  Edward   Jane

   Thomas
   (d. c.1537–1540)

Sir Francis of Stallingborough  Christopher,  Martha  Edward,  Anne  Jane
and S. Kelsey, Lincs  Gentleman of  (d. 1539)  Gentleman  (d. 1546)  (d. 1590)
Courtier (d. 1564)  the Privy Chamber   Pensioner and
  (d. 1543)   Cup-Bearer to
   Henry VIII (d. 1558)

SELECT PEDIGREES OF SOME LEADING NOTTINGHAMSHIRE FAMILIES
*(Names outlined are of people who figure prominently in this narrative.)*

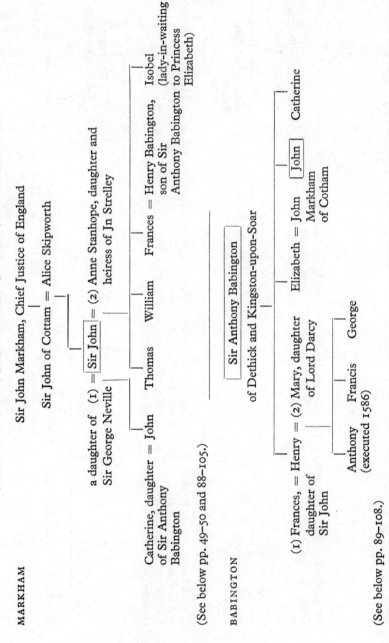

MARKHAM

Sir John Markham, Chief Justice of England

Sir John of Cottam = Alice Skipworth

a daughter of (1) = [Sir John] = (2) Anne Stanhope, daughter and
Sir George Neville      heiress of Jn Strelley

Catherine, daughter = John    Thomas    William    Frances = Henry Babington,    Isobel
of Sir Anthony      son of Sir    (lady-in-waiting
Babington      Anthony Babington    to Princess
     Elizabeth)

(See below pp. 49–50 and 88–105.)

BABINGTON

Sir Anthony Babington
of Dethick and Kingston-upon-Soar

(1) Frances, = Henry = (2) Mary, daughter      Elizabeth = John    Catherine
daughter of      of Lord Darcy      Markham
Sir John      of Cotham    [John]

Anthony    Francis    George
(executed 1586)

(See below pp. 89–108.)

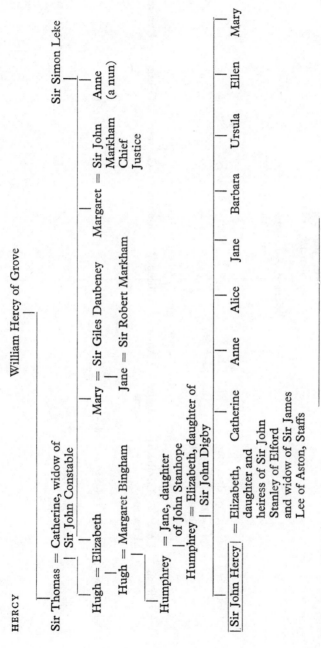

HERCY

William Hercy of Grove

Sir Thomas = Catherine, widow of Sir John Constable

Sir Simon Leke

Hugh = Elizabeth

Mary = Sir Giles Daubeney

Margaret = Sir John Markham Chief Justice

Anne (a nun)

Hugh = Margaret Bingham

Jane = Sir Robert Markham

Humphrey = Jane, daughter of John Stanhope

Humphrey = Elizabeth, daughter of Sir John Digby

Sir John Hercy = Elizabeth, daughter and heiress of Sir John Stanley of Elford and widow of Sir James Lee of Aston, Staffs

Catherine   Anne   Alice   Jane   Barbara   Ursula   Eilen   Mary

(See below pp. 90–107.)

LASCELLES

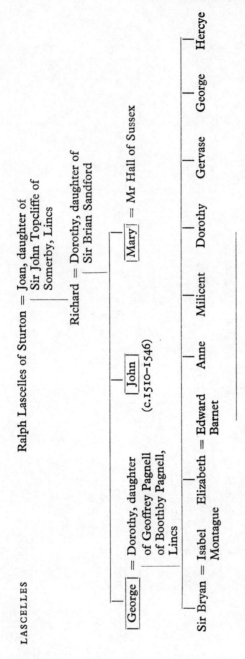

Ralph Lascelles of Sturton = Joan, daughter of
Sir John Topcliffe of
Somerby, Lincs

Richard = Dorothy, daughter of
Sir Brian Sandford

George = Dorothy, daughter
of Geoffrey Pagnell
of Boothby Pagnell,
Lincs

John
(c.1510–1546)

Mary = Mr Hall of Sussex

Sir Bryan = Isabel
Montague

Elizabeth = Edward
Barnet

Anne     Milicent     Dorothy     Gervase     George     Hercye

(See below pp. 91–108, 118–137 and 181–238.)

of all the pageantry and rejoicing that accompanied this ill-fated royal marriage* was William Ayscough.

After these stirring events the new knight returned to Stallingborough to order his estate and to play a full part in the management of the shire. He held office as sheriff twice more in 1504 and 1508 and was busy on many commissions in Lincolnshire. His son, another William, was placed at court and before his death (in 1509) the head of the family had seen his heir suitably married to the daughter of an influential courtier, William Wrottesley of Reading.[8]

The young couple set up home on the estates at Nuthall in Nottinghamshire which had come into the family through Margaret Tailboys. But young William Ayscough was little at home during the early years of the Tudor century. He was at court, attached to the household of Prince Henry, a boy not much younger than himself. The Prince had already captured the admiration of all about him. An athletic young man but no empty-headed boor, he excelled as much at conversation with learned doctors as at contests in the tilt yard or the tennis court. He loved gaiety but was no wastrel. He was interested in the new humanist ideas wafting across from the Continent. A spirit of physical vitality and intellectual freedom prevailed in his household and his servants counted themselves highly fortunate to be allowed to bask in the light cast by this rising sun. In common with most Englishmen they rejoiced in the prospect of a new reign, hoping that it would bring an end to the long night of civil strife under the Plantagenets, and the miserly oppressions of Henry VII. With the dynasty now firmly established, the power of over-mighty subjects checked and with a model prince to inherit the throne, they felt confident of the future.

That future arrived on 21 April 1509 when Henry VII died and passed the crown on to his son, aged seventeen years and ten months. Old Sir William Ayscough did not survive to see the new reign; he died on 26 March. Thus the new head of the household scarcely had time to assume his new responsibilities before his presence was required at the coronation in June. William Ayscough decided not to move house to Stallingborough; it was too far away across the Lincolnshire Wolds and marshes for a man whose visits

---

* 'Ill-fated' it certainly was. Within six months Arthur was dead. After protracted negotiation Catherine was married to the King's unwilling second son, Henry - the future Henry VIII.

home were infrequent and who, when he was at home, had to be much about the King's business. The east coast manor remained the principal seat of the family, however, and Lincolnshire was the county to which William and his descendants 'belonged'. It was at Nuthall that William and Elizabeth's children were born. They were overjoyed when their first was a boy, christened Francis. Another son, Edward, and a daughter, Martha, soon followed. But the young father was not able to spend much time with his children during their infancy. He was still much required at court.

Those early years of 'Bluff King Hal' were busy and enjoyable. While Henry felt his way in domestic and international politics, the business of running the nation's affairs was largely left to older and wiser advisers. The court became the scene of frequent jousts and pageants, banquets and hunting parties; for the young blades of the court it was an exciting – if expensive – time.

Even important affairs of state seemed to be embarked on in a lavish and hearty spirit. Such an affair was the King's first foray into international politics – the French campaign of 1513. The youthful Henry VIII, prompted by a simple piety and chivalric delusions, had entered into a Holy League with the more wily elder statesmen of Europe, Ferdinand of Spain and the Emperor Elect Maximilian. The ostensible object of this alliance was that of assisting the Pope against the military advances and political intrigues of the King of France – who was also proving himself a nuisance to Henry by encouraging the Scots to renew their border incursions. In accordance with Henry's obligations to the League a force of fourteen thousand men was shipped across the Channel in the summer of 1513. A newly-emerged power at court, Thomas Wolsey, was in charge of the arrangements for provisioning, transporting and accoutring the army, and everything was planned on a lavish scale – it was to be war in the grand manner, as befitted the honour and prestige of the young Apollo who occupied the throne. This advance guard of the army began at the end of June a siege of the small town of Therouanne. On 30 June, the main assault force, superbly equipped and magnificently attired, under the leadership of Henry himself, left Calais to join up with the remainder of the army and overthrow the town. The King and his Royal Almoner (as Wolsey then was) had planned the campaign on an impressive scale with no eye to economy, much as they might have planned one of the pageants, banquets or seasonal entertainments at West-minster or Richmond. Sixteen thousand copies of the 'Statutes of War' were issued, which set forth the inviolable code of arms which was to be observed: 'Everyone, except he be a bishop, is to bear a Cross of St George, sufficient and large',[9] was but one of the injunctions laid upon the participants in this 'lofty and chaste performance'.[10] The core of the army was a body of German mercenaries and the armaments comprised an unprecedented battery of cannon prominent among which were the mighty siege pieces euphemistically known as 'the twelve apostles'. It was an enterprise in which, according to one recorder, 'the business of bashing men's heads seemed out of place'.[11] And so the young monarch and his gorgeously caparisoned retinue swept on to invest Therouanne, a small town whose size and strategic importance leave room to doubt whether it was worth the money, sweat and blood expended on its overthrow.

In all likelihood William Ayscough was already before the walls of the town having gone over as a commander of one of the Lincoln-shire levies in the advance guard under the command of the Duke of Suffolk. Since his own equipment and that of the men under his command had to come up to the grandiose standards set by the planners of the expedition, it is not surprising that Sir William found it an expensive business. In fact he had to part with 'the manor of Nethertointon and lands in Saucethorpe, Tangton and Hagworthingham'.[12]

On 16 August the French reinforcements were routed in an engagement which came to be known as the 'Battle of the Spurs' because of the speed of the French withdrawal. On 23 August the town fell and Henry received the official surrender. There now came a pause in this magnificently staged campaign – reminiscent of a battle scene by Uccello, intricate in design and resplendent with heraldic colour – before the army moved on to invest Tournai. It was an opportunity for pious thanksgiving and the distribution of rewards and honours to the deserving captains: ' . . . at Touraine in the Church, after the King came from Mass, under his banner in the Church', Henry made several new knights, among whom was Sir William Ayscough.[13]

Seven years passed between that memorable campaign and the year 1520 when Sir William Ayscough found himself preparing to

journey into France once more – this time on a still more extravagant royal venture. The stage-manager once again was Thomas
Wolsey, the Ipswich butcher's son who had become Cardinal,
Papal Legate, Archbishop of York, Lord Chancellor of England,
confidant of the King and manager of the affairs of the nation. It
was scarcely eighteen months since he had won international
prestige for himself and a pause in the tense 'cold war', which had
followed the making and breaking of Anglo-French peace in 1514,
by engineering a magnificent treaty of universal peace and Christian
brotherhood between Pope Leo X, Maximilian I, King of the
Romans and Emperor Elect, Charles I of Spain, Francis I of
France, Henry VIII of England and all the lesser Christian monarchs of Europe. This eirenic edifice had come crashing to the
ground within a few months on the death of Maximilian. This
sparked off the rivalry of Francis and Charles for the crown of
the Holy Roman Empire, and provided the opportunity for a
revival of the age-old Valois-Habsburg struggle. The crowning of
Charles V as Emperor had meant the combining of the Spanish
and Austrian Habsburg estates and the creation of the biggest
empire Europe had seen since the time of Charlemagne. It was no
secret that both of the powerful continental monarchs now coveted
the support of England. At Henry's court there were those, notably
his wife Catherine of Aragon, the young Emperor's aunt, who
favoured an alliance with Charles V. Equally there were those who
considered that England's best policy lay in cementing friendship
with France and restricting the power and influence of the
Habsburg Emperor. The pro-French party was led by Wolsey,
and it would seem that the Cardinal had got his way. The gathering
to which Sir William Ayscough had been summoned was nothing
less than a sumptuously-staged meeting of the French and English
kings and their courts at a specially prepared site.

And so, in May 1520, a still-youthful figure bade farewell to his
wife before travelling the familiar road to London. Elizabeth could
not come down to the gate to see her husband set off, for she had
just been delivered of another child – their fifth. Besides Francis, a
sturdy lad of eight or nine, Martha and Christopher had survived into
a healthy childhood and had been joined by another brother,
Edward. Now they had a new baby sister, christened Anne,
and their mother was still in bed recovering from the birth. It was
thus in their chamber that William took leave of his wife.

He made his way, with a few servants and his baggage horses, past rich pastures and open fields, where peasants were already tending the new crops, to Nottingham. Across the river, where sea-going ships nodded their tall masts, through the Trent valley and up on to the Great North Road at Grantham. Climbing out of the town the party had a long view over the fenland and marsh of Kesteven and Holland. Beyond those vast flat expanses lay other Ayscough lands and responsibilities, entrusted to the care of Sir William's bailiffs. But now he was called away southwards by duty and honour.

For it was a high honour indeed to be numbered in the royal retinue on this grand occasion. Only those close to the King and those who had influence with Wolsey had been chosen to accompany Henry to the Field of Cloth of Gold. Many had sued and bribed to gain a place in either the King's or Queen's personal retinue, only to be disappointed. Wolsey's final list included ninety-seven knights chosen from every shire of the realm. Lincolnshire was represented by Sir William Ayscough, Sir William Hussey, Sir Christopher Willoughby, Sir Thomas Burgh and Sir William Hansard.[14] All were men in the prime of life, all courtiers, all either possessed of, or heirs to, large estates. Thus in that early summer of the twelfth year of the reign of King Henry VIII did Sir William Ayscough take his place among the leading gentlemen of England threading their way by lanes and highways towards Canterbury where the royal carnival was to assemble. Thence to Dover and so across the Channel to France and the Val Doré between Ardres and Guines where a myriad workmen were already completing the preparations for this lavish royal fiasco.

For fiasco it was. The object behind it as far as Wolsey and Francis I were concerned was to cement a firm alliance between their two countries. But Henry of England was far from being convinced that an agreement with France was in England's best interests. The period of Henry's quiet submission under the Cardinal's tutelage was passing. The Valois monarch was not the only sovereign wooing England: for Charles V an English alliance and the security of the Channel which that would bring were also desirable. Moreover, the Queen's party at court was as pro-Spain as it was anti-Wolsey. Its members urged the importance of Antwerp, in the Spanish Netherlands, to England's wool trade, they stressed the treacherous friendship of France with Scotland, they played on the family ties between the royal houses of England and Spain. The King agreed to meet Charles V and on 26 May the Emperor arrived to spend Whitsun with his aunt, Queen Catherine, at Canterbury – a 'family gathering'. Henry treated the young man as a son and though no formal alliance was concluded between them, they agreed to meet again after Henry's impending visit to his brother of France. Wolsey knew that in the face of all this activity, he had to work hard to bring off his plans. He hoped to dazzle his master into acquiescence with a magnificent tourney and sumptuous entertainments amidst richly-hung pavilions, cunningly conceived fountains, elegant palaces and beautifully decorated chapels.

Sir William Ayscough was well aware of all these diplomatic undercurrents as he attended the King at Canterbury. In all probability he had met up with his old friend and companion in arms Sir William Hansard on the journey. Although slightly older, Sir William Hansard had been closely acquainted with the head of the Ayscough family since the latter's childhood at Stallingborough, for part of the Ayscough estates lay at Keelby and bordered on some of Sir William Hansard's land. On 31 May Sir William Ayscough set sail for France, a member of the King's retinue of 4544 persons comprising every rank from duke to the humblest knight's servant.

On 7 June began two and a half weeks of pageantry, jousting, dancing and feasting in a setting which was the result of keen rivalry between Wolsey and his French counterpart. Amidst the elaborate courtesies, the Cardinal attempted, with limited success, to bring Henry and Francis to the conference table, but the royal carnival ended on 24 June without appreciable progress having been made. On that date the assembly broke up and most of the English contingent began to make its way back across the Channel. Henry, however, remained on the Continent and Sir William Ayscough was among the much smaller retinue chosen to accompany the King on 10 July to Gravelines where Henry met the Emperor and escorted him back to Calais for their conference.[15] It took only four days to achieve a treaty whereby each participant promised to make no alliance with France for two years. Wolsey did not attempt to divert the will of his royal master (in any case, Charles had already given the Cardinal a *douceur* in the form of a pension of 7,000 ducats and a promise to use his influence on Wolsey's behalf when the next papal election occurred).

When, at last, he returned to England, Sir William was able to spend the greater part of a year at home. On 6 November 1520 he was appointed Sheriff of Lincolnshire and as such had to spend much time on the business of the shire. The first Tudor had broken the power of most of the greater and lesser feudal magnates of central and southern England whose independence had survived the Wars of the Roses. This left a vacuum in the administration and government of rural England, a vacuum which King and council hastily filled with servants loyal to the central government. This meant that traditional offices such as that of sheriff became more important and the influence of the gentry families who filled those offices similarly increased. This was part of a social revolution steadily taking place throughout the sixteenth century – a revolution which placed power, wealth and authority in the hands of the gentry, which created a middle class of moderately wealthy land-owners, who owed their position to the crown and lacked the power, as individuals or as a group, to rise against it. The position of this middle class was further consolidated by grants of land – first from among the sequestered estates of Yorkist supporters and later from among the territory of despoiled abbeys.

If 1521 was a busy year for Sir William Ayscough, it was also a sad one. In that year Elizabeth, his wife, died. In fifteen years or more of married life she had brought forth and reared six healthy children. Probably there were others who did not survive birth or infancy, for there was scarcely a family in Tudor England which did not experience a high rate of infant mortality. In the summer of 1521 Elizabeth was brought to bed with her last baby. It was a third girl, Jane. Did Elizabeth die in childbed? It is more than possible that she did; lack of adequate maternity care was a common cause of death. It may be that she succumbed to the sweating sickness which swept England with unwonted ferocity the following winter. With a heavy heart William buried her at Stalling-borough where other Ayscoughs lay awaiting the last trump.

It was certainly the sweating sickness which carried off an old friend and comrade in arms early the following year. On 11 January 1522 Sir William Hansard died at his home at South Kelsey at the age of forty-three. He left a widow, Elizabeth, his only son and heir, William, and two daughters, the teenage

Elizabeth and young Bridget. The new head of the household was nineteen or twenty years of age and newly married to Agnes, the daughter of another prominent Lincolnshire gentleman and courtier, Sir Robert Tyrrwhit of Kettleby. The Hansards buried and mourned their father and slipped into a new routine of living which was not much different from the old. But death had not done with the South Kelsey household. On 15 April it claimed William Hansard. The younger William also died of the sweating sickness which was rife throughout the area. One of the royal commissioners sent into Lincolnshire to check on the numbers of men and arms being kept for the King's service complained, 'There is much harness in houses infected with sickness, with which no one will meddle.'[16]

This death was a triple tragedy to the Hansards. The sorrow and anguish of parting with a much loved young son, brother and husband was intensified by the helplessness and vulnerability felt by the all-female household now left at South Kelsey and by the fear that the male line of the Hansards – intact since before the Conquest – was ended. There was one chance that the last mentioned tragedy might be averted: at the time of her husband's death young Agnes Hansard was four months pregnant. She was now carrying within her the heir – or heiress – to all the Hansard estates. For months Agnes was fussed over with well-intentioned cossetting while Dame Elizabeth prayed devoutly for a grandson. In October the young widow gave birth to a daughter – christened Elizabeth – and the Hansard lands were destined eventually to pass into other hands. In fact they would be at the disposal of whoever obtained the wardship of the child. As an heiress and a minor, she was automatically declared a royal ward and, as such, a prospective source of wealth to the crown.

The rights of wardship, which involved custody of a ward's lands and the authority to sell his or her marriage, was the most remunerative of all the feudal sources of revenue remaining to the crown. Henry VII, as he set about laying the financial foundation of his dynasty, had been careful to exploit his feudal dues to the full. He issued commissions for the seeking out of concealed wards' lands, appointed a surveyor of the prerogative rights, and finally – in 1503 – appointed a special master of the wards to control both the direct exploitation of wardships and their sale to interested parties. The second method quickly became the more usual and profitable of the two. The Court of Wards became a bustling department where bureaucrats did a brisk trade in lands – and persons. By 1522 it was a centre for wild speculation and a hotbed of intrigue and corruption. So a household of women was left entirely to the avarice of rich neighbours and the whim of the current Master of the Wards – Thomas Wolsey.[17] This was the situation at the beginning of 1523, when Sir William Ayscough intervened.

Sir William had been back at court for the greater part of 1522. During the two years since the Field of Cloth of Gold, relations between England and France became more and more strained and in May 1522 the Emperor Charles V paid another visit to Henry VIII in order to conclude a military alliance. He landed at Dover on 26 May. Sir William Ayscough was in the party that rode out with the King to meet the Habsburg at Canterbury.[18] During the following weeks he was with the court at Westminster, Greenwich, Richmond, Hampton Court, Windsor and Winchester where he helped to organize the sumptuous royal entertainments which systematically de-stocked each of the manors at which the court stayed. Despite the many duties which kept him busy during the summer (Charles V left on 6 July) and autumn, Sir William kept himself in touch with affairs in his county and particularly with events at South Kelsey. As soon as he heard of the birth of Elizabeth Hansard he began petitioning Wolsey for the wardship of the heiress. At the same time, he proposed marriage to Sir William Hansard's widow.

But there was someone else who had an interest in the wardship of Elizabeth Hansard – someone who thought he had a better claim. Sir Robert Tyrrwhit was the child's grandfather and her closest male relative. He too wished to protect the bereaved family and to have the administration of the Hansard estates. The two Lincolnshire knights vied with each other for the coveted prize. Each urged friends at court to speak on his behalf to Wolsey. But in the last analysis the wardship went to the man prepared to pay the best price, and that man was Sir William Ayscough. By being the highest bidder for the wardship of Elizabeth Hansard, Sir William had gained the administration of thousands of acres of fair lands, with the choice that they would eventually pass into his own family. He had also gained a lifelong enemy in the person of his aggrieved and envious neighbour, Sir Robert Tyrrwhit.

There were obvious advantages on both sides to a merger of Ayscough and Hansard interests. There were the children of both marriages to be considered. For the smooth running of both households it was desirable for the bereaved partners to marry again. Much better for Elizabeth to marry an old friend and neighbour than to entrust herself and her family to an ambitious stranger. For Sir William the Hansard house and estates were a very tempting prize, situated as they were between the Ayscough properties in Lincolnshire and Nottinghamshire. South Kelsey was a pleasant spot, with good land, and command of a long stretch of the river Ancholme with all fishing and fowling rights. It was centrally situated and within easy reach of Gainsborough, Market Rasen, Kirton in Lindsey and Caistor. This was important for a man involved in county administration, for it was to the market towns that he had to resort frequently in his capacity as justice of the peace or commissioner. The inconvenience of both Nuthall and Stallingborough must have been borne in upon him before, especially during his year as sheriff in 1521. Furthermore South Kelsey was near the main Lincoln–Barton-on-Humber road and access to the county capital was easy. Now he could administer the Hansard lands as if they were his own and in due course he could ensure that they would indeed pass into his family. For it would be arranged that when Elizabeth came of age she would marry Sir William's own heir, Francis, thus uniting the two fortunes.

Sir William's new territorial plans soon became clear. When the wardship was purchased and his second marriage celebrated, he moved without delay to South Kelsey. Once established there, he immediately began to consolidate his land and put it to the best advantage. In 1524 he managed to lease from Michaelhouse, Cambridge, neighbouring property in South Kelsey and Wingal Priory for forty years at twenty-five shillings a year.[19] His right to Wingal was unsuccessfully challenged in 1526 in no less a court than Star Chamber by 'Patrick Dixon, Robert Broxholme and others'.[20] Yet again, two years later, he was having to give evidence before an inquest at Lincoln Castle that he held 'view of frankpledge and other rights to a manor in South Kelsey'.[21] In short, Sir William Ayscough was pursuing his rights with dynastic determination and creating for himself and his family a position of power, wealth and influence greater than that held previously in Lincolnshire by his predecessors. Apart from his houses at

Memorial brass of Sir William Ayscough and his wife in St Peter's Church, Stallingborough.

Sir William Ayscough's Will, 1540.

Lincolnshire's once great abbeys, Thornton (*above*) and Crowland.

Stallingborough, South Kelsey, Nuthall and Basford, he had a substantial residence at Spalding. This house, Ayscoughfee Hall[22] (so called because the land on which it stood was held in knight's fee from the crown), afforded a useful base for a couple of months every winter when the larders were well stocked with local wild-fowl. Sir William held land, not only in every corner of Lincoln-shire and Nottinghamshire but in most of the neighbouring counties also. Wills, legal documents and records of lawsuits alone show that the Ayscoughs had property in Kilham (Yorks.), Lockington (Leics.), Royston (Yorks.), Blacktoft (Yorks.), as well as in their home counties.[23]

Sir William also acted as steward for a number of monastic houses. Like most wealthy English landowners he condescended to act as a patron of the great abbeys in return for an annual fee. The office of steward involved little work but it did mean that the reli-gious could call upon the support of a powerful local personality if ever they were in difficulties. Sir William was steward of the Stallingborough estates of Thornton and Selby Abbeys, steward of Nun Cotham Priory and chief steward of Newsome. He pre-sided at their manorial courts and acted generally as a good friend of the religious. For these services he obtained a total sum of £6. 6s. 8d. a year.[24]

He also acted as a good friend to the city authorities of Lincoln. On more than one occasion he was called on to advise and support them when they were encountering financial or legal problems.[25]

Of the manor house which Sir William found at South Kelsey nothing now remains. It was a moated and fortified dwelling dating from the twelfth century. When Francis Ayscough came into his inheritance in the middle of the century, he pulled down the traditional Hansard home and replaced it with a modern Tudor building. There exists a record of a letter of 1552 from Sir Francis Ayscough to Sir William Cecil, the Principal Secretary of State to Edward VI, suggesting that the Church of St Mary's, Grimsby be pulled down and that Cecil should have the lead (worth £200, in the writer's estimation). Sir Francis, for his part, 'would crave the stone and timber at a reasonable price'.[26] In 1566 Sir Francis was active on a commission enquiring into articles of church furniture which might be considered unduly superstitious or idolatrous by the Elizabethan regime. Existing documents in the Lincoln archives show the progress of this 'last wave' of Tudor Reformation

C

as it swept one hundred and fifty of the county's parishes. Among 'popish' articles taken away from churches to be destroyed or put to secular use were the altar stones of Market Rasen and Waddingham, which Sir Francis appropriated.[27] These records indicate how Sir William's son obtained some of his building materials.

Though not completed until the reign of Elizabeth, the new Ayscough home provides some indication of the state of the family fortunes.[28] The Tudor Hall was large at a time when there were few extensive gentry houses in the county. It was built largely of brick which could probably be obtained cheaper than the excellent Lincolnshire stone from such quarries as Stamford and Ancaster. The Hall was built on the old, square, medieval plan, had a courtyard and was protected by walls and moat. In fact fortified dwellings were generally out of fashion by the mid-sixteenth century. In most parts of the country they were no longer necessary and, in addition, they were frowned on by royal authority.

Even during the reign of Elizabeth a new house in Lincolnshire needed the security of a moat. The power of the great magnates had been broken; there were few men in the realm powerful enough to pose any serious threat to the stability of the Tudor regime. But there were many men of rank who were feared by their neighbours and who could successfully defy the royal justice in their own areas. Such a man was Lord Willoughby d'Eresby. From his house on the border of the fen, bands of liveried retainers were sent out on cattle raids and punitive expeditions against those who had offended the lord of the manor. Violence and scant regard for law on the part of their betters encouraged anarchy among Lincolnshire's yeomen and peasants. There was, particularly among the fenlanders, a long-standing tradition of independence. Feudalism had never gripped this area very tightly in its deadening grasp. Most of the farmers were proud leaseholders and freeholders, jealous of their rights and ambitious for their advancement. They frequently banded together for mutual protection or to stage a joint demonstration. Sometimes they, too, took the law into their own hands.

To some outsiders there was little difference between the Lincolnshire peasantry and the men of property. A visitor from London described them thus:

Knights and esquires are meeter to be baileys; men void of good fashion, and, in truth, of wit, except in matters concerning their trade, which is to get goods only.[29]

Such a sweeping condemnation could not with justice include Sir William Ayscough. He was no rural clod, but a cultured gentleman trained at the court of a Renaissance prince. All the men with whom Henry VIII surrounded himself were expected to be able to discourse on politics, theology, law, new discoveries in the realm of geography and empirical science, poetry and fashion. Sir William Ayscough, the well-travelled courtier, was able to hold his own in conversation on any of these topics. He was not a scholar, but, having been at the centre of things for so long, he could not fail to be aware of the exciting and disturbing new ideas that were creating a ferment in academic circles. Indeed some aspects of the 'New Learning' affected him deeply, as they did most of his colleagues. He was being forced to re-examine old attitudes and beliefs – particularly religious beliefs.

'For many educated men the early sixteenth century proved a period of intense mental crises and revisions, a period of exposure to ideas as remorseless as those which later accompanied the French Revolution.'[30] Before 1520 'heresy' had been a word which carried not only moral opprobrium but social stigma. The heretic was an artisan troublemaker, considered by the ruling classes, who had a vested interest in the Tudor peace, as much a rebel against law and order as against the dogmas and dictates of the Church. Traditional Lollardy, the mainstream of British heresy, had hardly ever received the allegiance of educated or influential people. It was over a hundred years since the movement's most notable martyr, Sir John Oldcastle, had been captured in Wales, dragged to London, hastily tried and carried to St Giles' Fields where he was 'hung and burnt hanging' (December 1417).[31] Since then influential and responsible members of society had left the movement well alone.

This does not mean that all well-born gentlemen and nobles were faithful and uncritical sons of Mother Church. Far from it. Ecclesiastical and lay authority often came into conflict and gentlemen were as aware as anyone else of the failings of the clergy. It was a Yorkshire gentleman, Wilfrid Holme, who unburdened himself on the subject of the religious life in these words:

None entereth to religion with any true devotion,
For the most part be infants, and put in by coaction,
And none of free will, except for promotion,
Or else for despair to do satisfaction,
And some very sloth to do no worldly action,
Professing obedience, poverty and chastity,
To which three essentials they make their contraction,
And to many trifles more the which is but vanity.

And so for their poverty, there is neither knight nor Lord,
Earl, marquis nor duke like them in abundance:
And as for their obedience, all men can record,
They are high rebellious against true allegiance,
Having both their King and God at defiance:
And as for their chastity the visitors know well,
For Sodom and Gomorrah had never such ordinance,
Their pollution and ways I shame for to tell.[32]

As long as bishops and abbots were administrators of large estates and held various secular jurisdictions, there were bound to be clashes between them and the landed classes. But it was a long step from anti-clericalism to heresy for a gentleman with lands and a name to lose. As long as Lollardy appeared to lack intellectual respectability and official sanction, few of the wealthy were likely to be enticed into its ranks. But if an age ever dawned when doctrines for which Lollards had been burned began to be voiced by academic theologians and when the government made statutory offences of sins for which the Church had long been criticized, then might the class divisions which had hitherto insulated the gentry from heresy be broken down. In the 1520s such an age began to dawn.

It was, in fact, in the year 1520 that disquieting events began to be noticed. In that year the son of a Shropshire gentleman, in London for his education, wrote home to his father, 'Sir, as for news there is none, but of late there was heretics here, which do take Luther's opinions.'[33] It was barely three years since the Wittenberg monk had made his first challenge to papal authority in the celebrated ninety-five theses. But in those three years, his pent-up religious experience and revolutionary theology burst forth in a spate of books which had passed, via German and Dutch printing presses, to London and many of England's eastern ports.

Thus the literate and curious were able to lay their hands on the treatise *On Good Works* which set forth a belief in the necessity of faith alone for salvation, the supreme importance of the Bible, and the freedom of the Christian soul from all ecclesiastical laws and sanctions. They were able to read *The Address to the Christian Nobility of the German Nation*, which exhorted all princes to rule fully in their realms and throw off the shackles of papal control. They might pore over *The Freedom of the Christian Man* in which Luther further expounded his conviction that no pope, bishop or priest could stand between the believer and his God (a conviction which he dramatically illustrated by publicly burning copies of the canon law in 1520). But most forthright and inflammatory of all the secretly read and carefully guarded Lutheran scripts was *The Babylonian Captivity*, which was nothing less than a devastating attack on the entire sacramental system of the Roman Church; it overthrew transubstantiation, drastically altered the nature of penance, denied completely the sacramental understanding of ordination, confirmation and marriage and denounced the monastic life as worthless in the eyes of God.

Luther's writings were soon followed by those of the more extreme Swiss reformer, Ulrich Zwingli. They added similar fuel to the same fires. His *On Divine and Human Justice* explored the relationship between Church and State, stressing the need for complete harmony between them but confining Church leaders to the possession of spiritual authority alone. *On True and False Religion* set forth the basis of Christian faith as a personal relationship between the Christian and his Saviour which called for no other kind of mediator. It showed the need for a complete re-interpretation of Catholic doctrines to make them agree with this fundamental proposition.

That the fires of the Continental Reformation quickly took hold in English academic and business centres is proved by the energetic action taken by the authorities to quench them. In 1521 Cuthbert Tunstall (soon to become Bishop of London), recently returned from a diplomatic mission in Germany where he had seen how quickly Lutheranism was spreading, wrote to Wolsey lamenting the popularity of some of Dr Martin's views in London. He declared his fear that *The Babylonian Captivity* might soon be circulating freely despite all the efforts of the Bishop's vigilantes, who were searching ships' cargoes and swooping on the houses of suspect citizens. Yet the ecclesiastical ferrets of Bishop Fitzjames did have some success: on 12 May a spectacular bonfire of banned books was staged in St Paul's churchyard and was presided over by Cardinal Wolsey himself. Such displays could frighten only timid souls. The convinced converts, the aggressive anti-clericals, the curious, the adventurous and those whose high position put them above criticism continued to demand the reformers' tracts and made it worth the while of entrepreneurs to persist in taking the risk of handling the forbidden volumes.

German and Swiss scholars did not hold the monopoly of new ideas. In 1523 William Tyndale came to London seeking the patronage of Tunstall, the new Bishop, to help him further his passionate ambition to translate the New Testament into English. He was disillusioned by his experiences in the capital.

> And so in London I abode almost a year, and marked the course of the world, and heard out praters (I would say preachers) how they boasted themselves and their high authority; and beheld the pomp of our prelates and how busy they were, as they yet are, to set peace and unity in the world (though it be not possible for them that walk in darkness to continue long in peace, for they cannot but either stumble or dash themselves at one thing or another that shall clean unquiet all together) and saw things whereof I defer to speak at this time, and understood at the last not only that there was no room in my Lord of London's palace to translate the New Testament, but also that there was no place to do it in all England. . . .[34]

So it was abroad that Tyndale produced the English New Testament which was to have the greatest single impact of any book in bringing about reformation in England. It would be impossible to overestimate the influence of the new vernacular translation, and especially of the later editions which carried prefaces and marginal notes setting forth the translator's interpretations and contemporary applications of the Scriptures. Setting his heart on the conversion of his fellow countrymen, Tyndale followed up the New Testament with other works: *The Parable of Wicked Mammon* and *The Obedience of a Christian Man*. The latter, which enjoined obedience to the two authorities of Holy Scripture and divinely appointed monarchs, greatly influenced the course of the English Reformation and was favourably received by Henry VIII. By 1520 Tyndale was engaged in a polemical literary battle with Sir Thomas

More and, as his views became more and more extreme, so return to England became impossible. In his Continental refuge he was joined, from time to time, by other like-minded countrymen, some of whom such as John Frith and George Joye, made their own contributions to the early literature of the Reformation.

These scholarly but dynamic writers made the first breach in the walls of British upper class respectability and conservatism. As early as 1519 Erasmus could write to Luther and report that some 'very great people' in England were admiring his writings. Country gentlemen like Sir William Ayscough, inspired either by genuine zeal or curiosity, bought Tyndale's New Testament even though (or perhaps because) the Church frowned. The great ones of the court read it and so the great ones of the shires read it also.

In this changing climate of opinion old Lollard tracts were republished, some dressed up in a more academic disguise. The leaders of the movement made a definite bid for the support of a more sophisticated section of the populace. Every effort was made to prove that what the English and Continental reformers were saying was nothing more than the old truth proclaimed and guarded by generations of faithful Wycliffites. Oldcastle's memory passed through the cleansing fire of popular re-appraisal and he emerged, purged of the stigma of treason and rebellion, as a holy, upper-class martyr. The bid for more influential support is clearly seen in the choice of old tracts that the Lollards made for republication.[35] Two of the first tracts to be re-printed abroad and smuggled into England in the 1520s were *A Book of Thorpe or of John Oldcastle* and *A Popular Dialogue Between a Gentleman and a Husbandman*. In the latter work the gentleman is made to express a significant approval of certain old tracts:

> Now I promise that after my judgement
> I have not heard of such an old fragment
> Better grounded on reason with Scripture.
> If such ancient things might come to light
> That noblemen had once of them a sight,
> The world yet would change peradventure.[36]

Yet it was the academic centres in Cambridge, Oxford and London rather than the court which were the main seed beds of upper-class heresy. Men of Sir William Ayscough's generation were, for the most part, already too old to have their basic attitude to life completely transformed by doctrinal novelties. While they had not reached the stage of automatically discarding 'new-fangled notions', they had inherited family and other responsibilities and were not prepared to hazard all for the sake of a principle. But by the 1520s it was fashionable for these men to send their sons to the University. A few terms at Oxford or Cambridge would, it was supposed, better fit the young men for their future careers as courtiers and local administrators. Students were then as they have always been, enthusiastic listeners to anything new – particularly anything which offered a challenge to authority – and so the universities became centres of heresy.

The academic revolution had started around the turn of the century when the first wave of humanism swept over Oxford and Cambridge. Fresh light was brought to the study of Scripture by John Colet at Oxford, whose lectures on Romans in 1496–7 had cast aside the medieval scholastic methods of study and exegesis, and by Desiderius Erasmus at Cambridge, whose Latin and Greek translations of the New Testament had encouraged scholars to study afresh the Scriptures now shown forth in their original warm colours, stripped of centuries of Vulgate corruptions and scholastic glosses. By 1520 Greek lectures were a regular and popular feature of University life and pupils were firmly set on the dangerous path of examining the Bible for themselves without the commentaries of the schoolmen to guide them or the firm hand of ecclesiastical control to restrain them.

These concessions had not been easily won by liberal academics and there were still many authoritarian churchmen who resented the free and enquiring atmosphere of the university lecture rooms. Their fears seemed to be realized when zealous reformers made it their business to circulate heretical writings among the students. At Oxford a certain Thomas Garrett was to the fore in this method of proselytizing. His approach was simple and effective: he would seek out young men studying Greek, Latin or Hebrew and provide them first with harmless literature to help them in their work. When this diet had been digested Garrett would next wean his clients on to more exciting and dangerous fare. By 1527 Dr London, Warden of New College, was urgently drawing the attention of higher authority to the size and activities of the Protestant cell in the University. In February 1528 the Bishop of Lincoln, in whose diocese the University lay, was outraged to hear that no less than eighty-seven different heretical works were being sold there. Cardinal Wolsey was at first disposed to easy-going tolerance in matters concerning mere scholars but even he was moved to anger when he learned that the taint of heresy had spread to his own proud new foundation, Cardinal's College. The hounds of ortho-doxy were slipped from the leash and Garrett and his colleagues were harried and at last tracked down far from Oxford's walls. They were forced to recant and, when the authorities were convinced that their change of heart was genuine, most of them were set at liberty. But not before three unfortunate Protestants had died in the dank prisons of Cardinal's College. Meanwhile persecution had its age-old effect: it only encouraged the spread of heresy.

The infection had been carried to Cardinal's College by some of the Cambridge scholars whom Wolsey had chosen to serve his new foundation. It was Cambridge which was the real cradle of acad-emic Protestantism. There the leading dispenser of heretical books was Robert Barnes, Prior of the Augustinian house and lecturer on the New Testament of Erasmus. He played a leading part in meetings which took place at the White Horse Inn. Here the works of Luther, Tyndale and other heretics were discussed and soon the hostelry earned itself the nickname 'Little Germany'. Apart from Barnes, the Cambridge Protestant cell included at different times many of the future architects of the English Reformation – Cranmer, Latimer, Tyndale, Frith, Joye, Parker and Coverdale – as well as many unknown young men destined to become royal officials, landed gentlemen and ambassadors. From the universities also ordained men and members of preaching orders went out, with royal or episcopal licences, on preaching tours in many dioceses. Such a one was Thomas Bilney who carried the new heresies throughout East Anglia before providing Cambridge University with its first martyr in the Lollards' Pit at Norwich in 1531.

It was to this Cambridge – a university in a state of intellectual ferment – that young Francis Ayscough was sent to spend some of his most impressionable years. Already more than half-prepared by the liberal atmosphere of his home, Francis readily absorbed the new ideas preached from university pulpits and discussed in the students' halls and hostels. He became, like so many of his generation, an emancipated young man of the New Learning; an angry young man out of sympathy with the medieval, catholic establishment; a Protestant – although that word was not yet used in England to cover most of the varieties of new religious thought and experience.

One prominent Cambridge scholar who was still lecturing at Jesus College while Francis Ayscough was up was an old acquaintance and neighbour of the family. The Cranmers were of lesser gentry stock and held land in south Nottinghamshire and Lincolnshire. Their family seat was at Aslockton, barely twelve miles away from Nuthall on the road from Nottingham to Grantham. They also had an estate at Algarkirk near Spalding. Before 1531 Sir William Ayscough little regarded the unpretentious Cranmers, though Francis was impressed by Master Thomas Cranmer, the quiet doctor of divinity who insisted that all his scholars should be well-versed in the Bible and not mere students of a millennium of scholastic glosses. In 1531, however, the obscure fellow of Jesus was lifted out of his quiet fenland haunts into the glaring limelight of the royal court. He had been brought to the attention of the King as one who might be able to find a way out of the impasse of Henry's relations with the Pope. Rapidly the bewildered Cranmer found himself employed on ambassadorial missions, taken into the King's confidence, showered with honours and finally appointed Primate of all England. He was destined to become the first Archbishop of Canterbury in the independent church of England. Under these circumstances, Sir William Ayscough bethought himself again of his 'old friend' and exact contemporary Thomas Cranmer. He had to find a place for his second son and planned to place Edward in the household of some nobleman or leading minister who, in due course, would introduce him to the royal court. Once there, the young man would be in a position to sue for lands and favours from the King and establish his fortune. Thus it was that young Edward became a page in the household of Thomas Cranmer and the Ayscoughs forged another link with the reform movement.

Sir William Ayscough maintained his connections with the court and was kept well informed of the dynamic events taking place there, but his mind was much more occupied with family and county affairs. The large family at South Kelsey was made larger when a son, Thomas, was born. But some of the other children were already leaving home. The older Hansard girls were the first to go on their marriage to wealthy neighbours. Elizabeth married one of the Girlingtons – a merchant family who had recently bought land at Normanby. In the early 1530s Bridget became the wife of Thomas Moigne, a young lawyer who had just returned from the inns of court to take over the family estates at Willingham. Shortly afterwards he was appointed Recorder of Lincoln and seemed well on the way to making a good career for himself. Sir William next had to place young Christopher's feet on the ladder leading to wealth and rank. This he managed with excellent results. We do not know with whom Christopher first saw service but he progressed quickly and by 1536 had gained a much-coveted position as Gentleman of the King's Privy Chamber.

In the education of the women of his household, Sir William Ayscough showed how enlightened a man he was. The common feeling about the training of girls was that they should be instructed in the arts of kitchen and parlour. They were to be transformed into efficient wives and little else. It was not thought necessary that they should be able to read and write, for the man was the thinker of the family and a woman who presumed to debate with or instruct her spouse was anathema. Such opinions may well have been shared by Dame Elizabeth Ayscough but, if so, her charges were shielded from a cramping conservatism by Sir William. Martha, Anne and Jane Ayscough and Elizabeth Hansard grew up to be – by the standards of the age – very well-educated women. Where they received their instruction, we do not know. They may have been farmed out, like the boys, to the households of noblemen or courtiers. It is, perhaps, more likely that a young scholar fresh from one of the universities was brought to South Kelsey as a tutor. Certain it is that the girls became fluent readers and writers of English and probably of Latin. They avidly read the books and tracts which the Ayscough boys occasionally brought back to South Kelsey with them on their return from more interesting and exciting places.

On their visits home from Cambridge, Westminster and Lambeth, Sir William's sons must have come full of news of the progress of religious change. Francis could report that students were encouraged to read the Bible for themselves. Scholastic glosses and traditional interpretations of Scripture were thrown overboard. Degrees and lectures in canon law were abolished. Edward had stories to tell of his master's deliberate encouragement of Latimer and other 'suspect' preachers, of his advancement of heretics to ecclesiastical office and of angry visits to the Archbishop by outraged orthodox churchmen. The gossip from court would be of the rise to power of the upstart Thomas Cromwell, replacing the upstart Wolsey, of the triumph of Anne Boleyn and her patron the Duke of Norfolk and of the encouragement given by the Queen's faction to the new ideas. Above all, Christopher was able to bring home details of the King's breach with Rome and his establishment as Head of the Church in England.

Protestant influences were thus strong in the Ayscough household in the early 1530s and, as the general drift of royal policy seemed to be towards Reformation, Sir William saw no harm in letting his children read the Bible and even heretical tracts. Though he held office for some of the monasteries, he had never been a friend of powerful and pompous abbots and prelates, and so he threw his support fully behind the work of the official Reformation in Lincolnshire. For government policy had been moving rapidly since Sir William's last stay at court. In 1527, Henry VIII's desire for a divorce from his Queen, Catherine of Aragon, had led him into a conflict with the Pope. One thing had rapidly led to another. Observing the swelling river of anti-clerical, anti-papal criticism, the King turned its energy into the formulation of a mass of legislation passed by the 'Reformation Parliament' (1529–1536). This culminated in his masterstroke – the Act of Supremacy – which finally cut the gordian knot of Anglo-papal relations.

For the time being the even tenor of life at South Kelsey Hall was undisturbed (though far from uninfluenced) by these events. Sir William Ayscough and his family enjoyed years of peace and prosperity. They were to be the last such years many members of that household were ever to see. 1536 brought turmoil and bloodshed to Lincolnshire. Thereafter Sir William, Francis, Edward, Christopher and, above all, Anne were to be involved in a sequence of events which were to end in stark tragedy. But all that was in the future. Now we can leave the Ayscoughs for the time being, basking in the sunshine of good fortune. We turn our attention to another panel of the tapestry, occupied by a lonely man, much more closely bound up with the religious movements in England between 1520 and 1536.

# 2

# *King's Bishop*

---

ON 5 May 1536 John Longland was in his sixty-third year
and celebrating the fifteenth anniversary of his consecration as Bishop of England's second-largest diocese. It was
highly characteristic of the man that part of that day should have
been spent in the study of his palace at Woburn composing a long
letter to Thomas Cromwell, the King's Secretary. The subject of
his letter was the eradication of heresy.

Ever since assuming responsibility for the diocese of Lincoln in
1521 Longland had been as vigilant in the seeking-out of heresy as
he had been in the defence of the privileges of the Church and the
improving of the educational and moral standards of his clergy.
For the Bishop of Lincoln was an ecclesiastical martinet; efficient
in administration, persistent (some said 'ruthless') in the execution
of his duty and demanding of his subordinates.

The spread of native Lollardy and imported heresies he viewed
with particular alarm. And, indeed, he had good reason for concern;
for there was at least one area in his sprawling diocese where
Wycliffite doctrines had for decades been firmly rooted. The mono-
lithic diocese of Lincoln was only smaller than the neighbouring see
of York. A wide arc of authority from the Humber to the Thames,
it sprawled over eight counties.[1] It was the Chilterns, in the south
of this diocese, which were such a prolific breeding-ground of
heresy. Aylesbury, Buckingham, Amersham and the villages of the
gentle hillsides – from time immemorial all had sent men and
women to the stake or to carry their penitential faggot around the
market cross. Bishop Smith had tried to prosecute the Chiltern
Lollards out of existence between 1506 and 1508. Between those

years over eighty were brought to trial and convicted. Most recanted, and a few bore their beliefs through flame and fire. Yet it was vain for the Bishop's officers to hope that they had purged their parishes of the stigma of heresy. The busy pluralist, William Atwater (Bishop 1514–1521), pursued a milder policy, hoping, no doubt, to kill by kindness what the weapons of the canon law had failed to slay. His toleration was appreciated: 'My lord that is dead was a good man, and divers known-men were called before him, and he sent them home again, bidding them that they should live among their neighbours as good Christian men should',[2] – so reported Richard White of Beaconsfield. But the Bishop's policy failed of its object. Penitents relapsed into their old beliefs. Families and sometimes whole villages remained as compact, defensive Lollard groups. Worst of all – proselytizing was on the increase.

Longland thought with anger of the insidious ways in which heresy spread from house to house, village to village, shire to shire. The apprenticeship system and the inevitable journeys involved in industry and trade contributed to the easy dissemination of religious 'novelties', but in addition there were missionaries who had devoted themselves to preaching and teaching. What was it Thomas More had written about the Lollard preacher? He was a man who lived 'everywhere and nowhere . . . for he walked about as an apostle of the devil from shire to shire and town to town, through the realm, and had in every diocese a diverse name. By reason whereof he did many years much harm before he could be found out.'[3]

As the ascetic figure gazed from his study window at the spring thrusting into his Buckinghamshire acres, he could reflect that he had done his utmost to grasp the quicksilver heresy. Nor had he flinched from widespread unpopularity in the execution of his plain duty to Mother Church. The House of Commons had had him in the forefront of their minds when they complained in their 'Supplication Against the Ordinaries' (1532) against bishops who were over-zealous in the seeking-out of heretics. And the tide of criticism had mounted steadily over the years. It was but recently that Cromwell himself had received a report from one of his agents that 'poor people be indicted for small matters of pretended heresy, as by the Bishop of Lincoln in his diocese'.[4]

Within months of his consecration Longland had instigated a

fresh attack on the Chiltern Lollards. He obtained a royal mandate to all civil authorities 'to assist the Bishop of Lincoln in executing justice upon heretics of whom there are now no small number in his diocese'.[5] During the autumn and winter of 1521–2 Longland's officers examined over three hundred suspected Lollards. And what an exasperating business heresy trials were, the judges trying everything in their power (including, sometimes, bribery) to obtain confession and recantation from the accused, ever reluctant to resort to the ultimate penalty. While the accused for his part denied, prevaricated, twisted words, went back on his oath and raised legal quibbles. Yet the result had been gratifying: many hitherto unknown nests of heresy had been discovered; Longland had been able to give information to brother bishops about suspects in other dioceses; there had been a total of fifty abjurations and only six obstinates had had to be handed over for burning. Thus numerous souls had been saved from perdition and the spread of Lollardy had been checked – for a while.

But Longland's ecclesiastical hoe had barely scratched the surface of Chiltern society. Even if the persecutors had succeeded in eradicating Lollardy among the ranks of the simple and the poor, their victory would have been a hollow one. For more substantial citizens, prosperous yeomen and businessmen who as employers and parish officials held together the fabric of rural society, were now infected. There were men like Richard Saunders of Amersham, who was rich enough to buy his penance in 1521 and whose wealth protected him from interference even though his neighbours knew that he and his wife read heretical books.[6] Those who offended the Saunders paid dearly for it as Thomas Houre discovered. After telling Alice Saunders that he would no longer favour heresy, he ceased to be employed by Master Saunders and was later dismissed from his post as holy water clerk. Nor was Houre the only one to be brought to beggary by locally powerful Lollards.[7] Sustained and encouraged by their brethren in London and Essex (for Lollard activities in the capital and around Colchester also gave the authorities considerable trouble) the Chiltern Lollards not only persevered under persecution, they prospered. Their numbers and influence grew, they met regularly for Bible reading and prayer, their proselytizing became more open, those who could not read learned proof-texts by heart and repeated them parrot-fashion to others. So, in the spring of 1536, the ageing but still energetic and zealous Bishop Longland could look out of his window at Woburn on to the gentle Chilterns and reflect that the country between himself and the Thames was still alive with heretics despite fifteen years of vigilance.

The proximity of the Chilterns to Oxford and the lively flow of native heresy along the London road had probably encouraged the spread of new ideas in the University. This, too, had been Longland's care as diocesan since 1521 and as chancellor since 1532. His watch over the orthodoxy of the fellows and students had been perpetual. He had for an agent the obnoxious Warden of New College, John London, to whose sadistic, lustful and sycophantic soul the opportunity to indulge in spying, bullyings and threatening was as manna in the wilderness. To curry favour with the Bishop he eagerly turned bookshops upside-down, grilled penniless students, informed against academic rivals, imprisoned suspects. To satisfy his own appetites he took bribes of money from the rich while claiming from fearful womenfolk favours of a more basic nature as reward for his silence. London's excesses were notorious and were soon to bring him into disfavour. For the time being, Longland, who was well acquainted with the man's coarseness and brutality, felt that he had to use even such vile instruments as the Warden of New College to eradicate the greater evil of heresy.

Yet, as a scholar himself, he always felt a certain sympathy for young men of the universities who became entangled in the evils of unorthodoxy. For Longland was no backs-to-the-wall reactionary, frightened of every manifestation of independent thought. As a student at Oxford around the turn of the century he had absorbed the teaching of John Colet, whose firm disciple he became. In common with many first-generation English reformers Longland applauded the move 'back to the Bible'. He frequently vowed that he had learned more from the Greek New Testament and other writings of Erasmus than from all the traditional commentaries in his library. Unlike many of his ecclesiastical colleagues, Longland set great store by preaching and early took pains to cultivate a gift for pulpit oratory. It was this that had particularly attracted the attention of the King, who appointed him royal confessor in 1520.

Longland found Wolsey's easy-going tolerance towards heretics both irritating and dangerous. During the burst of persecution at Oxford in 1527–8, heretics had been allowed to escape or been pardoned because Wolsey had been lacking in vigilance. John

Taverner, choirmaster and organist at Cardinal College, had been acquitted of a charge of concealing heretical books because he was 'but a musician'. John Frith, a man of really pernicious opinions, had escaped to the Continent with the connivance of Wolsey's officers. On Frith's subsequent return to England the authorities had had to burn him (1533).

Then there had been the case of George Joye, fellow of Peterhouse, Cambridge. Longland had taken a personal interest in that young man's case in 1527. Joye had been reported to him as a man holding erroneous opinions about the priesthood, about auricular confession and about faith and works. Moreover he had been causing disturbances among the undergraduates. Prior Ashwell of Newnham, Longland's informant, reported, 'I have heard some reports that when he has been among lay persons at feasts or youngsters in the country he has put forward many lewd opinions among the people. Some good folks would murmur and grudge at his sayings and some would rejoice at them.'[8] Longland had urged Wolsey to summon the errant Cambridge don to London, which he did. But then the Cardinal seemed to lose all interest in the young man. Longland, therefore, decided to interview Joye himself, but before an opportunity presented itself the suspected heretic had decided that discretion was the better part of valour. He fled from London and by the time Longland was able to send after him, he was well on the coast road. The Bishop did not mind English heretics escaping to the Continent, as long as they stayed there. Perhaps he thought, mistakenly, they could do little harm to English Christians from Antwerp or Germany; at least while they were there the authorities were saved the trouble of bringing them to trial. Even so, the spread of heresy in the academic world was alarming. Perhaps it was about this time that Longland began to have serious doubts about the whole reform movement which had started so innocuously in the closing years of the fifteenth century. Like many of his contemporary bishops and theologians, he knew that the Church was in need of reform – but . . . ? He was uneasy about the way things were developing.

Longland was one of the last 'statesmen bishops' of the medieval pattern. As confessor and advisor to the King, his presence at court was required almost continuously. Within these limitations he was a conscientious diocesan. Besides, being at court had distinct advantages. As Henry VIII's reign wore on, the privileges and

D

rights of the Church came under ever closer scrutiny and Longland often found himself having to use his influence with the King
and his councillors to fend off royal encroachments on ecclesiastical
preserves. Yet the fact remains that the Bishop of Lincoln was not
able to spend as much time in his diocese as he would have liked.

The northern part of Longland's vast bishopric saw him very
infrequently. In 1523 the episcopal palace at Lincoln was reported
as being in a semi-derelict state (a situation which the Bishop had
to rectify very quickly when the King declared his intention of
stopping there during his northern progress in 1541). Fortunately
the northern parts were less troublesome. He was well supported
by his leading clergy; men like George Henneage, Dean of Lincoln,
who, as one of Longland's chaplains, well knew the Bishop's mind
and, as a member of one of the leading gentry families of the area,
could count on considerable local support in carrying out his
Bishop's policies. The lesser clergy were almost entirely men of
peasant stock, unlettered and, in many ways, unsatisfactory but
all rigidly conservative and enemies of heresy. Particularly was
this so in the Lincolnshire fen where the long parishes, stretching
further and further towards the sea to keep pace with reclaimed
farmland, boasted numerous subsidiary chapels and where the
priests formed a leading social caste. The fenland from Longland's
point of view was the 'safest' part of his diocese. Not that any of
his northern parishes showed much proneness to heresy – or, at
least, they had not in the past.

Such cases as there had been were isolated and rare. Some
ten years previously there had been a group of clergy and laymen
in southern Lincolnshire infected with Lutheranism but Longland's
vigilant chancellor, Dr Prynn, had acted swiftly in suppressing
their erroneous opinions. As a result Henry Aglyonby, John
French and 'one Algar, alias Jones' recanted their belief in the
priesthood of all believers, their denial of purgatory and their
rejection of the primacy of St Peter.[9] Lutheranism had reared its
ugly head again at Barrow-on-Humber in 1528. Henry Burnett, a
merchant, had returned from a trading voyage to Amsterdam and
Bremen provided not only with German goods but with German
ideas. He excitedly told his friends about the Lutheran services he
had attended. His hearers were astonished at his tales of a land
where mass was not celebrated and where the congregation actually
participated in worship in their native tongue. They were appalled

to hear that he had eaten meat on fish days and scandalized when he continued the practice on his return to his home town. Flushed with the excitement of religious freedom, the wisdom of outward conformity occurred to him too late. When he went to his parish priest to confess, the cleric threw up his hands in horror and referred the suspected heretic to higher authority. By this time two of Burnett's fellow travellers and colleagues had been arrested in Hull and accused by the York diocesan officers of holding Lutheran opinions and owning an English version of the gospels. It was a very frightened Henry Burnett who found himself on trial before Chancellor Prynn at Lincoln. He feverishly denied having been won over by foreign heretics, avowed his holy dismay at the non-Catholic practices he had observed in German churches and gave eager assurances of future good conduct. The man obviously did not have the makings of a heretic and Prynn felt quite justified in dismissing him with a caution.[10] A handful of cases such as these during a decade and a half were nothing to worry about.

Yet Longland did not allow himself to be complaisant even about the northern parts of his diocese. Only recently news had come to him of a relapsed heretic re-arrested in Leicester. This was Lawrence Dawson, a serving-man who, despite his earlier recantation, now firmly and stubbornly denied any belief in the priestly miracle of the mass. Longland knew – and the knowledge caused him nothing but pain – that he would have to burn the fellow. He also knew that for every Dawson who was caught there were fifty who successfully concealed their foul heresies from the parish clergy. Leicester, Stamford, Grantham, Barton-on-Humber, all had their Protestant cells, whose members were in close contact with heretics of nearby areas.

Longland's ecclesiastical neighbour, the conservative, Archbishop Lee of York, had his problems in plenty in the towns of Nottinghamshire and south Yorkshire – Nottingham, Newark, Worksop, Doncaster, Rotherham and Hull. Here were heretical 'centres' almost on a par with Aylesbury and Colchester. The Great North Road, the navigable waterways of Trent and Ouse, the Pennine passes – all were busy thoroughfares carrying men and ideas to the ports, the monastic centres, the market towns and the nascent industrial concentrations of the north.[11]

But it was at Doncaster that a much more prominent troublemaker was drawing attention to himself. John Bale had been a contemporary of Thomas Cranmer at Jesus College, Cambridge, and a member of the clandestine 'Little Germany' group. At the age of twelve he had been sent to the Carmelite house at Norwich and by 1530 had risen to be prior of the Doncaster Carmelites. His espousal of the new views appears to have attracted little attention before that date. In 1531 he spoke out against Catholic ceremonial and had to be admonished. Chastened, he managed to contain himself for three years. Then, in August 1534, he began not only to preach reformed doctrines with vigour but also to vilify – with equal and unseemly gusto – the warden of the Doncaster Grey-friars, who had presumed to contradict his teaching. Within weeks the whole town was buzzing with the controversy between the two men and discussing the doctrines they represented. Such a scandalous state of affairs could not be allowed to continue and both contenders were hailed before Archbishop Lee. But the man had friends in high places. It was said he had appealed direct to Crom-well. Small wonder 'Bilious Bale' got off scot free – no doubt to make mischief elsewhere. Oh yes, Master Bale was a man who needed watching.

That was the trouble, these new men had influence. Whoever heard of heretics with friends at court in the old days? Now, since the King had become Supreme Head of the Church, everything had gone haywire. Queen Anne openly reading her illuminated, vellum copy of Tyndale's New Testament.[12] Queen Anne inter-ceding with Cromwell for the release of suspected heretics.[13] Cromwell, the all-powerful Cromwell, needed no second bidding to set them at liberty and even to license them to preach around the shires.

As Bishop Longland sat on that spring morning in 1536 and wrote his letter (one of many despatched to the same recipient) to a man he disagreed with, despised and yet had to co-operate with, he was troubled in his conscience. England – his England – was a divided country; divided over religion; divided over its attitude to the King's policies. The English Church was in schism from the rest of Christendom. Over the last decade he had seen the country drift closer and closer towards the rocks of Lutheranism and other foreign heresies. The question he asked himself was, 'Am I partly to blame?' God knew he had done all in his power, no man had done more, to stamp out heresy, but was that enough? Had he, in other ways, compromised his principles for fear of incurring the

King's displeasure? He was not ambitious for office or wealth. He had always sought to live an exemplary life of simplicity, almost of asceticism, but could it be that he was too jealous of rank, position, royal favour to make a decisive stand against mistaken policies? But where should he have made his stand? At what point had things begun to go wrong?

Did John Longland, on that anniversary in 1536, as he must have done on so many occasions, think back over the sequence of events that had led England to its present, unhappy situation? Had it not all started in about 1524? In that year Henry was thirty-three and had been married to his virtuous and popular Queen, Catherine of Aragon, for fifteen years. During all those years of matrimony Henry had been, by the standards of the day, a dutiful and loving husband. But during those years Catherine had given birth to six children – and buried five. The only survivor had been a girl – Mary. By 1524 the virile King of England had had to face the fact that he had no male heir and that his wife, now thirty-nine, was unlikely to provide him with one. This, in the troubled state of national and international politics, was more than misfortune; it could wreck the dynasty. Henry was genuinely troubled. He fell to asking why God had allowed this to happen. Was it a judgement on him for marrying his deceased brother's widow? Was not such a union forbidden in the Book of Leviticus? Had the Pope, who had granted a dispensation for his marriage with Catherine, the power to set aside the dictates of Holy Scripture? These questions had lain on Henry's conscience and he had unburdened himself to his confessor. The problem had then become Longland's and Longland, after much consideration, had encouraged the King to consider his marriage invalid in the sight of God.[14] That had been the beginning of the long drawn-out negotiations with Rome and other European capitals, the appeals for support to scholars and authorities at home and abroad, the international tensions, the failure and consequent downfall of Wolsey, the frustrations and delays which all led to the eventual drastic solution.

The unpopularity of the divorce came home to Longland most forcibly when, in April 1530, he went with two other commissioners to Oxford to obtain the support of the University for the King's cause. The royal servants found a hostile body of teachers and students awaiting them. Several days of arguments, threatenings and, at last, third-degree type interrogations passed before a suitable decision could be obtained and, even then, the majority favouring the government's policy was scarcely overwhelming – thirty-seven for, twenty-five against.[15] Longland and his colleagues had got their decision but only by bludgeoning the University leaders with threats. And the students had made quite clear their opinion about intellectual coercion by government agents. As the commissioners rode out of the city the undergraduates lined the route and pelted them with stones.[16]

After that events had proceeded inexorably as though moving towards some awful, predetermined end. Wolsey had been held responsible for the negotiations with Rome. Later in that same year, he had fallen from power – and from life. Again Longland had welcomed the ministerial changes brought about by the Cardinal's death. Wolsey, as well as being over-tolerant of heretics, had been a worldly, pomp-and-luxury-loving prelate of a type that Longland disapproved of. But the man who had replaced Wolsey as chief minister had soon shown himself to be a rabid anti-clerical and a positive patron of heretics. Thomas Cromwell had conceived and put into the King's mind thoughts of a Machiavellian simplicity and ruthlessness such as would never have occurred to his predecessor.

The trouble was that Longland basically agreed with the premises underlying Cromwell's policies. Longland had always been quite clear in his mind that the Pope's authority should be restricted to the spiritual realm and that kings and princes in their domains exercised sovereignty as from God over all their people. The King's complaint, in 1532, that the clergy of England 'be but half our subjects, yea and scarce our subjects' by virtue of the oath to the Pope taken at institution was just, and Longland had been to the fore in urging the clergy of his diocese to submit themselves to their divinely-appointed sovereign. Thereafter the axe-blow parliamentary statutes had fallen, severing, one by one, the cords binding the English Church to the see of St Peter. When Henry had cast off his Spanish wife to marry the capricious, self-willed and heretically-inclined Anne Boleyn, Longland must have asked himself whether it was for this that he had encouraged the King's matrimonial doubts in 1524. But the Boleyn marriage, like the rise of Cromwell, was part and parcel of 'the King's great matter', and Longland knew that he could not escape his share of the responsibility for it.

Yes, the doubts in Longland's mind had certainly grown to oppressive proportions by the end of 1534 when the Act of Supremacy had been passed, proclaiming Henry VIII Supreme Head of the Church in England, and the Act of Succession had bastardized Princess Mary by proclaiming the marriage of Henry and Catherine illegal. Yet the Bishop of Lincoln had pursued a consistent policy. In his sermons he had upheld the royal supremacy and, in June 1535, he had enjoined all his clergy to do the same. The stand taken against the oath of succession by his old friends Sir Thomas More and John Fisher had shocked him. Should he have stood with them? But he could not, in all conscience, say that he shared their beliefs.

That in itself was disturbing; Longland found himself increasingly at variance with men of high principles and known holiness of life. How lonely was the life of a bishop. How episcopal authority cut a man off from his fellows. Longland might share the anxieties and fears of most good English Catholics, yet, being a pillar of the establishment, he could not voice them and was looked on by his fellow Christians as a wholehearted supporter of every new move made by the government. In his loneliness he did not even have anyone he could turn to for advice. He had to make his own decisions and live with his own conscience.

But if Longland's conscience troubled him, this was as nothing to the attacks made upon him in his own diocese. Not only was he, on the one hand, accused of being over-zealous in the persecution of heretics; he was, on the other, vilified by conservatives as an arch-supporter of the divorce and the Supremacy and Succession Acts. Never, in fifteen years, had he known his diocese to be in such a troubled state. Scarcely a month went past without report being made to him of fresh attacks upon Queen Anne or the King's ministers. Three years before, there had come a shocking report from the normally quiet extreme north of his diocese, at Barrow-upon-Humber.

... A naughty person of Antwerp resorted to this town of Barrow during the Easter fair with images and pictures in cloth to sell. Among these cloths he had a picture of our Sovereign Lord the King (whom our Lord preserve). And this day setting up the same picture in the market place to sell, he pinned upon the body of the said picture a wench made in cloth, holding a pair of balances in her hands. In the one balance was two hands together and in the other balance a feather, with a writing over her head saying that love was lighter than a feather.[17]

Matters had become even worse since Queen Catherine (or the 'Dowager Princess' as royal edict demanded she be called) had been housed at Kimbolton, Huntingdonshire, in Longland's diocese. Her house there became a centre of pilgrimage and a potential trouble spot. Thither resorted men like the hermit Hugh Lathbury who on 2 June 1535 had had to answer to the royal justice for attempting to stir up sympathy for the ex-queen. Lathbury had openly boasted of his journey to Kimbolton and on into Lincolnshire, where he had discovered much support for 'Catherine, Queen of Fortune'; so much so that he could claim 'she would make ten men against the King's one'. Furthermore, the justices had reported, 'he trusteth that she shall be hereafter Queen again'.[18] There had been much truth in the hermit's contention; Catherine had considerable potential support, especially in the fens and midlands. Even Henry had acknowledged this when he remarked to his Council:

> The lady Catherine is a proud, stubborn woman, of very high courage . . . she could quite easily take the field, muster a great array, and wage against me a war as fierce as any her mother Isabella ever waged in Spain.[19]

For every troublemaker who was reported to the authorities, there were hundreds of more discreet men and women who yet took every opportunity of complaining about the King's shameful treatment of the Lady Catherine – and about those they believed had 'put him up to it'. Indeed, Queen Catherine had been a good woman. And yet it was perhaps as well for all concerned that she died in January 1536.

But the death of Catherine of Aragon did not mean the death of Longland's unpopularity in his diocese. The 'brisk and giddy-paced times' continually stirred old grievances and raised new ones. Henry's expulsion of the Pope had led other men to think that they could, with equal impunity, defy all ecclesiastical authority. Everywhere that Longland turned in his diocese there was some individual or group challenging his courts, his priests, his chancellor, the ancient and inalienable rights of his episcopal oversight. Troublemakers all, taking advantage of the Church's temporary instability during a period of re-adjustment and reform. Troublemakers – like the lewd fellows of Newark.

The town of Newark had grown steadily over the years, prospering because it stood at the junction of a main highway, the Great North Road, and a navigable river, the Trent. As it developed it had sought its independence from the lords of the manor, the Bishops of Lincoln. But none of Longland's predecessors had agreed to let Newark have a charter and Longland had no intention of relinquishing control over a lucrative source of diocesan income. But now, after a long period of calm, matters between the town and the Bishop had come to a head again. It had begun, a year before, in a dispute between the town fathers and the Bishop's bailiff, Anthony Foster, over a piece of demesne land. When the two parties met, an ugly scene quickly developed. Bitter feelings had led to hard words and hard words to harder blows, until the supporters of the two parties were fighting in the streets. Only with the greatest difficulty had the unseemly brawl been brought under control. The disturbance had been brought to the attention of the local justices, chief among whom was Sir John Markham of Cottam, the greatest landowner in the district. Markham was very much a man of the new learning and no friend of the ecclesiastical establishment. His impartiality in dealing with the disturbance of the peace in Newark had been suspect and Anthony Foster, believing that little help was to be obtained from the secular authorities, had busied his bruised hands and aching head in drafting a letter of complaint to his master.

Longland, who was nearby, in his house at Liddington, Rutland, at the time, had taken the matter up with Sir John Markham.

'I . . . am sorry my neighbours of Newark deal so unkindly with me and my officer,' he had written to Markham on 22 April. 'I suppose there has not been so great a riot of late days within the realm and so little done to punish the offenders. My bailiff, Anthony Foster, shows how you and other gentlemen there have made him have the matter in gentle hearing [i.e. decided by the local justices of the peace], which I think is the best way, for it will be pain to the offenders if it come to the hearing above [i.e. into a higher court] and to the determination of the law.'[20]

Markham had refused to take the hint. When the dispute came up before the local magistrates, their decision had favoured the citizens. The Bishop's officers were furious and, with Longland's

backing, took the matter up in the King's courts. It had by now
become a quarrel between the Bishop and Markham. Longland had
been determined to prevail against the gentleman, not only
because he had believed his case to be just but because he had felt
he had to strike a blow for ecclesiastical privilege against the
encroachments of the state.[21]

But if Longland could muster influence in support of his case,
so could Markham. He had appealed to his old friend and neighbour, Archbishop Cranmer, who in turn sought the aid of the most
powerful man in England under the King.

> Sir John Markham has always stated that you are his special good
> master ... I have known Sir John in his county above thirty years.
> ... The bailiff of Newark boasts that Sir John shall be committed to
> prison before he can make his answer. (Cranmer to Cromwell
> 3 November 1535.)[22]

With Cromwell against him, Longland had been unable to get
justice in the Court of Chancery when the case came up early in
1536. He had had to assent to an unsatisfactory compromise over
the land issue while Markham and the men of Newark celebrated
what they claimed as a victory. Relations between the civil and
ecclesiastical authorities in the town were still strained and were
obviously going to remain so.[23]

But the chief problem on Longland's mind in the spring of 1536
was that of troublesome preachers. Here again, the Bishop felt at a
disadvantage, for had he not always advocated the need for more
preachers? Had he not tried to raise the educational standards of his
clergy so that at least some members of his large flock might
occasionally receive pulpit instruction from their parish priests,
instead of uncomprehendingly watching them mutter their way
through a Latin mass sabbath by sabbath? But the problem of
improving the parish clergy was almost insoluble. Archbishop Lee
of York, Longland's neighbouring diocesan, had stated the
problem quite clearly in a complaint to Cromwell, recently
appointed Vicar General by the King:

> Many benefices be so poor, £4, £5, £6, that no learned man will take
> them, and therefore we be forced to take such as be presented, as long
> as they be honest of conversation and can competently understand what
> they read and minister sacraments and sacramentals, observing the
> due form and right. .... And in all my diocese I do not know secular

priests that can preach, any number necessary for such a diocese, truly not twelve, and they that have the best benefices be not here resident.[24]

This being the situation Longland had welcomed the King's decision early in 1535 to send out preachers under royal licence. The task of these itinerant sermonizers was to convince the people of the reasons lying behind the royal supremacy and to denounce 'the pretended authority of the bishop of Rome'. However it was one thing to license a preacher and quite another to maintain any control over what he said from distant pulpits. When Longland had learned the names of some of the preachers soon to be touring the dioceses he was appalled. They included such men as Robert Barnes and John Bale, known heretics whose beliefs extended beyond the official repertoire of moderate Henrician reform. Longland knew that he certainly should have protested at the decision to send some of these men into his diocese.

If he did not, it was largely because he wished to avoid incurring the royal displeasure, as Edward Lee of York had done. Lee had shown some hesitation about letting appointed preachers into his diocese. For this and for scant enthusiasm himself in preaching the royal supremacy, he had been bitterly attacked by Cromwell and had had to submit to an examination of his beliefs by the King's visitor, Richard Layton, at the end of 1535. Still Lee had fought for his right to safeguard the orthodoxy of his diocese. In October and November 1535 he pruned out certain preachers, recommended by Cromwell, whose sermons were causing dissension. By the following January he was still not satisfied about the situation:

There is . . . another friar here of the Grey sort, of whom I am now informed, whom I shall . . . discharge. For he preacheth new things and that very slanderously to the offence of the people . . . I admitted some preachers at the request of Dr Brown, who pretended to me that they were discreet and well learned, and should do the King good service. Other preachers of novelties here be none that I know of, nor have been, saving two or three, that pretended to have the King's authority.[25]

So he had written to Cromwell on 24 January 1536, and he had concluded his letter by requesting permission to silence all 'preachers of novelties', even if they had a licence from the King or his Vicar General.

His protest had availed him nothing, for the prevailing wind at the turn of the year was blowing in a different direction. Cromwell paid much closer attention to reports like the following sent to him from York Diocese by Richard Layton:

> I should advise you to set forth the King's authority as Supreme Head by all possible means. There can be no better way to beat the King's authority into the heads of the rude people in the North than to show them that the King intends reformation and correction of religion. They are more superstitious than virtuous, long accustomed to frantic fantasies and ceremonies, which they regard more than either God or their prince. They are completely alienated from true religion.[26]

Nothing could illustrate more clearly the extreme course upon which Cromwell was set. Longland had the same problems in his diocese as Lee had in York – heretics licensed by the King, unlicensed preachers roaming the parishes unchecked, others posing as licensed preachers, rumours circulating of violent reformation to come, all resulting in the spread of heresy and the growth of Catholic resentment on a hitherto unprecedented scale. Yet Longland had failed, once more, to make a stand. He had stood by helplessly, watching the tares of chaos sown in his fields by strangers and enemies.

Indeed, in some ways, Longland had even more cause to complain than Archbishop Lee. There were two preachers touring his diocese in 1535–6 whose influence was particularly insidious. One was Thomas Swynnerton, alias John Roberts, an outspoken, dyed-in-the-wool heretic if ever there was one. Educated at both Oxford and Cambridge he had been studying during the early days of the impact of continental Protestantism. In 1534 he had attracted Cromwell's attention with his book *A Muster of Schismatic Bishops of Rome (otherwise naming themselves popes)*. This treatise went beyond an attack on the papacy and argued that the Word of God alone is necessary to salvation, without all the worldly trappings of traditional Christianity. He asserted that the Christian soul need recognize no other spiritual authority than the Bible. This man travelled widely and rapidly (within the space of a few months in 1536 he appeared in Lincolnshire, Suffolk, Essex and London) disseminating his dangerous doctrines.

The other troublesome preacher was none other than Thomas Garrett with whom Longland had had to deal years before at Oxford. He was still acting as a colporteur of heretical tracts and books as well as preaching novelties. He, too, proceeded on his hortatory way unmolested. He later appeared in Worcestershire, where he enjoyed the protection of the reforming Bishop, Hugh Latimer.

Thus, in May 1536, Bishop John Longland might well reflect, without pride, that for ten years he had stood back and watched his diocese and his country slip into the abyss of religious anarchy and heresy. He had even – always with the best of intentions – contributed to that slippery decline. But now, perhaps, the chance had come to redeem that disastrous decade. Now, at long last, a ray of light had appeared. News had just reached him from London of Anne Boleyn's downfall.

Longland had been at court during the early months of the year when Cromwell, never more sure of himself, had been planning his most audacious coup so far – the seizure of monastic land and wealth for the crown. But those closest to the King, as Longland was, could sense an imminent change. Henry was tiring of his wife. Anne, like her predecessor, had successfully brought forth only one living child – a girl christened Elizabeth. The King was dissatisfied and his first passion had cooled. He realized (did his confessor help him to the realization?) that he had broken relations with Spain, cut his country off from the rest of Christendom, placed himself (once dubbed 'Defender of the Faith' by a flattering Pope) under excommunication and created religious havoc in his country – and all for . . . what? Yet by Easter, when Longland preached before the King, no change had taken place. Shortly after the festival the Bishop had left court to come to his palace at Woburn.

And now, on this his consecration anniversary, the hoped-for news had been brought to him. On the evening of 2 May Anne Boleyn had been arrested and conveyed to the Tower of London. Lodgement in the Tower could mean only one thing. Anne's days as a Queen – and as a mortal woman – were numbered. And if Anne fell, would not Cromwell fall, too? Well, even if he did not, there was a strong chance that he would be forced to modify his policies. Now was Longland's opportunity to rid his diocese of troublesome preachers. And after that, perhaps he could once more take up the sword against heresy, before it was too late. So, the Bishop of Lincoln wrote his long letter, describing the spread of heresy in his diocese, accusing men like Swynnerton of exceeding their commission and asking for redress.

Within a few days the Vicar General's reply arrived. He thanked the Bishop for his letter and would do all in his power to deal with the grievances of which he wrote.[27]

# 3

## Knights Defensive

———✦———

**B**UT there was no Catholic reaction. Henry married another Queen who favoured the new learning, Jane Seymour. Cromwell, after a slight hiatus, pressed on with his policy of reform and, throughout the country tension continued to mount. That tension reached its breaking point in the autumn of 1536. For seven years the mass of England's conservative and Catholic people had borne with decreasing patience the doctrinal and social changes of the official Reformation. They had grumbled against Cromwell, Cranmer and the 'heretical' bishops. They had expressed sympathy for the repudiated Catherine and her bastardized daughter. They had been increasingly alarmed as the threads connecting the English Church with the papacy had been snapped one by one. Many had been appalled by what they considered the blasphemous assertion of royal supremacy. Some had resisted the new doctrine unto death and were secretly revered as martyrs around the simple hearths of the faithful. When Fisher, More and the monks of the London Charterhouse had perished in the summer of 1535, tumultuous indignation had been mingled with the widespread mourning. Yet still there was no organized reaction.

If Conservative forces were slow to gather themselves for resistance there were many reasons for this – not least among which was the simple fear of reprisals. Yet a more fundamental cause of the apparent Catholic lethargy was that it was not until well into 1536 that the full implications of royal supremacy were realized by the English people. Until then, their own lives were little affected by the ecclesiastical changes made by their superiors. The first real warnings came in 1535. In accordance with his new powers as

Vicar General, Cromwell arranged a visitation of all the benefices of the English Church. Between January and September royal commissioners roamed every diocese demanding complete accounts of parish incomes and possessions from the priests and church-wardens. The object of this *Valor Ecclesiasticus* was the accurate assessment of the Church's wealth so that it might be fully and accurately taxed by the government.[1] The unfortunate commissioners charged with this snooping were, for the most part, the leading local gentry. Much of the unpopularity of royal policy rubbed off on to them. The knights and gentlemen of the shires thus found a wedge being driven between them and their people. For many who had a sneaking dislike for the new royal policies, there was also the additional discomfort of a troubled conscience. But the *Valor Ecclesiasticus* was only the beginning. Before all the reports were in, a second visitation had been set afoot. In July specially chosen clerical and lay agents were touring the monastic houses of the realm, enquiring into their spiritual condition – and their wealth.

In market place, church and tavern, men speculated together as to what these investigations might mean. Speculation begat bewilderment and wild rumour: taxes on Church property were to be increased; shrines were about to be despoiled of their jewels and precious metals; royal officers were coming to seize reliquaries, holy statues and the traditional objects of devotion; the King was going to grasp all the land of the monasteries and turn the religious adrift in the world; the very parish churches themselves were in danger. Such rumours bred an atmosphere of tense resentment. Men began to reckon there was a limit to what the King could get away with. If necessary his agents must be prevented from despoiling the churches and depriving the dear departed of the prayers of the monks. For, though bitter criticisms were levelled at the religious by rich and poor alike, there were few who were prepared to see the entire monastic system swept away.

The monastic visitors did not complete their commission until well into 1536 and even then they had scarcely investigated half the religious houses in the realm. The East Midlands were almost entirely by-passed in December 1535 when Richard Layton and Thomas Leigh, Cromwell's agents, sped northwards on a lightning tour of over 120 houses in the Diocese of York. The visitors were back in London by February and from their hastily compiled

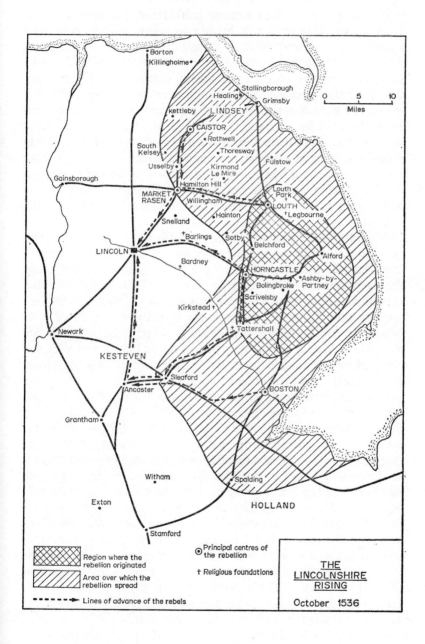

Barton
Killingholme

Stallingborough
Healing
Grimsby

Kettleby
LINDSEY
CAISTOR
Rothwell
Thoresway
South
Kelsey
Usselby
Kirmond
Le Mire
Fulstow
Gainsborough
Hamilton Hill
Louth
Park †
MARKET
RASEN
Willingham
LOUTH
† Legbourne
Snelland
Hainton
† Barlings
Sotby
Belchford
LINCOLN
Bardney †
Alford
HORNCASTLE
Bolingbroke
Ashby-by-
Partney
Scrivelsby
Kirkstead †
† Tattershall
Newark
KESTEVEN
Sleaford
Ancaster
BOSTON
Grantham

Witham
Spalding
Exton
HOLLAND
Stamford

0     5     10
Miles

Region where the
rebellion originated

Area over which the
rebellion spread

Lines of advance of the rebels

⊙ Principal centres of
the rebellion

† Religious foundations

THE
LINCOLNSHIRE
RISING

October 1536

E

evidence, gathered from a mere half of the country's religious foundations, Cromwell was, within ten days, able to compile a damning case against English monasticism. On 11 March 1536, Parliament was asked to approve the dissolution of all the smaller religious houses – those with an annual income of less than £200. Many of the monasteries and nunneries now threatened with extinction were but shadows of their former selves; income was inadequate for the needs of the religious and for the maintenance of the fabric. But others were tiny cells of devoted people living in voluntary poverty. Annual income was clearly no yardstick for measuring spiritual health. Many men knew or suspected the Act for the Dissolution of the Smaller Monasteries for what it was – a first step in the secularization of the Church's wealth by the Crown.

Armed with the assent of Parliament, Cromwell's next move was the despatching of yet another commission. On 24 April, government lawyers and local gentry were appointed as commissioners for each county. They were to make a fresh, more accurate, valuation of the property of the doomed houses. Furthermore, they were to quiz all superiors about the spiritual condition of their brethren: Are there any who wish to forsake the religious life altogether? Would any be prepared to take a benefice as a secular clergyman? Would those maintaining their vows mind being moved to another house of the order? Few of the gentry approached their inquisitorial task with relish. Whatever their complaints and criticisms about the monasteries or their hopes of benefiting from the dissolution, when it came to the point of making recommendations to the government, many commissioners shrank from suggesting the eclipse of a foundation which had been a neighbour of their forefathers for centuries. In the event, the reports which came back to London were far more favourable than Henry would have liked. Many commissioners sent in appeals for the preservation of houses for which they felt a certain responsibility or affection. For this reason some of the monasteries and nunneries were spared. But the visitors were followed after an interval of some weeks by other royal agents who came to receive the submission of doomed houses. The cowled inhabitants passed across their thresholds for the last time. Carts creaked away towards the London road laden with movable spoils. Sounds of hammering and destruction filled the air as lead from the roofs and glass from the windows were systematically removed. And the local people looked on with dismay and apprehension.

Cromwell was far from unaware of the rising tide of discontent; both he and the King took measures designed to stifle criticism during the summer months. The bishops were set to re-define the major doctrines of the Church of England and on 11 July produced ten *Articles of Faith to Establish Christian Quietness*. These 'Ten Articles' had a generally Protestant flavour while yet seeking to offend Catholic feeling as little as possible. In fact, by a mixture of ambiguity and silence they sought to appeal to all. To make sure that they did not become ammunition for rival sermonizers, on the very next day the King forbade all preaching in England (with minor exceptions) until Michaelmas (29 September) and even thereafter all preachers were to shun interpretation of the Articles 'after their fantastical appetites'. Royal injunctions to the parish clergy ordered them to preach four times a year against the usurped authority and false claims of the Bishop of Rome and to teach their congregations to recite the Ten Commandments, the Lord's Prayer and the Creed *in English*. If the Supreme Head of the Church and his Vicegerent in Spirituals thought that these measures would quiet the consciences of all English Christians and stay any rebellious spirits, they underestimated the strength of traditional beliefs and customs in at least some parts of the realm – such as the backward and priest-ridden fenland.

It would be incorrect to view the rebellion in Yorkshire, the so-called Pilgrimage of Grace, as purely and simply an upsurge of militant piety on behalf of the old religion. Unpopular taxes, local and regional grievances, poor harvests as well as the attack on the monasteries and the Reformation legislation all contributed to the creation of a tense atmosphere in many parts of the country. The leaders of revolt were able to pluck many strings of discontent in stirring the commons 'agin the Government'. Although we can distinguish throughout the Pilgrimage as a whole a certain fundamental provincialism striving to make itself heard against the distant incomprehensible yet disturbing policies emanating from the capital, the actual complaints made by the rebels were many and varied. It was this lack of cohesion and clear objectives which was ultimately responsible for the failure of the rebellion.

But when all this has been said it seems clear that the original impetus to rebellion in Lincolnshire was religious. By that I do not mean that England suffered a minor holy war started by intransigent Catholics fighting to preserve specific doctrines and to uphold Papalism or even monasticism. What inspired the Lincolnshire rebels and imparted an odour of sanctity to their proceedings was the need to preserve traditional customs and some of the material trappings of the old religion. The most active agitators in the fenland and the regions bordering it were the parish priests who obviously had a greater stake than the commons in the religious establishment.[2]

Fen and marsh in south and east Lincolnshire formed a very real barrier which largely cut off the men of this area from their neighbours. Parts of the fenland were, indeed, inaccessible to outsiders, since the only approach to them was by sunken causeways across the waterlogged wastes, which were known only to the inhabitants. Not that there were many outsiders who wished to visit the damp and windswept fen. Many shared the view of Walter Graves, a friend of Cromwell's who wrote in 1535 after two years' teaching in Crowland 'the climate is so unwholesome that I would rather die than spend a third summer there'.[3] Patterns of life and thought had changed little over the centuries. It was a land of independent peasant farmers, where feudalism and obedience to social superiors had been virtually unknown. In these flat lands where grey-green fields and straight black dykes met grey skies along a low horizon, the fenlanders were perpetually occupied in a struggle to reclaim saltmarsh from the sea and to keep floodwaters away from their own fields. Yet the living was good; high quality pasturage was plentiful and, as well as relying on their herds and a few crops, the people could turn to the rivers and dykes for food and marketable produce. East and south Lincolnshire was a region 'for fowl and fish exceeding any other in the Realm; wherein at some times and seasons of the year, hath been taken in nets in August at one draught, above three thousand mallards, and other fowls of the like kind'.[4] The wealthy days of Boston and other ports were already passed. The Hanse merchants, discouraged by taxes, restrictions and the growth of the English cloth industry, had, one by one, left the Steelyard. But the region was far from being 'depressed'. Trade in local produce kept the market towns and harbours busy and throughout the villages and towns of the fenland there were, in the magnificent decorated and perpendicular churches,[5] evidences of an affluence that was only slowly fading.[6] There were few gentlemen settled in this area and the leaders of society were the richer yeomen and the priests, almost all of whom were of peasant stock and, to a man, faithful to the old ways.

Their anger had mounted steadily over the months and years since 1529. By the autumn of 1536 there was scarcely any topic of conversation in the villages and towns between Spalding and Grimsby except the new heresies being spread by the King's evil advisers and the rumour, now grown to a certainty, that all churches and abbeys were to be despoiled. Parish priests were agitating their flocks. In some places the coming 'commotion' threw up leaders from among the common people. Messages passed from village to village and a peasant solidarity began to emerge. Merchants whose business took them occasionally across the Humber reported that common feeling was the same in Yorkshire. Thus passed the months of August and September in an atmosphere of growing tension.[7]

Then, in the last days of September, the Lincolnshire men received exasperating news: no less than two new bands of commissioners were on their way. The royal tax-collectors were coming to take up the second part of the subsidy voted in 1534 and Dr Raynes, the Bishop's Chancellor, was about to enquire into the spiritual state of the parish clergy and to read the royal injunctions to them. Now events came rapidly to a head. At Louth feeling ran particularly high. There was agitation at the dissolution of the Cistercian abbey of Louth Park and open demonstrations when the royal agents went on to dispossess the nuns of Legbourne. There were minor clashes between the King's men and the locals but on 21 September many of the commissioners observed St Matthew's Day by attending mass in Louth church. During the service, one of the serving men of the official party remarked loudly that the parish's fine silver alms-dish would be meet for the King's use. It so happened that Louth was the wrong place to make that sort of remark. The churchmen of Louth were more sensitive than most to any threat to the fabric or treasures of their house of worship. Between 1501 and 1515 they and their fathers had toiled, had given, raised and borrowed money to stretch a fine new spire two hundred and ninety-five feet towards Heaven.[8] This was the crowning achievement in the work of rebuilding, redecorating and

re-equipping the church of St James which had occupied the energies
and devotion of two generations of Louth citizens.[9] They were
enormously fond and proud of their church and it is no wonder
that they were violently alarmed at the insinuations of the men
from London.

Michaelmas came and with it the traditional holiday and the
extra services and processions of the Church. The Louth Christians
flocked to their church to gaze with a possessive anxiety upon the
images, the vestments, the reliquaries, the banners and the silver
crosses venerated by generations of their forefathers. As one of the
singing men said, 'Go ye and follow the crosses, for if they be taken
from us, we are like to follow them no more.'[10] On Sunday 1
October, the clergy of the district began to gather in Louth at the
request of the Chancellor who was on his way thither with the
royal commissioner to read the injunctions. The priests encouraged
the townsmen and appeared to give the sanction of Mother Church
to their complaints. Throughout that day crowds gathered and
before nightfall they had chosen a representative to lead them in a
determined resistance to the King's men. At their head was
Nicholas Melton, henceforth to be known as Captain Cobbler. The
people's first concern was for the safety of the church valuables.
They marched to St James's and forced the not-unwilling churchwardens to yield up the vestry keys. The plate and jewels were then
removed to a place where they could be constantly guarded by
armed men. The unpopular Chancellor Raynes, meanwhile, had
failed to appear. Either because of genuine illness or because he
had heard of the disturbances ahead, he had turned off the road at
Bolingbroke, where he found the old royal castle a suitable refuge.

John Heneage, the King's commissioner for the Suppression of
Legbourne Nunnery, was not so fortunate. Riding, unsuspecting,
into Louth on Monday morning with but one servant, he was
suddenly confronted by an angry mob. Setting spurs to their
horses he and his man were able to gain the church and thus,
almost certainly, saved their lives. Even so, they were dragged out
when the citizens arrived and forced to swear an oath of loyalty to
'God, the King and the Commons'. The same fate befell the
Chancellor's trembling Registrar, sent on to Louth ahead of his
master later that day. Next, Heneage was forced to send for all his
men from Legbourne, who were promptly clapped into Louth
prison. When the clergy gathered together it was not to hear the

King's injunctions but to see them publicly burned and to be sworn to the cause of the rebellion. They then hastened back to their parishes to stir up their people. Throughout that day the sound of steeple bells could be heard floating across marsh and meadow as the villagers of first one place then another were summoned to hear their vicars and curates explain the stand that they must take for liberty and for the old religion.

Meanwhile the leaders in Louth decided on their next step – they must secure the support of the gentry. They had little love for the wealthy landed squires, most of whom lived in different parts of the county anyway, but they knew that they would achieve little without experienced leadership when it came to treating with the King and his representatives. They also knew that, left alone, most of the gentry would flock to the support of the government and raise armed men to suppress the rebellion. The coercion of their social superiors was therefore vital.

Many of the leading gentlemen were at that time involved with the subsidy commission. Two groups were, in fact, due to meet the next day (3 October), one at Caistor and one at Horncastle, to collect the tax. Therefore messengers were sent to Horncastle (where, in any case, feelings ran high and the people were already making preparations to raise the standard of revolt) and a body of men made ready to ride out to Caistor early the following day.

At South Kelsey Hall, Sir William Ayscough made ready to meet his fellow commissioners at Caistor. When he heard of the disturbances to the east and south his concern was slight. His own country was fairly quiet, though there were many, as he knew, who resented the changes foisted on them by the government. However, there was nothing new in that. All men had their grievances with the present regime. After four years of wrangling, Parliament had just been induced by the King to pass the Statute of Uses which considerably complicated the purchase and tenure of land from the Crown and from wealthy tenants-in-chief. It paved the way for interminable litigation and made it very difficult for gentlemen to provide for their younger sons. On the whole, however, Sir William favoured the drift of government policy. The dissolution of the lesser houses worried him little and there was the prospect of territorial gain from the sequestered estates. Not that he had as yet made eager suit for land like some of his neighbours.

Indeed, the grasping Edward Skipworth and the Heneage clan had already been rapped over the knuckles for their importunity.[11] Still, he was not without influence at court: even though Sir Robert Tyrrwhit, Sir William's old enemy, held an important position in the King's household, Christopher was in favour at court. Archbishop Cranmer spoke well of Edward and his promotion to the royal service was only a matter of time and opportunity. The Ayscoughs had everything to gain and nothing to lose from stringing along with the Tudor regime.

Sir William did not take religious controversy very seriously. Just as he was tolerant of the opinions held by members of his own family, so he refused to be very alarmed when cases were reported to him of men wrangling in the ale-houses or even coming to blows over doctrinal differences. But serious disturbance of the peace – whether instigated by Catholics or Protestants – was another matter. Men might believe or disbelieve what they liked, but law and order were sacrosanct.[12] When news reached him on Monday evening of the disturbances at Louth he sent out servants with messages to his fellow commissioners suggesting that they should all meet at nine o'clock the following morning at a point a mile outside Caistor to take stock of the situation.

So, on Tuesday morning, the Lindsey commissioners converged on Caistor: Thomas Moigne, Sir William Ayscough's stepson-in-law riding up from Willingham probably in company with Thomas Heneage of Hainton; Sir Edward Maddison, a remarkable octogenarian, had only a mile or so to come from Fonaby;[13] Sir William Ayscough from South Kelsey; Sir Thomas Missenden from Healing and the rest of the company (Lord Burgh, William Dalyson, William Booth and Thomas Partington) travelling up from Kettleby with Sir Robert Tyrrwhit, whose guests they had been overnight. They were all nervous, for they had heard rumours from the troubled area they were approaching. They gathered under the lea of Caistor Hill in the chill of the morning, long before the early mist had dispersed, and pooled their knowledge of the commotion while their horses cropped the grass. The latest news seemed to be that the earlier rumours were grossly exaggerated. However, it was obviously important to find out exactly what was happening in Caistor and so messengers were sent ahead. They quickly reported back that all seemed quiet and that the representatives of the neighbouring wapentakes were waiting to render their subsidy accounts to the commissioners, as they had been ordered. Encouraged, the party set off together up the flank of Caistor Hill. Scarcely had they reached the top when new and much more alarming news reached them. Ten thousand men were marching up from Louth across the wolds and were within a mile or two of Caistor. Moreover, the mood of the town had changed within the last half hour; the commons were out and preparing to welcome the Louth party.[14] The commissioners stopped to take stock once more. For several minutes they debated their best line of action. The delay was to prove disastrous. Some of the gentlemen were in favour of beating a hasty retreat. It was William Dalyson who urged bolder – and apparently wiser – counsels. If they made off without any message to the people of Caistor, he said, they would simply be encouraging the rebels. They would be better advised to go into Caistor, to persuade the commons to disperse before the mob from Louth arrived, and to explain, with as much dignity as they could muster, that the collection of the subsidy would be postponed for the time being. The others saw the need to make some show of authority but were not prepared to expose themselves to the dangers of the town. The commissioners therefore decided to summon representatives out to Caistor Hill and address them where there was a good all-round view and they could not be surprised by the arrival of the Louth men. A messenger was sent into the town and the gentlemen waited – fidgeting and casting anxious glances across the heath to the south-east. After some delay the messenger returned – alone. He had argued with the townsmen but their mood was now truculent and they had sent him back with the answer that they did not choose to come. The dilemma of the gentlemen was now acute. They could either go forward in pursuance of the King's business or they could retreat in the interests of their own safety. They were fortunately saved from an agonizing decision by the arrival of a body of a hundred or so men from Caistor, under the leadership of their chosen captain, George Hudswell, who had thought better of their attitude towards the royal commissioners.

The gentlemen now tried to do their duty boldly and faithfully. Thomas Moigne, their spokesman, explained why the collection of the tax was to be delayed: 'Notwithstanding ... the King's most gracious and favourable goodness there were divers (people) that had unlawfully assembled them together, to what intent we knew not. Wherefore, we intending to avoid the danger of further trouble, would not at that time sit upon the said commission until the King's further pleasure were known therein.'[15] The Recorder then went on to explain that the fears and rumours which had given rise to the commotion were baseless. The people were not going to be overtaxed and would have the opportunity to appeal against their assessment. As for the notion that their churches were about to be despoiled or destroyed, '. . . they might be sure that the King's grace would not do so; he being Supreme Head of the . . . Church might not of his honour see the same Church destroyed . . .'.[16] Moigne talked hard and fast. Gradually he won the commons over. And then, suddenly, a new sound, bursting upon the air, ruined all. The bells of Caistor began to ring, calling the people to join forces with the rebels. An advanced guard from Louth had arrived and all chance of conciliation was lost. Pausing only to make arrangements to meet the next day and to send an urgent message to Lord Hussey, the Lord Lieutenant, the gentlemen set spurs to their horses and fled.

They scattered in all directions. Tyrrwhit and Partington set off in the direction of the former's house at Kettleby. Thomas Moigne attempted to go no further than his bailiff's house at Usselby, where he lay low. Lord Burgh fled to a friend's house and was hidden there. Thomas Heneage reached Hainton but stayed only long enough to have food and collect a fresh horse before putting more ground between himself and the disturbed area. The rest of the commissioners galloped off with Sir William Ayscough towards the stout walls of South Kelsey Hall. Unfortunately, they had left their flight too late.

From the top of Caistor Hill the Louth leaders saw Sir William's party of twenty horsemen speeding westwards. They gave chase and came up with them after a couple of miles. The gentlemen even now might still have made good their escape had not their own servants, emboldened by events at Caistor, forced the party to halt. Sir William Ayscough therefore turned his horse and waited for the rebels' spokesman, William Morland, a dispossessed monk of Louth Park. Morland was clearly uneasy in the role in which the commons had cast him. He spoke civilly – even deferentially – with the august and widely respected Squire of Stallingborough and South Kelsey. He requested that the gentlemen return to Caistor. Sir William was dubious. 'Trowest thou that if I should come

amongst them I should do any good, and be in surety of my life?'
he asked. Morland, anxious to show good faith, replied, 'Let two of
your servants lead me between them, and if they do any hurt to
your person, then let me be the first that shall die.'[17] There was
now a large crowd of horsemen on the narrow road and all eyes
were fixed on the two spokesmen. Taking advantage of the
situation, Thomas Missenden slipped from his horse and slithered
away among the tall gorse bushes covering the heath. He was not
missed until the whole party had turned back towards Caistor and no
search was made for him. So Ayscough, old Sir Edward Madison
and William Booth of Killingholme were led back to Caistor Hill.
There they found the entire hilltop covered with the rebels from
Louth, Caistor and the surrounding countryside. The commons
were rejoicing in the capture of Tyrrwhit and Partington but they
were angry that the other gentlemen – particularly Lord Burgh – had
escaped. So furious were they that they caught hold of one Nicholas
among Sir William Ayscough's party and beat him to death – for no
better reason than that he was a servant of Lord Burgh's.

When these pleasant preliminaries had been concluded Sir
William demanded what the rebels wanted of the gentlemen they
*had* captured. 'First you must be sworn', was the answer. A Bible
was fetched and one of the priests solemnly took the gentlemen's
oath of loyalty to God, the King and the commons. Then,
Morland carefully explained the objects of the commons which the
gentlemen were now sworn to pursue also. The Louth men had had
time to thrash out their demands and they were as follows:

1 The King might enjoy the title of Supreme Head of the English
   Church and that Church should remain severed from the Church
   of Rome *but* the King must promise to suppress no more
   religious houses.
2 The King might have the subsidy voted in 1534 and might
   collect the ecclesiastical revenues of first fruits and tenths *but*
   he must not take any more money from the people.
3 The King must yield up to the commons his evil and heretical
   advisers, namely Cromwell, Cranmer, Longland, Hilsey
   (Bishop of Rochester), Goodrich (Bishop of Ely), Latimer
   (Bishop of Worcester) and Browne (Bishop of Dublin).

Quite simply what the commons wanted was that the gentlemen
should present these demands to the King.

During the afternoon scarcely a half hour passed without the
sound of distant church bells being heard. News came in that one
by one all the towns and villages around were joining the rebellion.
Market Rasen, Grimsby, Fulstow, Kirmond le Mire, Rothwell,
Thoresway, Alford – defection was complete throughout the
eastern parts of the county. And reports coming in from Horncastle – a second centre of the rebellion – were very encouraging to
the commons leaders.

It took no time at all for the five gentlemen at Caistor to decide
that for the moment they were powerless and that their only
possible course of action was to play for time. This they were to do
very successfully for the next ten days. Never for a moment did
Sir William Ayscough and his colleagues sympathize with the
rebels, whom they looked on as a disorganized and presumptuous
rabble. They realized that if they could hold out for long enough,
appearing to take the mob's side, if necessary, then either support
would arrive from the King or impatience, hunger and discord
would whittle away the rebels' resolve.[18]

Meanwhile the leaders had decided to make Louth their temporary headquarters and, late in the afternoon, the gentlemen were
conveyed thither. They received honourable and comfortable
lodging with one of the wealthier citizens – Guy Kyme, a merchant
and member of a very ancient Lincolnshire family. They were glad
to sit down to supper in Kyme's house after a long, wearying day
and would have been even gladder to retire early but Morland and
Captain Cobbler insisted that a letter be sent to the King that
night. The gentlemen thus put their heads together and concocted
the following letter to their sovereign:

> Pleaseth your highness these be to advertise your Grace that this
> third day of October we by the virtue of your gracious commission
> directed unto us for the raising of your second payment of the subsidy
> to your grace granted by Act of Parliament assembled us together at
> the town of Caistor within your county of Lincoln for the execution
> of the same. There were assembled at our coming within a mile of the
> town two thousand of your true and faithful subjects and more by our
> estimation and the reason of their said assembly was, as they affirmed
> unto us, that the common voice and fame was that all the jewels and
> goods of the churches of the country should be taken from them
> and brought to your Grace's Council, and also that your said loving and
> faithful subjects should be subject to new taxes and other importunate

charges, which they were not able to bear by reason of extreme poverty. And upon the same matter they did swear us first to be true to your Grace and to take their parts in maintaining of the commonwealth and so conveyed us with them from the said Caistor unto the town of Louth, twelve miles distant from the same, where . . . we yet remain until they know further of your gracious pleasure. We humbly beseeching your Grace to be gracious both to them and to us to send us your gracious letter of general pardon or else we be in much danger that we be never like to see your Grace nor our own houses, as this bearer can show, to whom we beseech your highness to give further credence. And further your said subjects have desired us to write to your Grace that they be yours – bodies, lands and goods – at all times where your Grace shall command for the defence of your person or your realm.

> Robt Tyrrwhit    William Ayscough
> Edward Madison
> Thomas Partington[19]

It was close on midnight before the message was ready. Then it was committed to John Heneage (still kept in custody at Louth) and Edward Madison to take to London. They rode hard – astonishingly hard when we realize that Madison was in his eighty-second year – and reached court by nine o'clock the following morning. Meanwhile secret messages had been sent by two of the gentlemen who had escaped. From his hiding-place Lord Burgh wrote to the King and to two of the magnates of neighbouring counties who might be able to muster forces – Lord Darcy in Yorkshire and the Earl of Shrewsbury in Nottinghamshire. Thomas Moigne at Usselby sent word to the Lord Lieutenant, Lord Hussey, at Sleaford, who immediately wrote back asking for more information and sent to warn the mayor of Lincoln. It seemed that the delaying tactics of the gentlemen at Louth would bear fruit very swiftly. On 4 October they were able to persuade the commons that it would be treason to take any further action before the King had sent a reply to their letter. Thus, at Louth, the principal centre of the rebellion, the gentlemen had slowly begun to capture the initiative. Unfortunately their work was undone by events at Market Rasen and Horncastle.

Market Rasen had joined in the rising late on the Tuesday and the leading townsmen had organized themselves very quickly. Bands of men had immediately been sent out to raise the neighbouring country. All that evening and the following morning the bells in the villages around had been rung. One party of Market Rasen men had been near South Kelsey when they came up with a serving man, George Eton, wearing the livery of Lord Hussey. They stopped him and forced him to hand over messages he was carrying. When the letters were opened and their contents read, the rebels were filled with alarm. One was a letter from Hussey offering help to Sir William Ayscough and the other was the mayor of Lincoln's reply to Hussey assuring him of the support of the city fathers in staying the revolt. Enraged at the duplicity of Ayscough the party rode up to South Kelsey Hall. There they found Francis, now a young man of about twenty, Thomas, a boy still in his teens, and the women and girls of the household. Dame Elizabeth Ayscough was terrified by the angry words and demands of the men, the more so since she knew that her own servants sympathized with the rebels. The Market Rasen men said that they could not trust Sir William and they therefore intended to take Francis and Thomas with them as hostages. All Elizabeth's pleadings were in vain and at nightfall the young men rode off with the rebels, taking with them the Ayscoughs' most trusted servant, William Bard.

When the party reached Caistor and reported to the commons leaders, there were angry scenes. Some of the rebels were all for killing their three captives on the spot. When wiser counsels had prevailed, the wilder spirits contented themselves with riding over to Willingham the next morning to bring in Thomas Moigne. That unfortunate gentleman had at last arrived home late on Tuesday to find his wife, Bridget, seriously ill. He was now thrown into an agony of indecision. It would be folly to stay at Willingham, yet he could not desert his wife. Apart from sending a letter to Sir William Ayscough asking for advice and help, Moigne did nothing but 'walked up and down in my house . . . until it was seven of the clock.'[20] His hesitation was stupid and, in the opinion of the judge who tried him five months later, criminal. He had still taken no action whatsoever when the large body of men from Market Rasen rode into the courtyard, swore him to their cause using a Bible from his own chapel and took him, with the other prisoners, on to Louth. When the contents of the confiscated letters were reported, there was a fresh outcry of anger and anxiety at Louth. The bell was rung to summon the people and rumours began to fly around that both Hussey and Burgh were on their way with large armies. The rebels decided to organize themselves into an army and pressed the gentlemen to send for their harness and take military command.

The position of the gentlemen was complicated by the news from Horncastle where their counterparts had taken a very different stand. Events had taken a sinister turn there. On 3 October the commons had risen in revolt, choosing Nicholas Leach, parson of Belchford, and his brother William as their leaders. They immediately sent for the subsidy commissioners. The Sheriff, Sir Edward Dymock, was staying at Scrivelsby with his father, Sir Robert Dymock, and his brother Arthur. With them was Nicholas Sanderson of Reasby. These gentlemen, along with Thomas Littlebury and Sir John Coppledyke, showed a remarkable willingness to join with the commons. Sir William Sandon alone among the local gentry had to be forced to make the journey from his home at Ashby-by-Partney to Horncastle. A group of men was sent to Bolingbroke where they swore Chancellor Raynes to their cause. They did not force him to accompany them to Horncastle because he was a sick man.

The next day we find Sir Edward Dymock, the Sheriff, personally taking the lead.[21] Despite his position he seems to have allowed himself to be swayed by his sympathies into making common cause with the rebels. He was devotedly Catholic and so were most of the other gentlemen of the area. Certainly no trace of reluctance can be seen in his attitude towards his role in the rising. His first act was seriously calculated to win the support of an important section of the mob – the clergy. They had been angry and disappointed the previous evening when the deputation had returned from Bolingbroke without Raynes. Dymock now ordered that, ill or not, Raynes should be fetched before him. No sooner had the Chancellor appeared, weak and trembling after his enforced ride, than the crowd, egged on by their priests, who had waited years for this moment, dragged him from his horse and tore him limb from limb. It is difficult to believe that Dymock had not foreseen that something like this would happen. He must, therefore, bear a large share of the blame for this needless brutality. Not content with this, he went on to give the people another taste of blood. A certain Thomas Wolsey, servant to one of the commissioners, was dragged before him and accused of spying. His name and his connections with the court were enough to damn him, and Dymock ordered his immediate execution. Without further delay the mob strung him up to the nearest tree.

But Dymock and the gentlemen had other proof to offer of their wholehearted espousal of the rebels' cause. They had drawn up a list of grievances for presentation to the King. At the muster on Wednesday afternoon the Sheriff, on horseback, brandished the parchment before the crowd and shouted, 'Masters, you see that in all the time we have been absent from you we have not been idle. How like you these articles? If they please you say "yea". If not, you shall have them amended.'[22] Some of the articles were similar to those drawn up at Louth but others clearly reflected the attitude of the gentry. There was a demand for the repeal of the Statute of Uses and the King was bidden to put from him not only 'heretical bishops' but 'low-born ministers', such as Cromwell, Christopher Hales (Master of the Rolls) and Richard Rich (Chancellor of the Court of Augmentations). These articles were warmly received by the commons, though many of them cannot have understood the references to the Statute of Uses and certain members of the Council. The other activities at Horncastle on 4 October included sending a deputation to Lord Hussey at Sleaford and another party to find out what Lord Burgh was doing. Morland, who had ridden down from Louth, was sent back with a copy of the articles.

Meanwhile, Hussey, the one man who should have been doing his utmost to organize opposition on behalf of the King was too agitated and undecided to pursue any coherent line of action. He was in Sleaford with three hundred men at his command but could not decide whether to advance on the rebels, or stay at Sleaford and try to prevent the spread of disaffection, or join up with other loyal forces. If he had struck quickly, he might, even with such a small band of soldiers, have nipped the Horncastle rising in the bud. To stay at Sleaford and do nothing was as good as a signal to the people of Holland that the representatives of law and order were powerless. Baron Hussey's reluctance to move against the rebels is certainly capable of another interpretation, as the government urged at his trial some months later. He was intractably Catholic in sympathies and strongly opposed the religious changes which had largely given rise to the revolt.[23] Yet it is extremely doubtful that he would be foolish enough to allow a sneaking sympathy for the aims of the insurgents to stop him carrying out his clear duty to the King (of whom he was an old and trusted servant). By the evening

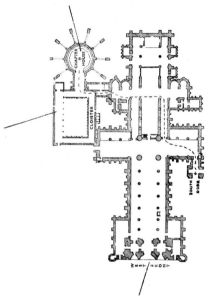

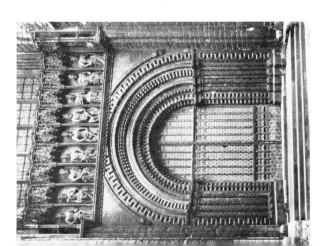

Lincoln Cathedral, to illustrate the events of October 1536.

Centres of the Lincolnshire Rising. St James's, Louth, showing the great spire, and one of the church's treasures, the Sudbury Hutch, with its carved portraits of Henry VII and his Queen.

*Below:* St Mary's, Horncastle, and *(left)* the scythe blades said to have been used in the rebellion.

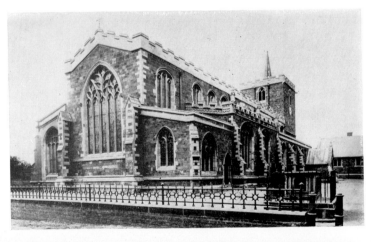

of the fourth the insurrection had spread over a wide area of the
fenland. When the deputation from Horncastle arrived at Sleaford,
Hussey refused to join the commons but also made no pretence of
his inability to stop the revolt.

At Louth the position of the gentlemen was becoming precarious.
Sir William Ayscough was able to persuade the commons that he
had not been in contact with Lord Hussey but a group of twelve
men was nevertheless chosen by the commons' leaders to ride to
Sleaford to discover exactly what the Lord Lieutenant was doing.
In the afternoon the gentlemen were forced against their will into
dividing the host into wapentakes, a commissioner in charge of
each. They were then required to send for weapons to arm the
contingents. Now the whole host was restless to be on the move
and only with the utmost difficulty could the gentlemen restrain
them. When Morland returned from Horncastle with news of how
the commissioners there had wholeheartedly taken up the commons' cause, suspicion broke out afresh that the Lindsey gentlemen were playing them false. As night fell there was an ugly mood
throughout the town and the camps outside the town. At midnight
a false alarm spread that the gentlemen had betrayed them and
escaped. Before the rumour could be scotched someone had fired a
beacon on the nearby heath. Within the hour answering fires
blazed up and down the countryside. By the morning of 5 October
all of eastern Lincolnshire was up from the Humber to the
Wash.

As fresh contingents continued to pour into the two main
centres, the hosts of Louth and Horncastle moved west towards
Lincoln. On the evening of 5 October the Louth insurgents met
with other groups on Hamilton Hill just outside Market Rasen.
By nightfall this part of the rebel army totalled ten thousand men.
The Horncastle host moved like a mighty band of solemn pilgrims
along the edge of the fen. They had made themselves a large
banner symbolizing their pious intentions and this now fluttered
before them as they marched. The dedicated host called at the
abbeys of Kirkstead, Bardney and Barlings and forced the superiors to provide them with food and men. Edward Dymock sent a
message to Dean Heneage[24] at Tattershall College to send him
food and money.[25] The next day he summoned the Boston host to
join him at Ancaster on 8 October. Dymock had clearly cast himself in the role of leader of the revolt – but he had yet to meet up

F

with the Lindsey gentlemen who viewed the whole undertaking in a very different light.

They, meanwhile, were marching from Market Rasen to Lincoln at the head of an unruly and already divided host. There were arguments all the way along the road. The Louth leaders disagreed not only with the gentlemen but also among themselves about the best course of action. At Lincoln they found that someone at least had made careful preparations. Guy Kyme had arranged for some pieces of artillery to be brought from Grimsby. Having reached the county town the commons found looting and other diversions to occupy them for a few hours. Longland's palace, though already in a semi-derelict state, was completely ransacked.

News had reached the court on the morning of the fourth and the King hurriedly sent relays of messengers to the troubled area to report on the situation while at the same time trying to organize military resistance. To reconnoitre he chose members of his court who came from Lincolnshire and the surrounding area. Thus, late on 4 October, John Heneage was sent back with Robert Tyrrwhit the younger and Sir Marmaduke Constable of Yorkshire. They reached Sleaford on Thursday afternoon, found the whole area hostile and Hussey completely hemmed in. Constable went on into his own county to see what was happening there, while the two Lincolnshire men sped back to London. Twenty-four hours later Christopher Ayscough, Sir William's second son, reached Spalding whither he had been sent by Cromwell. By that time the situation had deteriorated much further as his alarming report showed. He reckoned that there were forty thousand rebels in Lincolnshire and that the movement was in danger of spreading southwards. 'About Stamford, Spalding and Peterborough they are very faint in rising against the rebels.' Only the persuasions of Sir John Harrington of Exton had eventually brought to the surface the loyalty of the Lincolnshire–Rutland–Leicestershire–Peterborough border region.[26] Christopher reported that many people felt that now that the rebellion had started they must support it for fear of universal reprisals if it should fail. 'For it is reported that they shall pay a third part of their goods to the King and be sworn what they are worth, and, if they swear untruly, other men will have their goods.' In his opinion, Hussey was by now in a hopeless position; his tenants would not support him and it would only be a matter of time before he was captured by the Horncastle host.[27]

In this conjecture Christopher Ayscough was wrong. That very night (6 October) Hussey escaped from Sleaford disguised as a priest. He left his departure almost too late for within hours a party of five hundred men arrived from Lincoln to bring him in. They were led by Sir Christopher Ayscough of Ashby near Louth.[28] He was a distant relative of Sir William of South Kelsey and differed from him in both religious and political views. As one of the gentlemen who enthusiastically took up the rebels' cause, he found it very difficult to ingratiate himself with the King after the failure of the rising. Learning that the bird had flown, Sir Christopher frightened Lady Hussey into riding after her husband to persuade him to return to Sleaford. When she found him the next day he refused to go back. During the past week he had received increasingly strongly worded notes from George Talbot, Earl of Shrewsbury and Lord Steward of England who seriously doubted Hussey's loyalty. The last message had been virtually an order to report to Nottingham, where Shrewsbury was mustering all loyal men of the Midlands. The Lord Lieutenant dared not refuse this summons.

Shrewsbury did his best to make the forces mustering for the King sound impressive. In fact they constituted scarcely any less of a disorganized rabble than the rebel army. The Earls of Rutland and Huntingdon were also gathering their forces at Nottingham. At Stamford Sir John Russell, Sir William Parr and Sir Francis Brian were mustering support. Small detachments led by Richard Cromwell and Sir William Fitzwilliam were making their way up from the south. The King had chosen Charles Brandon, Duke of Suffolk and Thomas Howard, Duke of Norfolk to lead the royal forces and they were now on their way towards the troubled area. By 8 October, when all the Lincolnshire hosts met at Lincoln, the situation was critical. Yorkshire was known to be restless. The rebels held the initiative and their forces were united in one place. The loyalty of the men being pressed into service by the government was far from certain. Discontent with Cromwell's religious policy was widespread and there was no knowing whether it would flame out into open rebellion. Never had Henry VIII's throne been less secure.

Early on Sunday 8 October Dymock's men met up with the Holland host and they all immediately turned for Lincoln. If the Sheriff had remained in control and made his headquarters at

Ancaster, the outcome of the rebellion might well have been different. Under his determined leadership the commons might have
maintained the initiative and struck boldly at the disorganized
royal forces. Once Dymock reached Lincoln and came into contact
with the moderate and essentially loyal gentlemen of Lindsey, his
cause was lost. For the moment, however, everything seemed to be
playing into the hands of the extremists. The combined forces at
Lincoln were anxious to be on the move. Then, on Sunday
evening, a message came from Beverley, brought by one William
Woodmansay. It pledged the commons of south-east Yorkshire to
the support of the rebellion. Later on two men from Halifax rode
in with a similar message. This support excited the commons more
than ever and they clamoured for action.

Meanwhile the gentlemen were in conference together. They
had obtained lodgings in the cathedral close on the hill above the
town where the commons were staying. Dymock and his supporters
among the gentlemen were thus divided from the host and had to
face alone the angry remonstrances and stern warnings of Sir
William Ayscough and the Lindsey gentlemen. They argued
earnestly and angrily for hours. Ayscough repeatedly stressed that
it would be treason to advance before the King's reply had been
received. Dymock pointed out that the King had had plenty of
time to answer the commons' demands and had done nothing. At
length the extremists agreed to help restrain the host if a new set of
articles was sent to London. So a fresh list of demands was drawn
up and despatched by one George Staines. It was only with the
greatest difficulty that the gentlemen were able to persuade the
commons to accept their decision. In fact they had to be bribed:
the gentlemen agreed to let them spoil and loot the property of
anyone who would not join the host. So matters rested on Sunday
evening but the situation was so uneasy that the gentlemen thought
it prudent to spend part of Monday putting the late chancellor's
house in a state of defence, in case of a possible attack from the
city.

On Tuesday 10 October exaggerated reports of the royal musters
reached Lincoln. The commons grew agitated and the gentlemen
were in serious danger of being attacked. Fear of the mob broke
down the final barriers between the extremists and moderates
within the close; 'all the gentlemen and honest yeomen of the
county were weary of this matter, and sorry for it, but durst not

disclose their opinion to the commons for fear of their lives'.[29] When they heard that the Duke of Suffolk had reached Stamford, the men of Sleaford and the southern parts of the county wanted to go home before they found themselves in serious trouble. Many contingents began to drift away.

The real crisis for the gentlemen came about midday. From Stamford, Brandon forwarded the long-awaited royal reply to the rebels' demands, together with other letters demanding the immediate help of the Lincolnshire gentlemen in suppressing the rebellion. The letters were delivered to the gentlemen in the chapter house and crowds of rebels crammed in demanding to have them read out immediately. The gentlemen, therefore, had no chance to look over the royal message and decide how to present it to the people. The papers were thrust into the hands of the unfortunate Thomas Moigne while the evil-smelling crowd pressed close upon him, some peering over his shoulder to see for themselves the words of their King. The royal message was far from concilatory:

> Concerning choosing of Councillors, I never have read, heard, nor known that Princes' Councillors and Prelates should be appointed by rude and ignorant common people; nor that they were persons . . . of ability to discern and choose suitable Councillors for a Prince. How presumptuous then are ye, the rude commons of one shire, and that one of the most brute and beastly of the whole realm, and of least experience, to find fault with your Prince, for the electing of his Councillors and Prelates; and to take upon you contrary to God's law, and man's law, to rule your Prince, whom ye are bound by all laws to obey, and serve, with . . . your lives, lands, and goods, . . . you, like traitors and rebels have behaved, and not like true subjects, as ye name yourselves.
>
> As to the suppression of religious houses and monasteries . . . know what unkindness and unnaturalness may we impute to you, and all our subjects, that be of that mind, that had rather such an unthrifty sort of vicious persons should enjoy such possessions, profits, and emoluments, as grow of the said houses, to the maintenance of their unthrifty life: than We, your natural Prince, Sovereign Lord, and King, which doth and hath spent more in your defences, of his own, than 6 times what they be worth.
>
> As touching the Act of Uses, We marvel what madness is in your brain, or upon what ground ye would take authority upon you, to cause Us to break those laws and statutes, which, by all the Nobles,

Knights, and Gentlemen of this realm, whom the same chiefly toucheth, hath been granted and assented to; seeing in no manner of thing it toucheth you, the base commons of our realm. . . .

As touching the subsidy, which ye demand of Us to be released, think ye that We be so faint hearted, that, perforce, ye of one shire (were ye a great many more) could compel Us with your insurrections, and such rebellious demeanour, to remit the same? or think ye that any man will or may take you to be true subjects, that first maketh a show of a loving grant, and then, . . . would compell your Sovereign Lord and King to release the same. . . .

And thus We pray unto Almighty God to give you grace to do your duties, and to use your selves towards Us, like true and faithful subjects, so as We may have cause to order you thereafter; and rather obediently to consent amongst you, to deliver into the hands of our Lieutenant 100 persons, to be ordered according to their transgressions at our will and pleasure rather than by your obstinacy and wilfulness to put yourselves, lives, wives, children, lands, goods, and chattels, besides the indignation of God, in the utter adventure of total destruction, and utter ruin by force and violence of the sword.[30]

It is scarcely surprising that Moigne's firm voice, reverberating among the vaults and columns of the chapter house, suddenly faltered on reaching one of these passages or that he tried to gloss over the King's anger and to read from a different part of the letter. The Vicar of Snelland was standing at his elbow following every damning word with a keen eye. As soon as he saw the Recorder's deception, he snatched the letter and brandishing it aloft raised the cry of treachery. There was uproar for several minutes. Swords were drawn and several men were for killing the gentlemen on the spot. Only when these wilder elements had been pushed out into the cloisters was order restored to the meeting. An angry and frightened assembly then heard the unexpurgated text of the King's letters from the lips of the parson of Snelland. The commons were stunned and the meeting broke up in confusion.

Meanwhile the frustrated and angry troublemakers who had been pushed out of the chapter house had decided to carry out their plan to kill the gentlemen. They sauntered round to the main door and stood on the steps below the rows of carved saints in the west façade, as the commons poured out, talking together in agitated groups. Their hands were ready on their sword hilts as they waited for the gentlemen to follow. No one took any notice of the would-be assassins except one alert by-stander, a servant, who realized what their plans were. He hurried back into the cathedral, pushing through the emerging crowd, and went quickly to the chapter house. His master was still talking with other gentlemen but broke off to hear the man's tidings. Something of this sort had not been unexpected and it did not take the gentlemen long to decide what to do. Leaving the chapter house they passed into the cathedral. They moved swiftly through the chapels to the north of the chancel and reached the massive shrine of St Hugh, glimpsing the rich gleam of gold and silver within as they hurried on. They gained the south transept without arousing suspicion and were quickly through the south door, across the close and safely locked and bolted within the chancellor's house before their enemies realized what had happened. They were in no doubt now about their course of action. They had two objectives only – one was to stay alive and the other was to make their submission to the King as soon as possible. They immediately sent a message to Suffolk beseeching him to intercede with the King for a pardon for themselves and the rebels.

As for the host, their zeal and numbers were beginning to diminish. The corrosives of hunger and fear had already eaten into their ranks. Some of the rebels had crept away to their homes or into hiding. Many of the yeomen and lesser gentry had gone off to join the King's forces. The process of disintegration was accelerated on Wednesday morning when the gentlemen rode out from the close to meet the host in the fields. They took advantage of the prevailing confusion and disillusionment to make it clear that they would not stir without a reply from the King to their request for pardon. There were still firebrands among the crowd who tried to stir the people up but most of the rebels realized that without the leadership of their wapentake captains they were powerless. The gentlemen were thus able to return to their fortified lodgings unmolested.

In the evening Thomas Miller, Lancaster Herald, arrived with a proclamation from the Lord Steward, Talbot. He spent the night in the close and the gentlemen were able, at last, to obtain fairly accurate information about the royal forces. The moderates knew that their delaying tactics were on the verge of success and their only problem – albeit a large one – was whether they could persuade the King that they had acted honourably and loyally. The following morning the rebels were ordered to come up the hill to listen to Lancaster Herald read the proclamation from the castle garth. In sullen silence they heard Shrewsbury's message that they were to disperse immediately, every man to his own home. After desultory argument and a vain attempt by William Leach to whip up resistance, the commons agreed to disband.

The gentlemen wrote out a formal submission to Suffolk in which they asked whether they should stay where they were or come to Stamford with armed men. The document was carried by Edward Dymock accompanied by his father and brother. The Dymocks clearly had the greatest need to make personal submission and cast themselves on the royal clemency. They reached Stamford at midnight on the twelfth and Brandon saw them immediately. In his reply to the formal submission he told the men at Lincoln that they must use their own discretion about whether to stay or move. He could only hold them on surety until he knew his royal master's gracious pleasure. He immediately sent a messenger to London with a list of the gentlemen who had surrendered. He reported to the King that in his opinion they had all acted as loyally as their difficult circumstances permitted.

On 13 October the remainder of the host drifted away from Lincoln. Word was sent to Beverley informing the Yorkshiremen of the sadly altered state of affairs. The men of Horncastle trooped disconsolately home to put their superfluous banner in the church. The city and the county waited anxiously for the royal reaction.

Four days later the Duke of Suffolk rode into Lincoln having waited to receive fresh orders from the King. The people turned out to watch him and his men clatter through the streets but they did not come to show respect. Brandon complained that very few of the citizens raised their bonnets to him. It was soon obvious that the country was far from quiet. During the next few days he examined the gentlemen and sent most of them home 'with good words'. But he had clear instructions to send to London any whose conduct seemed suspicious and that meant that Henry wanted one or two notable scapegoats. He had also fixed on the arbitrary figure of one hundred of the commons who were to be executed.

In the singling out and punishment of offenders during the next five months, it was expediency and not justice which prevailed. The King was more interested in making an example of a certain number of rebels than in winkling out all the ringleaders. Furthermore, he had no desire to decimate the ranks of the gentry upon whom his government relied so heavily. Added to these considerations of policy was a much more pressing one. Lincolnshire was still in an ugly mood and by 16 October Yorkshire was in open revolt. Norfolk and Shrewsbury hastened northwards with thirty-eight thousand men leaving Suffolk with only a small force. He simply dared not risk provoking Lincolnshire into a fresh uprising by undue severity. On 19 October Brandon received instructions from the King, who needed all the men and weapons he could muster, to tell the gentlemen that all who flocked to the royal banner would be spared bodily harm. Many of them hastened to raise men and harness and speed northwards. The Dymocks and others who knew themselves to be particularly vulnerable were doing all in their power to avert calamity. This included disposing of any who might testify against them. Edward Dymock presented one such to Suffolk as a traitor and suggested his immediate execution. A few of the commons' ringleaders, including Captain Cobbler, were swiftly captured and hung but other offenders were rounded up slowly and imprisoned in Lincoln or sent to London. The only gentlemen to be arrested were Hussey and Moigne. By 26 October a hundred and forty prisoners were detained at Lincoln. On 14 November those still at liberty were at last released from their suspense when a general pardon was issued to all except the prisoners.

The captives were kept awaiting trial until the following spring when a commission presided over by Sir William Parr came to Lincoln for the purpose. One hundred prisoners who had survived a winter in Lincoln Castle's dungeon were examined and found guilty. All their property was confiscated but the lives of sixty-four of them were spared. The only notable trial was that of Thomas Moigne. Being a lawyer, he defended himself very skilfully but, of course, to no avail. The report sent to Cromwell reveals all too clearly what was meant by 'justice' in those cases where the King had a particular interest: '. . . for three hours Moigne held plea with such subtle allegations, that if Sergeant Hinde and the Soliciter had not acquitted themselves like true servants to the King and profound learned men, he had troubled and in a manner evict all the rest' (i.e. he would have disturbed or even convinced the other commissioners).[31] On 7 March Thomas Moigne was hung, drawn and quartered at Lincoln. The remaining offenders were executed at the next market days, some at Horncastle (9 March) and some at

Louth (10 March). Twelve men were tried in London on 26 March and executed at Tyburn on 29 March. Sir William Hussey had been freed after an examination at Windsor in October 1536 but the government found cause to arrest him again the following May. On the fifteenth he was tried at Westminster with his old friend Lord Darcy, who had been implicated in the Yorkshire rebellion, the Pilgrimage of Grace. He was beheaded – probably at Tyburn – in June.[32]

When we examine the list of those who were finally executed for complicity in the Lincolnshire Rising, we find on it few of the real ringleaders and an appreciable number who were either scapegoats or were included for reasons of state. The Dymocks escaped scot free, as did the Littleburys and Coppledykes, who were involved with them in leadership of the Horncastle host. Moigne and Hussey were foolish and inept, but they were not traitorous. If the Pilgrimage of Grace had not occurred, probably no Lincolnshire gentry would have suffered. The element of high-born leadership in the northern rising had been pronounced and by the spring of 1537 Henry VIII, ever sensitive to the danger of over-mighty subjects, felt the time had come for another demonstration. Henry needed the nobility and gentry of the shires, and his government was always reluctant to prosecute members of the upper class, but the troubles of 1536 had taught him the necessity of dividing them as much as possible from the common people.

Of the others who paid with their lives for the Rebellion, the fate of some was just; Captain Cobbler, Guy Kyme, Nicholas and William Leach, William Morland, Brian Staines (the instigator of Dr Raynes' murder) were among those who deserved harsh sentences. Others, by any modern criteria, did not merit death. Robert Harrison, Abbot of Kirkstead, was executed with three of his monks. Matthew Mackerell, Abbot of Barlings and four of his canons met the same fate, as did six monks of Bardney. It is clear now, and it was clear at their trials in 1537, that the religious only took a very limited part in the Rising and only had anything to do with it at all because they were coerced by the mob. But the monasteries were under a cloud in the time of the rebellion and the conviction of abbots for treason paved the way very conveniently for confiscation of the lands and property belonging to their abbeys.

And so Lincolnshire expiated its sins with the lives and goods of fifty or more of its people, accepted the religious changes imposed by the King, settled back into the seasonal routine and tried to remember 'the commotion time' as nothing more than a bad dream. Some of the gentry families were under a cloud for a while and some never regained favour as long as the King lived (the Ayscoughs seem to have fallen into this category).[33] Others recovered remarkably quickly and began profiting from the religious changes of the ensuing three years. Sir William Tyrrwhit, the new Sheriff, craved the, by no means inconsiderable, goods of Guy Kyme as recompense for expenses incurred during the Rising. John and Thomas Heneage received rich rewards for their services (which seem to have amounted to little more than escaping from the rebels' clutches). As the lands of first the lesser and then the greater monasteries came on the market these two families were able to acquire vast estates.[34] Almost all the gentlemen who profited from the Dissolution were those who had not had the misfortune to become involved with the rebels in October 1536 – the Harringtons, Skipworths, St Pauls and Carrs, to mention only a few. Two noblemen rose to prominence in Lincolnshire in the years after the Rising. One was Edward Fiennes de Clinton, Lord Clinton and Saye who acquired large estates in the Horncastle area. The other was Charles Brandon, Duke of Suffolk. He had recently married Catherine Willoughby, the heiress of Lord Willoughby d'Eresby, and thus obtained her lands in Lincolnshire. He received grants of monastic land from the King and was also forced by Henry to exchange some of his estates in Suffolk for land in Lincolnshire. Brandon made his home at Grimsthorpe in 1537 and became the most powerful man in the county.

The business of 'settling scores' went on for some time. The knights and squires of Lincolnshire did not bear the brunt of royal disfavour without in turn venting *their* anger on their tenants, who had been responsible for their embarrassment. But time healed all wounds. Cromwell was able to press on with more extreme measures of reformation in the years 1537–40. The conservative forces had shot their bolt in 1536 and he had little thereafter to fear from the agents of conservative reaction. Nevertheless he kept a sensitive finger on the pulse of the nation and particularly of the troubled areas. On 15 February 1539 John Marshall, one of his agents, reported from Lincolnshire:

> . . . the great ruffling is past and poor men may now live at peace by the great men. When they hear of papists' enormities to be redressed,

they whisper a little, but it is soon forgotten. People come reasonably well forward in the English paternoster since the uniform translation came down. Abbeys are now nothing pitied; the commons perceiving more common wealth to grow from their suppression, saving that they lose their prayers. ... Some men of reputation keep the days abrogated work days [i.e. saints days and festivals removed from the calendar], but many of the poor will not labour of those days as yet. Our valiant beggars be gone and unlawful games with them, except that in some alehouses men play at shuffleboard in default of the constables. The highways be cried out upon; every flood makes them impassable.[35]

The pulse rate was almost back to normal: the patient was responding to treatment.

# 4

# *Pawns in the Game*

———

THE summer sunlight streaming into one of the more comfortable chambers of the Tower of London was of no consolation to the well-dressed but dishevelled prisoner who sat one day in June 1540, scrawling a desperate letter to the King.

> Mine accusers your Grace knoweth. God forgive them. For as I ever had love to your honour, person, life, prosperity, health, wealth, joy and comfort, and also your most dear and most entirely beloved son, the Prince his Grace, and your proceedings, God so help me in this mine adversity, and confound me if ever I thought the contrary. What labours, pains and travails I have taken according to my most bounden duty God also knoweth. For if it were in my power – as it is in God's – to make your Majesty to live ever young and prosperous, God knoweth I would. If it had been or were in my power to make you so rich as ye might enrich all men, God help me . . . I would do it. If it had been or were in my power to make your Majesty so puissant as all the world should be compelled to obey you, Christ he knoweth I would . . . Sir, as to your common wealth, I have ever after my wit, power and knowledge travailed therein, having had no respect to persons (your Majesty only excepted) . . . but that I have done any injustice or wrong wilfully, I trust God shall be my witness, and the world not able justly to accuse me . . .[1]

The doomed writer was the one man whom half the people of England had longed – yet not dared hope – to see brought low. Until a few days previously he had seemed the most secure man in the realm. Now his titles and honours – Earl of Essex, Vicegerent in Spirituals and Vicar General, Royal Secretary, Keeper of the Privy Seal, Chancellor of the Exchequer, etc., etc., had been snatched from him, leaving him only with the names his parents had given him fifty-five years before – Thomas Cromwell.

Cromwell was hated in his lifetime as an upstart and a heretic who used his influence with the King to sweep away valued old institutions and limit the power of the traditional leaders of society. He has been accused by generations of later historians as an unprincipled Machiavellian, who subjected everything, including his conscience, to the empowering and enriching of his sovereign. These views have been modified in recent years and Thomas Cromwell has now emerged as a most remarkable phenomenon.[2] He had his faults, among which were an indifference amounting to callousness and a determination to pursue his policies with scant regard for humane considerations. But few rulers of England have been served by as devoted a minister and none by a more able administrator. Thomas Cromwell carried through in ten brief years a truly remarkable social, economic and governmental revolution for which there are few parallels in the history of this or any other modern nation. He made an efficient reality of centralized royal government, all-powerful in Church and State.

To watch this man at work, to read his voluminous correspondence, to study the reports of his agents – carefully preserved and filed in Mr Secretary's office – is to realize that he was the perfect civil servant, working calmly, efficiently, not tolerating muddle or failure in his subordinates, always clarifying, simplifying, improving, always fully informed of current events in Church and State. Let us, then, observe this master player, vigilantly crouched over the chess board of England, moving his pawns hither and thither, in pursuance of his grand strategy. Let us see how Thomas Cromwell continued and largely completed the work of reformation in the Church during the three and a half years following the Lincolnshire Rebellion and the Pilgrimage of Grace. We shall see that the boast underlying his abject appeal from the Tower was a true one. More than any man in England Cromwell took 'labours, pains and travails' for his King.

It seems clear that Thomas Cromwell was, in the strictest sense of the word, a Protestant. Much of Luther's teaching appealed to him and although he always had to be cautious in giving expression to his beliefs, he certainly patronized known heretics and 'preachers of novelties'. If we seek to define just what Cromwell did believe, we observe clear elements of rationalism and Erastianism in his Protestantism. He believed, as did all loyal and educated Englishmen, that 'the contempt of human law, made by rightful authority, is to be punished more heavily and more seriously than any transgression of the divine law'.[3] The strife resulting from the overlapping authority of Church and State, could only be finally stifled by making the King supreme in ecclesiastical affairs. Such a sweeping diminution of the authority of the Church could only be accompanied and supported by radical changes in the doctrines which had supported medieval Catholicism. Cromwell naturally inclined, therefore, to the rationalism of the humanists and reformers who sought to redefine completely the life and beliefs of the Church in accord with those principles which stood clearly revealed in the pages of post-Vulgate Bible translations. Cromwell's religion has long been the subject of debate among historians. The truth undoubtedly lies somewhere between the view that the Vicar General was a cynical, time-serving politician who cared nothing for spiritual values and the eulogy of John Foxe, who saw in Cromwell 'a valiant soldier and captain of Christ'. He had a layman's dislike of the traditional power and wealth of the Church and of the superstition that often passed for devotion among the simple. He befriended many reformers and extended his protection to critics of the ecclesiastical establishment. If he sought to restrict the temporal power of the higher clergy it was in order to recall them to their spiritual functions as well as to strengthen the authority of the Crown. We need not suspect Cromwell of hypocrisy when, in 1538, he responded to an ecclesiastical critic, 'I do not cease to give thanks that it hath pleased God's goodness to use me as an instrument and to work somewhat by me, so I trust I am as ready to serve Him in my calling as you are.'[4]

As far as the work of reformation was concerned, Cromwell had a twofold objective. He wanted to make his royal master all-powerful in the Church. He wanted to achieve that thorough-going reorganization of the machinery and doctrines of the Church which many of its leaders realized was long overdue, but which they were quite unable to bring about. We of the mid-twentieth century are perhaps in a position to sympathize with Cromwell's intolerance of ecclesiastical inefficiency and muddle. We, too, live in an age when most of our churches are self-perpetuating institutions out of touch with the mass of the people, yet incapable of radical change. The ranks of the clergy and laity are sprinkled with critics and frustrated reformers who long to see their denominations as spiritual and evangelizing forces in the world. But the hierarchies are only capable of producing reports and passing resolutions. Cromwell's tidy mind intended to sweep away muddle and enforce reforms from without.

The first of Cromwell's aims – that of making the King all-powerful in the Church in England – had largely been attained by 1537 and the failure of the conservative rebellions served to cement it. The second objective – that of complete reformation of organiz-ation and doctrine – would obviously take much longer to achieve. The Vicar General set about the task methodically; his *modus operandi* had both its negative and positive aspects. On the negative side Cromwell had to destroy resistance and disarm criticism. This he did by dissolving the remaining abbeys which were the main centres of conservative reaction, by seeking out and prosecuting ardent papists and by removing from churches objects of super-stition and popular devotion – objects which were ever present reminders of the old religion. Positively, he worked with Cranmer and the bishops to redefine the major articles of faith, he exhorted the parish clergy to educate their congregations in Christian fundamentals, he licensed preachers to tour the dioceses with reformed doctrines, and he caused the English Bible to be opened to all who could read it for themselves and who could, in their turn, instruct the illiterate from its pages.

To pursue this policy in a realm still essentially conservative called for a large army of Cromwellian agents. Preachers and sympathetic clergy made up a part of this army but there was still a need for secular representatives of the royal authority. There was no paid civil service in Tudor England. Instead, Cromwell relied in part upon servants and agents in his own employ and in part upon that large band of unpaid officials who served the Crown because they hoped for reward thereby and because they had a stake in the Tudor peace – the landed gentry. To see how the Vicar Gen-eral's policies were carried out in practice, let us follow the course of reformation in one of England's shires – the county of Nottingham, where Sir John Markham and his colleagues bore sway.

Thomas Cromwell, *after Holbein*, and a contemporary painting 'The Evangelists Stoning the Pope', which illustrates something of the passions roused by the Reformation, *by Girolamo da Treviso*.

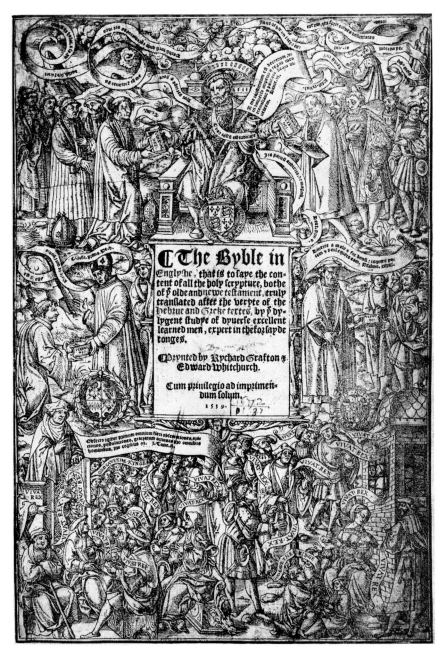

The title page from the Great Bible of 1539. Henry gives Bibles to Cranmer and Cromwell (top), who distribute them to the people (middle). Lower down, a picturesque group of laity cry out 'Vivat Rex' and 'God Save the King'.

First of all let us meet the prominent gentlemen of Nottingham-shire. Sir John Markham we have encountered already but only as a thorn in the flesh of the Bishop of Lincoln. He was in fact the most important single figure below the rank of nobleman through-out most of the county and the bordering regions of Lincolnshire. John Marshall reported to Cromwell – unnecessarily – in 1539, 'the parts of Nottinghamshire and Lincolnshire adjoining Newark upon Trent are much ruled by one Sir John Markham'.[5] He was a descendant of another Sir John Markham, Chief Justice of England (1460–1469) who died at a ripe old age in 1479. The family was an ancient one in Nottinghamshire as the names of villages in the East Retford area (East Markham, Markham Clinton, etc.) testify, but the principal family seat at Cottam was brought into the family by the Judge on his marriage to Margaret Leke. The grandson of the Chief Justice – another Sir John – married Alice, daughter of Sir William Skipworth of South Ormsby, Lincolnshire.[6] The eldest son of this marriage was the John Markham with whom we are con-cerned. He spent some years at the court of the young King Henry VIII before returning to Cottam in the mid-1520s to take over the family responsibilities in the county on the death of his father. He was summoned to Westminster as M.P. for Nottingham in the Reformation Parliament and served as Sheriff of Nottinghamshire in 1532, 1534, 1538 and 1545. As well as Cottam, Sir John held important estates at Southwell, Sedgebrook (Lincs) and in many parts of Nottinghamshire. His two marriages were with daughters of other wealthy families in the county and these further increased his landed wealth.

The Babingtons were an ancient family with extensive lands in Derbyshire and Nottinghamshire. In the 1530s the head of the clan was Sir Anthony Babington, who resided at Dethick, Derbyshire. He had four children who survived to adulthood but only one of them appears in this narrative. John was born about 1512. As a younger son, he had to seek his fortune away from home. Perhaps he spent some time at one of the universities or inns of court. If so, no record now remains. Certainly he came under the influence of the new religious doctrines circulating among educated people and certainly he eventually found a patron among the noblemen who thronged the royal court. It was as an ambitious young man favourable to religious change that he attracted the notice of Thomas Cromwell about 1536. Cromwell always found it useful

G

to have about him men from the shires, who knew their own country intimately. From about this time John Babington's name begins to figure on various lists of commissioners in Nottingham-shire. Here was a young man who had everything to gain by hitch-ing his star to Mr Secretary's wagon. His father was also a willing supporter of Cromwellian policy. Perhaps it was John who influenced Sir Anthony's religious views, for, by the end of his life the older man was certainly a convinced Protestant. His will, made in 1536, was one of the earliest which forsook normal Catholic expressions of piety in favour of distinctly Protestant sentiments: 'I commit and bequeath my soul to God, my Maker and Redeemer, trusting in his grace and by the merits of Christ's passion and resurrection in whose faith I do believe and by his grace will die to be one of the number of such as shall be saved.'[7]

Among Sir John Markham's close neighbours and closest friends were the Hercys of Grove and the Lascelles of Sturton-le-Steeple. Sir John Hercy was destined to be the last of the male line of an ancient family. Like the Ayscoughs and many of the groups who prospered under the early Tudors, the Hercys were prominent earlier in the service of the Lancastrian cause. Humphrey Hercy was sufficiently well favoured to be invited to attend the Field of Cloth of Gold in 1521.[8] He had made a very favourable marriage with the daughter of Sir John Digby, one of the leading gentlemen of Rutland, and the eldest son of that marriage, John, was placed in the court of the young King. In 1523 John Hercy began to be active in royal business in the shire.[9] By this time he had married a daughter of the Staffordshire branch of the powerful Stanley family. This union was destined to be barren – a source of great sorrow to John, the more so because he was the only son out of his parents' ten surviving children and was alone capable of perpetuating the family name. He was sheriff in 1537,[10] 1543 and 1548 and one of the leading figures in Nottinghamshire during the crucial years of the Henrician Reformation.

The Lascelles were of the rank of minor gentry but were rapidly improving their position during the middle years of Henry VIII's reign. The Nottinghamshire Lascelles probably originated as a junior branch of the Lascelles of Richmond, Yorks, but their known pedigree is very incomplete. Towards the end of the fifteenth century, one Ralph Lascelles of Sturton-le-Steeple

married Joan, daughter of Sir John Topcliffe of Somerby, Lincolnshire. By so doing he was forging links with an important and well-
connected family.[11] His son Richard[12] was able to look outside his
immediate locality for a bride and his choice settled on a daughter
of Sir Brian Sandford of Sandford, Shropshire.[13] By this time the
Lascelles estates in north Nottinghamshire had been enlarged with
the acquisition of the small manor of Gateford near Worksop. The
steady improvement of the family fortunes suffered a setback in the
autumn of 1520 when Richard died in his early thirties. His wife
had pre-deceased him so that he left an orphan family of three
young children; George, perhaps in his early teens, John and
Mary still scarcely more than infants. At this point the situation
was considerably eased by the help of their friends and neighbours,
the Hercys.[14] Humphrey and Elizabeth helped bring up the
Lascelles children and used their influence to advance their
interests. After Humphrey Hercy's death, his heir, John, took over
the patronage of the Lascelles family along with his other responsibilities. As a result George Lascelles was trained to take over the
management of his estates – a task for which he showed considerable flair. The Hercys then did all they could to introduce John and
Mary to more influential patrons who, in turn, might gain them
entry to the royal court.

Of the early formal education of the Lascelles children we know
nothing, but it is clear that, by the standards of the day, they were
well-tutored. The Hercys were in full sympathy with the more
advanced thinkers of the time, who were urging the complete overhaul of English educational systems, especially among the upper
classes. In this age, when new ideas were overturning old institutions and when, in any case, the destruction of the power of the
nobility and the Church was making social reform essential, criticism was mounting against the idea that sons of the wealthy should
be 'brought up in hunting and hawking, dicing and carding, eating
and drinking . . . in all vain, pleasure, pastime and vanity'. Rather
the reformers advocated that 'the good education of youth in
virtuous exercises is the ground of the remedying all other diseases
in this our politic body'.[15] More and more gentlemen hired tutors
for their children or put them in the households of those noblemen
who had a care for the liberal education of their charges. Whether
the Lascelles brothers were taught at home or in a noble household,
they certainly acquired a knowledge of English, Latin and, perhaps,

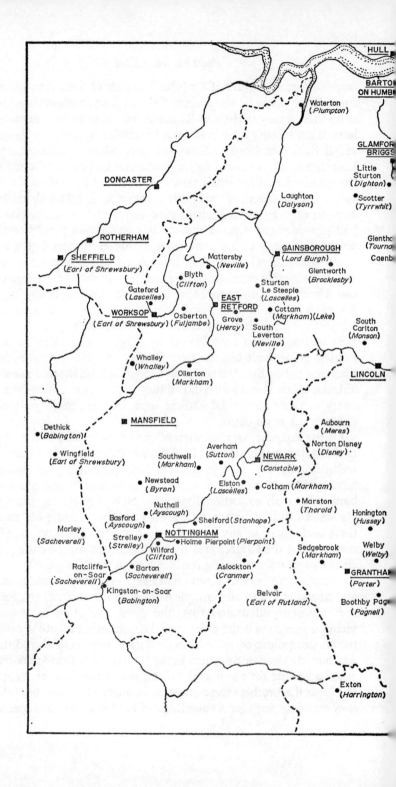

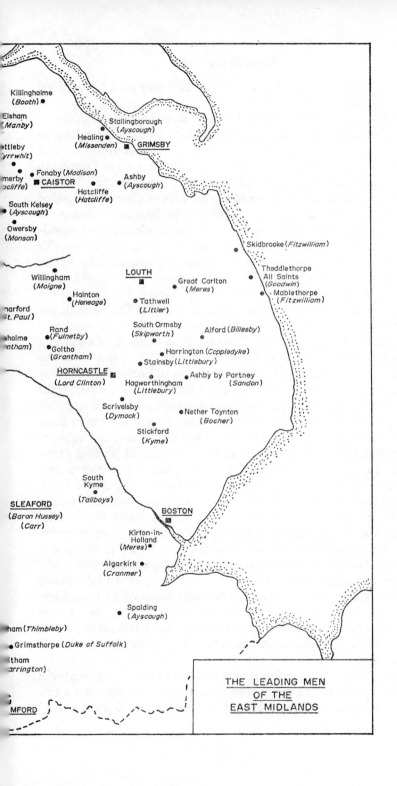

Killingholme
(*Booth*) ●

Elsham
(*Manby*)

Stallingborough
(*Ayscough*) ●

●ttleby
(*yrrwhit*)

Healing ●
(*Missenden*) ■ GRIMSBY

●merby
(*cliffe*) ■ CAISTOR

Fonaby (*Madison*) ●

Ashby
(*Ayscough*)

Hatcliffe
(*Hatcliffe*)

South Kelsey
● (*Ayscough*)

Owersby
(*Monson*)

Skidbrooke (*Fitzwilliam*) ●

Theddlethorpe
All Saints
(*Goodwin*)

● Mablethorpe
(*Fitzwilliam*)

LOUTH
■

Great Carlton
(*Meres*)

Willingham
(*Moigne*)

Hainton
(*Heneage*)

Tathwell
(*Littler*)

●harford
●t. Paul

Rand
● (*Fulnetby*)

South Ormsby
(*Skipworth*)

Alford (*Billesby*)

●holme
●ntham)

● Goltho
(*Grantham*)

Harrington (*Coppledyke*)

Stainsby (*Littlebury*)

HORNCASTLE ■
(*Lord Clinton*)

Ashby by Partney
(*Sandon*)

Hagworthingham
(*Littlebury*)

Scrivelsby
(*Dymock*)

● Nether Toynton
(*Bocher*)

Stickford
(*Kyme*)

South
Kyme
●
(*Tailboys*)

SLEAFORD
(*Baron Hussey*)
(*Carr*)

BOSTON
■

Kirton-in-
Holland
(*Meres*) ●

Algarkirk ●
(*Cranmer*)

Spalding
(*Ayscough*)

●ham (*Thimbleby*)

● Grimsthorpe (*Duke of Suffolk*)

●tham
●rrington)

MFORD

THE LEADING MEN
OF THE
EAST MIDLANDS

Greek. John could speak court French and may even have gained some facility in German.[16]

George passed from book learning to the practical affairs of estate management at Sturton, but the time soon came for John to leave home. It is possible that he went first to Oxford and graduated there in 1530.[17] Certainly, he was eventually sent up to London to begin the study of law at Furnivall's Inn. Situated in the suburb of Holborn, Furnivall's was one of the ten inns of Chancery founded in the fifteenth century[18] to provide a preliminary training for intending students at the inns of court and an elementary grounding in civil law for the sons of gentlemen. Studies at Furnivall's embraced more than attendance at lectures delivered by young barristers: instruction could be had in music, dancing and other accomplishments essential to a courtier.[19] Here at Furnivall's John Lascelles spent several terms in the early 1530s following in the illustrious footsteps of such predecessors as Sir Thomas More.[20]

In London the young John Lascelles found himself in a seething cauldron of religious debate and heterodoxy. The capital was the most notorious centre of heretical groups in all England. Merchants smuggled the works of Tyndale, Frith and foreign reformers from the Continent and these were sold through a hundred agencies throughout the city. The Bishop's officers were tireless in their efforts to eradicate both the literature and the colporteurs. Between 1527 and 1532 purges carried out first by Tunstall (Bishop 1522–1530) then by Stokesley (Bishop 1530–1540) brought over two hundred heretics of London and the neighbouring parts of Essex before the diocesan courts. But heresy was hydra-headed; Lollardy, Lutheranism and the numerous forms of unorthodox Christianity flourished on persecution and martyrdom. London was unique as a centre where heresy crossed all social boundaries. In the grimy, narrow streets and courtyards, in the market places and open fields, in the overhung alleys by the river and along broad Cheapside, apprentices and rogues, fishwives and merchants rubbed shoulders with courtiers, ambassadors, scholars and students. Any young man new to the city who wanted to enjoy the illicit thrill of owning and reading a banned book would not find it difficult to lay hands on a copy.

John Lascelles' experience may well have been akin to that of a fairly close neighbour who came up to the inns of court just a few years afterwards. Robert Plumpton's home was Waterton Hall near the mouth of the Trent, some twenty miles from Sturton. This young man began at the Middle Temple in 1535. He had not been there very long before he came into contact with the new doctrines, in particular, with the 1534 edition of Tyndale's New Testament. He avidly read the text and the inflammatory preface, *W.T. to the Reader*, and the marginal glosses which attacked the Pope and clerical abuses. He attended sermons preached by friars and clergy infected with the new doctrines. The completeness of his conversion can be gauged from the letters he wrote home to his mother. On 12 January 1536 he sent her a copy of the New Testament with this advice:

> If it will please you to read the Introduction you shall see marvelous things hid in it. And as from the understanding of it, doubt not; for God will give knowledge to whom he will give knowledge of the Scriptures, as soon to a shepherd as to a priest, if he ask knowledge of God faithfully.'

Another, undated, letter, written in response to one from his mother urging him to beware of heresy, is even more ardent in its language:

> I would desire you for the love of God, that you would read the New Testament, which is the true Gospel of God, spoken by the Holy Ghost. Wherefor doubt not of it, dearly beloved mother in the Lord, I write not this to bring you into any heresies, but to teach you the clear light of God's doctrine. Wherefore I will never write nothing to you, nor say nothing to you concerning the Scriptures, but will die in the quarrel. Mother, you have much to thank God for that it should please him to give you licence to live until this time, for the Gospel of Christ was never so truly preached as it is now. Wherefore I pray to God that he will give you grace to have knowledge of his Scriptures.[21]

In these and other letters Robert Plumpton revealed a considerable familiarity with moderate Protestant doctrines. Some sections of his correspondence are mere paraphrases of Tyndale and others, no doubt, reflect very faithfully the zealous rhetoric thundered from some city pulpit.[22]

The inns of court were themselves among the most active centres of anti-clericalism in England. It was not just that they were places where impressionable, educated young men met. One of the features of the Church-State controversy which came to a head in the 1530s was the conflict between civil and canon law. Officers of the royal courts had for centuries complained about clerical evasions of civil justice and the activities of the ecclesiastical courts. These were, indeed, widely resented (one contemporary went so far as to describe the bishops' courts colourfully as 'the filthy quakemire and poisoned plash of all the abominations that do infect the whole realm')[23] but it was natural that the practitioners and students of the civil law should form the spearhead of the attack.

John Lascelles may have been converted to the reformed faith in London, but it is probable that he had acquired more than a passing acquaintance with religious novelties in his own country. The area around Worksop, East Retford and Gainsborough was one where religious dissent had long been strong and where indictable cases of heresy had cropped up from time to time. Anticlericalism was very noticeable in the county, especially in centres like Newark where ecclesiastical authority had rankled for years. Unlike Lincolnshire with its fifty-one religious houses, including great and powerful monastic centres such as Thornton, Crowland, Spalding and Bardney, and its thirty or more friaries, hospitals and minor religious foundations, Nottinghamshire could only boast ten monasteries, a nunnery and four houses of friars. In the smaller county of forest and gentle hills, monasticism was not such a bright and indispensable colour in the pattern of society. In Nottinghamshire parishes were larger and clergy fewer than in the neighbouring county so that, all in all, the Church wielded less power and authority than it did in Lincolnshire. The work of reformation in county Nottingham was likely to be, therefore, comparatively easy to accomplish.

In the Babingtons, Markhams, Hercys and Lascelles, Cromwell found men who were much more than obedient agents carrying out a policy to which they were indifferent or which they executed solely for motives of gain. In this group Mr Secretary had a nucleus of ardent supporters, men who were united by ties of blood and friendship,[24] and also by a common devotion to the new religion. The correspondence which passed back and forth between Cromwell and his representatives in Nottinghamshire leaves no room for doubt concerning the zeal with which Sir John Markham and his friends embarked on their duties.

As early as 1531 we find Sir Anthony Babington proceeding against one Roger Dycker on seemingly trivial grounds. All England was talking about the King's 'great matter' and Dycker, an old man of sixty-nine, set in his ways but by no means disloyal to the King (a letter on his behalf to Cromwell described Dycker as a veteran of many campaigns and 'sore bruised in the King's wars'), was among many who declared himself opposed to the divorce. 'So noble a lady, so highborn and so gracious, he would not forsake and marry another', the old man is reported to have said – a sentiment betraying bewilderment and naïvety rather than misprision. Nevertheless, these words were enough to spell trouble for Dycker when they came to the ears of the local justice of the peace, Sir Anthony Babington. The old soldier was arrested and hailed before the bench. Babington and his colleagues then decided that Dycker's crime was so heinous that the prisoner and his case must be remitted to London and a higher court. In the capital he languished for several months in the Marshalsea prison awaiting trial while his friends appealed to Cromwell and the Council on his behalf. Henry's government were very sensitive about the divorce and had given instructions to the commissioners of the peace to stifle every breath of criticism concerning the King's matrimonial arrangements. Yet there were many royal officers who would have treated Dycker's words as what they were, the harmless babblings of an old man totally ignorant of politics. On the other hand it was said of Babington and his colleagues that they 'do all this to undo him utterly'.[25]

In 1533 John Markham was taking the initiative in attacking a much more important centre of resistance to royal policy. The Franciscan Observant friars were causing considerable anxiety to the government by their open opposition to the divorce. Cromwell tried at first to bring the friars of Greenwich to heel. When that failed he made use of *agents provocateurs* to stir up trouble in their midst. But all the Observants in the other six houses within the country were in sympathy. The government was in a quandary and Cromwell was undecided how to act. The friars, a preaching order, were both popular and influential. To act against them would be to court widespread hostility. Yet if they were allowed to become bolder in their pulpit criticism, they might emerge as the mouthpiece of the conservative body of the people. This could not be permitted. When the divorce and re-marriage of Henry to Anne Boleyn had presented Christendom with a *fait accompli*, the opposition of the Observants became more vociferous.[26]

After the spring session of Parliament which had passed the

momentous legislation enabling the King to settle his 'great matter' without reference to Rome, the members dispersed to their homes. Sir John Markham made his way back to Cottam. He had scarce reached his own threshold when word came to him of trouble in Newark. He was not slow in taking action.

> At my coming home it was reported that a friar Observant had preached certain sermons in the parish church of Newark of a seditious and slanderous tendency. I enclosed the words in a schedule and rode to the Prior's house and, calling him before me, in the presence of his warden and brethren, I read them unto him, desiring to know whether they were his words or not. He admitted all, except four or five, which I have drawn through with a pen. I remit to your discretion what inconvenience will ensue if these men be suffered to preach and stir men in their confessions, considering their credit among the people.[27]

It is scarcely necessary to read between the lines of this letter to see indications of the conflict between ecclesiastical authority and the townsmen of Newark. Nor, knowing the sympathy that Markham had for the civic leaders, is it difficult to see why he proceeded against the Observants with such alacrity. His rebukes frightened at least two members of the community, who fled to Bristol, where royal officers were still seeking them a year later.[28] They were eventually arrested and charged with sedition. (One of them is supposed to have retorted, when referring to Princess Elizabeth's baptism, that she was christened in hot water 'but it was not hot enough'.)

By the end of 1534 all the Observant friaries had been suppressed. Yet Sir John Markham was not so busy with monastic centres of resistance that he had no time for humbler offenders. He followed up every case brought to him which suggested criticism of the King. For instance when a certain disgruntled Allan Hey denounced his wife to Markham because she 'railed against the Queen' this became the subject of a report to Cromwell.[29]

Markham and John Babington were on the commission for the *Valor Ecclesiasticus* in 1535 and during the course of their investigations they were responsible for instigating proceedings against another religious community. On 16 April they arrived at Beauvale Carthusian Priory. Beauvale had already lost its Prior, Robert Laurence, who was in the Tower of London awaiting trial for failure to recognize the royal supremacy. The commissioners were diligent in their examinations of the rest of the community. They found the Proctor, William Trafford, adamant in his rejection of the royal supremacy; 'I believe firmly that the Pope of Rome is supreme head of the Church catholic.'[30] In his report to Cromwell, Markham explains how he and his colleagues argued for hours with Trafford, putting all the reasons they could think of for the rejection of papal supremacy in England, but in the end they had to admit failure and ask what they should do with the Proctor of Beauvale '*in exemplum aliorum*'. The answer came back that he was to be sent up to London. So he was despatched to the capital on 7 May, a few days after the death of his prior. He was not, however, destined to share martyrdom with Laurence. The King, for whom prosecutions and executions were matters of politics rather than justice, had decided that further 'examples' were not necessary. The monks of the London Charterhouse, John Fisher Bishop of Rochester and Sir Thomas More, were all in prison awaiting certain death – there was no need to add to their number. Trafford was dismissed and continued in the life of prayer until there was no cloister left in England to house him.

And so it went on. A few weeks later we find Sir John Markham in company with the Earl of Rutland, John Constable and Richard Disney[31] examining the friars of Grantham. This group of Nottinghamshire gentlemen proved to Cromwell during the early years of the Reformation, that they were exceeded by no men in their devotion to duty or in their acceptance of official religious policy. The northern rising provided them with the crowning opportunity to prove their allegiance. To a man the Markhams, Babingtons, Hercys and Lascelles flocked to Nottingham in 1536 to the banner of the Earl of Shrewsbury.

Such men were of vital importance to Cromwell as he moved into the second phase of the Reformation in 1537 and he determined to keep in close contact with them. A document of about 1538 has been preserved which is in effect a 'memo' for the steward of Cromwell's enormous household.[32] Cromwell was constantly besieged by aspiring noblemen and gentlemen to find places for their sons, and the Secretary's servants found it difficult to know the exact standing in their master's eyes of each of the visitors, agents, hangers-on and suitors daily calling at the house. Cromwell therefore drew up a list in which men who were useful to him or

in whom he had taken an interest were divided into three categories: 'Gentlemen not to be allowed in my Lord's household aforesaid but when they have commandment or cause necessary to
repair thither', 'Gentlemen most meet to be daily waiters upon my
said Lord' and 'Gentlemen meet to be preferred unto the King's
Majesty's service'.[33] The names of John Lascelles and John
Babington were recorded in the first category. They were princi-
pally employed as messengers between London and the East
Midlands, their tasks being to convey orders speedily to the
leading gentlemen of the area and to report back to Cromwell with
the latest information.

Party ties did not override considerations of personal advancement, as is shown by the career of Mary Lascelles. At about the
same time as her brother was gaining access to Thomas Cromwell's
entourage her friends gained for Mary a position in Lord William
Howard's household. Lord William was a brother of the Duke of
Norfolk, Cromwell's bitterest enemy. She was a nurse to the nobleman's young family for two or three years. Then she entered the
service of his mother, the Dowager Duchess of Norfolk. Dame
Agnes Howard divided her time between her two great houses at
Horsham and Lambeth. Her large household included many
young ladies of noble or gentle birth 'farmed out' to her for
training in those practical and social accomplishments which young
gallants looked for in their prospective wives. Among them Mary
Lascelles settled down to a life of service in kitchen and hall. But
the days in a noble household were not passed in unending
drudgery. There were many genteel diversions; lessons at the
virginals, walks in the great park or, when the weather prevented
that, exercise in the hall, embroidery, and always there was that
most fascinating of all pastimes – gossip. The Duchess's household
was large. Even in the enormous houses at Horsham and Lambeth,
conditions were crowded and privacy scarcely even thought of. As
they sat over their needlework in the solar or lay on their straw
mattresses in the draughty dormitory, they discussed and giggled
over the affairs of their colleagues and of their elders and betters.[34]
One of those colleagues whose conduct was already beginning to
shock the more strait-laced ladies of the household was the
seventeen-year-old step-granddaughter of the old Duchess –
Mistress Catherine Howard.

While a future queen of England was inviting comment on her

nightly activities in a noble household in southern England, the
serious work of reformation was being enthusiastically carried out
in the Midlands. In the spring of 1537, when Lord Darcy had been
apprehended and was under examination for his part in the
Pilgrimage of Grace, George Lascelles found his duty to the King
and his own possible self-interest marching happily side by side.
On 12 April he hurried to Gainsborough to lay evidence against the
unfortunate nobleman and Robert Aske, the leader of the Pilgrimage. What information he had to give or how valuable it was to
the royal officers we do not know, but that he had hopes of substantial reward is quite clear. Lord Darcy owned the manor of
Sturton and other extensive lands in Nottinghamshire. They
would provide a fine nucleus for the enlarged estates of a family
hoping to establish for itself new wealth and prominence in the
county.

Later in that same year a most interesting heresy case occurred
which involved many of the leading personalities of the region.[35]
There was in Rotherham a group of heretics, of a largely traditional,
Lollard persuasion. Most of them were sufficiently circumspect to
keep out of trouble – until 1537. Then, perhaps emboldened by
the new trends in official religious policy, one of them, William
Senes, a choirmaster in the song school at Jesus College, spoke out.
On 4 May he was in the parish church when he saw a priest,
Thomas Pylley, in the chantry of Henry Carnbull, saying a mass
for the soul of the donor and sprinkling holy water on his tomb.
Senes ridiculed these acts as superstitious and soon found himself
engaged in debate with the clergy of the college. He urged the new
doctrines as enshrined in the English New Testament and said that
men were now freed from old papist errors. The argument rapidly
grew more heated. William Ingram angrily retorted that he believed
what his father had believed. This was too much for the ardent
disciple of Tyndale. 'Thy father was a liar and is in hell,' he
retorted. 'And so is my father in hell also; my father never knew
Scripture and now it is come forth.' From this point the contest
degenerated into a slanging match.

This event sparked off a controversy between the priests and the
members of Senes's group, more of whom became involved in
incidents during the following weeks. On several occasions Senes
was confronted with irate conservative opinion, but the contests
were not always between orthodoxy and heresy. In one conversation

the choirmaster accused his adversaries of disloyalty to the King.

Thomas Holden, a chantry priest, and Mr Drapper, a chaplain at Jesus College, apparently upheld the Lincolnshire rebels; ' . . . those was good lads, for they would put down those heretics Cromwell, Cranmer and Latimer . . .' Senes remarked that these were traitorous words and cited such notable figures as the Earl of Shrewsbury and Sir John Markham as among those who agreed with the King's policy and were carrying it out. The two priests were, by this time, thoroughly angry; they dismissed the Earl as 'nought' and Markham as a 'heretic'. These arguments ended in the usual way with such expressions as 'Sir John Lack-learning' and 'Whoreson knave' flying back and forth.

After several incidents the bailiff of Rotherham had to intervene in the interests of keeping the peace. He arrested Senes and two colleagues and set them before the Earl of Shrewsbury at Sheffield Castle. Senes was charged with holding heretical opinions and possessing banned books. The reception he received from the aged Earl was hardly encouraging.

'Come near, thou heretic and kneel near. Ha! Thou heretic, thou hast books?'

'Yea, my Lord. The New Testament I have,' replied the cowed Senes.

'The New Testament thou hast is nought,' retorted the angry and almost incoherent nobleman. 'Thou art an heretic, and but for shame I should thrust my dagger into thee!'

With little more ado the Earl had the unfortunate trio clapped in prison and handed their case over to the archbishop's court.

During the following weeks Senes's friends and relations did all they could to help him. An explanation of the whole proceedings was sent to Cromwell but, apparently, to little avail. Then, when all seemed lost, someone thought of John Babington. The young man, who was spending a few weeks in his house at Kingston-on-Soar, was known to have access to Cromwell and to be an enemy of the Catholic clergy. So a deputation was sent to Kingston bearing Senes's own account of events. Babington was easily convinced and only too pleased to have an opportunity to take action against priests whose loyalty to the Head of the Church was suspect. On 16 October he passed on Senes's letter to Cromwell with an appeal of his own to the Vicar General to exercise his prerogative of intervention. Babington's patronage did the trick; Cromwell immediately issued writs for the case to be removed from archiepiscopal jurisdiction to the court of King's Bench. There, it was apparently squashed. Once Senes had come to Babington's attention, it appears that he continued to enjoy the gentleman's patronage. Another letter from Kingston on 21 August following, asks Cromwell to procure for Senes the rectory of Laxton, Nottinghamshire. Whether or not this suit was successful, we do not know but we do know that the Rotherham choirmaster's enemies did not dare to touch him while his protector was alive. It is very significant that consistory proceedings against Senes began again in September 1540. Cromwell had died in June.

The year 1538 saw the climax of the Cromwellian Reformation. At no other time in the reign of Henry VIII did England seem more firmly set on the road to thoroughgoing Protestantism. Cromwell was receiving the voluntary submission of many religious houses whose superiors accurately read the writing on the wall and yielded up their lands and goods in the hope of gaining royal favour and fat pensions rather than wait until they were forcibly dispossessed. At the same time pockets of papalist resistance were ruthlessly sought out. 1538 saw a full-scale onslaught made on images, shrines and other 'objects of superstition'. Cromwell's agents throughout the country relentlessly tore down rood lofts and statues, ruthlessly exposed 'miracle-working' relics and shrines. For displaying a similar zealous iconoclasm against the 'holy' rood of Dovercourt in Essex in 1532, three men had been hung. On the positive side, the Vicar General issued fresh injunctions in September stressing the educative role of the clergy and announcing his grand scheme for the setting up of an English Bible in every parish church. Throughout much of the year King Henry, under considerable pressure from his Secretary, was toying with the possibility of an alliance with the German Lutheran princes of the Schmalkalde League, while in the closing months he openly snubbed the Pope and exterminated a group of noblemen whose Yorkist connections and conservative opinions constituted, in his view, a threat to his throne.[36] It is not surprising that, throughout the country where most people were unaware of the subtleties of royal policy, men and women thought that old beliefs and falsehoods had been swept away for good and that a Protestant age had dawned in the land.[37]

1538 was, therefore, a busy year for Cromwell's agents and supporters in Nottinghamshire. In the spring, we find Sir John Markham, Sir John Hercy, George Lascelles and John Babington working together on the commission of oyer and terminer[38] and using John Lascelles as their chief messenger. On 26 March they were in that old centre of trouble, Newark. In view of Markham's earlier experiences with the clergy of the town it is difficult to decide how unbiased are his accounts of the situation there. Certainly he seemed determined to create trouble for the Vicar of Newark, Henry Litherland. The commissions' complaints to Cromwell concerning this man were very serious. He had recently preached a sermon which seemed to 'rise and sound of a cankered and corrupt mind'. He was failing to assert the royal supremacy and condemn the Pope. He was exhorting his flock to maintain such customs as offerings to images and praying for souls in purgatory. He condemned as heretics all those who were taking down images and warned his people not to read English books – even if they had the King's approval. Cromwell was reminded that this same Litherland had been in Axholme and Yorkshire during 'the commotion time' inciting the people to rebel.[39] The suspected traitor was sent up to London for further investigation.

The next day, 27 March, the commissioners were reporting from Lenton Priory near Nottingham. They had been sent thither by Cromwell to examine a case of verbal treason that was already over a year old. However, the Vicar General had marked out the Cluniac priory as ready for dissolution and so the matter was reopened. The commissioners discovered, through informers in the community, evidence against three of its members. Prior Heath had allegedly spoken traitorous words as long ago as 29 June 1536. Two of the monks had been heard to condemn the King's suppression of the northern risings in December 1536. They were John Houghton and Ralph Swenson. In 1534 the Tudor autocrat had armed his government with an infamous Treasons Act which made disloyal wishes and intentions as culpable as actual deeds. The monks of Lenton were to discover just how comprehensive this Act was. Ralph Swenson had voiced the following opinion: 'The King . . . will keep no promise with God Himself, but pulls down His churches'; 'The King will hang a man for . . . speaking nowadays . . . but the King of heaven will not do so, and He is King of all kings; but he that hangs a man in this world for . . . speaking, he shall be hanged in another world himself'. George Lascelles carried the commissioners' report to London and was back within a few days with Cromwell's decision. On 16 April Markham and his colleagues were able to report that they had attended to the execution of 'the late Prior of Lenton and Ralph Swenson' at Nottingham. The property of the priory, of course, reverted to the crown by attainder.[40]

The commissioners did not feel bound to convict in cases to which they had not been directed by the government or which they had not ferreted out for themselves. In the early part of April 1538 Sir Nicholas Strelley sent a certain Nicholas Sanderson to Nottingham for examination by the judges of oyer and terminer. The charge concerned a verbal treason some two years old. When Markham and his colleagues acquitted the man, Strelley was furious and immediately wrote a strong complaint to Cromwell. Mr Secretary, however, upheld his commissioners.[41] A few days later, the judges were opposing the wishes of no less a personage than the Earl of Shrewsbury. Talbot, who was approaching the end of his earthly days, sent Nicholas Harrison, parson of Pleasley, to the commissioners on the grounds that he had 'misused himself in his words' against the King. Perhaps suspecting that the justices (Markham, Hercy, Roger Greenhaugh and Edmund Molyneux on this occasion) might not find Harrison guilty, the Earl sent a separate report to Cromwell on 28 April. His suspicions were well founded. The parson and his accusers were examined on 30 April and the commissioners came to the conclusion that Harrison did not merit punishment. 'The priest is aged and his wit and memory simple,' they explained. The worst offence his adversaries could lay to his charge was the opinion that: '. . . if the lords of England were as they have been as they be now but boys and fools, the King should not have pulled down so many abbeys as he hath done.' A fairly harmless sentiment, indeed, but under Henry VIII's laws quite indictable. The old man was committed to ward awaiting Cromwell's pleasure. Cromwell's pleasure was apparently to uphold the judgement of the Nottinghamshire commissioners rather than that of the Lord Steward of England.[42] Personal interests and rivalries frequently influenced the course of justice in rural England.

John Lascelles returned to Nottinghamshire early in May with Cromwell's reply to Sir John Markham's report and was able to

H

spend two weeks at home. On several occasions during those days he sat with his brother and John Hercy discussing religious issues. He could report that no one in the Council dared oppose the policies of that champion of the true faith, Thomas Cromwell. Mr Secretary had the confidence of the King as never before and the machinations of Norfolk and the Howard faction were powerless against him. Together this zealous trio thanked God for the deliverance of their land from papalism. Yet enemies of biblical Christianity still abounded, even among their Nottinghamshire neighbours. Hercy and the Lascelles pledged themselves to the extermination of the Catholic threat. When John returned to London on 28 May he bore a letter from cousin Hercy to Cromwell.

> I have been informed that Sir Edward Eland, Chaplain to Dr Knolys, Vicar of Wakefield, has been teaching young folks seditious songs against your Lordship and others. This he has confessed. Sir Edward says that he had it from one Berkeleyd of Bole . . . My cousin George Lascelles knows him well. Let me know your pleasure in this by your servant John Lascelles, to whom I beg you to continue good Lord . . . Have pity for the poor men of Cottam, sore vexed by Anthony Neville,[43] who, besides his own matter, threatens them with a lunatic priest put to them by the Archbishop of York's officers. They showed themselves loyal at the commotion time. I wish you would be pleased to take the Lady at Doncaster away, and send some good preachers into the country.[44]

By the summer of 1538 John Lascelles had probably been promoted to the category of 'Gentlemen most meet to be daily waiters upon my said Lord'. He now had regular access to Cromwell and was in a position to seek favours for himself, and his associates. It was an accepted convention of the sixteenth century that anyone who was a regular member of the royal court or the household of a powerful minister should use his position to advance his family's fortunes. Lady Lisle, for example, hoped by conveying small gifts to his majesty via her daughter Anne Bosset (who was established at court) to obtain much larger recompense. The poor girl was pestered ceaselessly by her impatient matriarch to know the success of her suit but, as she sought to explain, she really was placed in an awkward position: 'I have presented your quince marmalade to the King's Highness, and his Grace does like it wondrous well and gave your ladyship hearty thanks for it. And whereas I perceived by your ladyship's letter, that when the King's

Highness had tasted of your marmalade, you would have me to move his Grace for to send you some token of remembrance . . . I durst not be so bold . . .'[45] Such importunity was certainly fraught with hazards and disappointments. Yet John Lascelles's friends were on firmer ground. The information they sent via 'your servant' was more valuable than any amount of quince marmalade.

The Hercys, Babingtons, Markhams and Lascelles and their counterparts in every part of the realm were Cromwell's ears and eyes. From the carefully-sifted intelligence he received from them, he framed his policy. On 13 October Hercy reported 'the prior and convent of Worksop are so covetous they sell flocks of sheep, cattle, corn, timber, etc., and all our priors follow the example'.[46] Such news was alarming to Cromwell. It revealed what was, indeed, a widespread practice. The remaining monasteries, knowing that their days were numbered, were realizing as many of their assets as possible so that the King's men should not be able to lay hands on them.[47] The Vicar General knew that, if he was going to reach out for the remaining wealth of the religious, he could not afford to delay. On the following 12 January John Babington was sent word about a late friar of Bristol who had come to the Midlands spreading rumours about an impending Catholic invasion to be undertaken by the combined forces of the Emperor, the Pope and the King of France.[48] Cromwell was more accurately informed of events on the Continent than any 'ex-friar' but it could be very useful to know that such widespread fears existed and could be exploited.

This group of eager Nottinghamshire gentlemen thus served the Lord Privy Seal* very well and he was prepared to reward them. In October 1538 John Lascelles was able to hurry home with good news for cousin Hercy. Cromwell was well disposed towards him and would listen favourably to any request he wished to make. Hercy's reply was prompt:

> I understand by my cousin, John Lascelles, your benevolence towards me. I should be glad to obtain the stewardship of Tickhill and Conisbrough . . . I beg you will remember your servant Lascelles to have the preferment of Beauvale Abbey for the setting forth of a faithful brother, and you shall command me, having no children, to help him.　　　　　　　　　　　　　　　Grove 31 October 1538[49]

---

* Cromwell became Lord Keeper of the Privy Seal in 1536 and was frequently referred to by this title.

And so the rewards began to pour in. Those who had proved themselves industrious in the process of dissolution were the first to
benefit from it. George Lascelles's suit for a part of Darcy's attainted
lands had not yet been decided and when John returned to London
after Christmas he sought opportunities to remind his master of
his brother's faithfulness in laying evidence against the noble
traitor. In his letter of 12 January 1539 John Babington also urged
that Lascelles' suit should be granted. He explained how George
had been persistently ferreting out information about the threat
of foreign invasion and sending it back to Cromwell via brother
John.[50] But George Lascelles had to wait over a year more before
the coveted Darcy lands fell into his hands. Even then he was
lucky to get them. The grant was made out on 17 March 1540.[51]
He had scarcely taken possession when news arrived that his patron
was in the Tower.

That the Cromwellian regime should have survived long enough
for George Lascelles to receive his rewards was, indeed, fortunate,
for by this grant the Lascelles became one of the wealthiest
families in the county. Just how wealthy appeared quite clearly in
1545 when a dispute arose over some of George's land. A contemporary account tells us:

> A great suit was tried . . . at Nottingham, in which George Lascelles,
> Esq. claimed against Richard Townby, Esq. the manors of Gateford,
> Everton and Haworth, with the appurtenances, and one hundred and
> twenty messuages, forty tofts, one dovecote, one hundred and twenty
> gardens, one hundred and twenty orchards, two thousand acres of
> arable land, two hundred of meadow, one thousand of pasture, two
> hundred and fifty of wood, one hundred of moor, forty of turbary
> [i.e. land affording turf or peat for fuel] and forty shillings rent in
> Gateford, Everton, Haworth, Worksop, Groingely, Wellow, Bole,
> Babworth, Ordsall, Sturton, Eaton, W. Markham, Blyth, and several
> other places.[52]

George Lascelles and his family, who moved at about this time, to
a fine house at Elston in south Nottinghamshire, knew that they
owed everything to Thomas Cromwell. They were among the few
people in England who mourned his passing and revered his
memory.

There was no sign throughout the whole of 1539 that Cromwell's
career in the royal service – and, indeed, his life – was drawing to a

close. The year saw the consummation of his ecclesiastical policy. The last of the monasteries fell or were doomed to fall. The Great Bible was set up in parish churches throughout the realm. After many shifts of policy, Henry at last allowed himself to be steered towards a marriage alliance with the German princes. Having already completely re-organized the principal offices of state, the indefatigable Secretary embarked on a sweeping overhaul of the royal household. He loved his King and by the end of 1539 he had made Henry the richest king ever to have sat on the English throne. He loved work and throughout 1539 he was working harder than ever before. He loved being at the centre of the nation's affairs – and in 1539 there was no sphere of English life which he did not control.

Yet, in 1539, Cromwell also had his disappointments, and his enemies began to allow themselves to hope. The most serious challenge to his religious policy came in June, when the Act of Six Articles was passed through Parliament. It was utterly conservative in tone, re-affirmed essential Catholic doctrines and provided harsh punishments for 'heretics' who rejected them. It was not followed by the all-out onslaught on the new men for which the conservative bishops hoped but the reactionaries did now have a powerful weapon which could be used against anyone – high or low – who dabbled in religious 'novelties'. Five hundred people in the Diocese of London were immediately arrested on charges involving the new Act – only to be pardoned by the King. Yet Cromwell's enemies on the Council now began to believe in the possibility of success. The proud, tight-lipped, narrow-visioned Duke of Norfolk and the incrediby cunning 'fox' Stephen Gardiner, Bishop of Winchester schemed industriously to undermine the Lord Privy Seal's policies. Where Cromwell worked hard to bring off a German alliance, they strove for a rapprochement with Catholic France. When Cromwell succeeded in temporarily cementing Anglo-German relations with the marriage between Henry and Anne of Cleves, they set before the King's eyes the young, vivacious and well-drilled Catherine Howard.

As the year opened Cromwell's ecclesiastical plans were proceeding very smoothly. The wealth of the abbeys and of despoiled shrines was pouring in in a steady stream and the royal finances were completely transformed. From the shrine of St Thomas à Becket at Canterbury alone, Henry made a haul of two enormous chests of jewels and twenty-four wagon-loads of plate. For Cromwell's part, it rejoiced his bureaucratic heart to see this vast treasure being put at the disposal of the government instead of lying in dim vaults for the sole purpose of exciting superstitious awe from generations of shuffling pilgrims. There was no longer any need for the cautious policy he had originally adopted towards the monasteries. In 1536 it had seemed that ecclesiastical resistance and the practical problem of providing for the dispossessed religious would only make it possible for the crown to appropriate some of the monastic houses. But the Court of Augmentations,[53] set up to administer confiscated lands and pay pensions to the ex-monks and nuns, had swiftly got into its stride under the control of the ambitious, unscrupulous but efficient Richard Rich, and had been able to cope with an increasing volume of work. The failure of the northern risings had broken the resistance of the conservatives and also provided excuses for further confiscations. By attainder and by voluntary surrender, numerous monastic estates had fallen into the King's hands since the first Act of Dissolution. But the superiors of some houses were obdurate and Cromwell realized that the time had come to make the final moves in his game of expunging the religious life from English soil. Once the old and unproductive had been swept away, the Vicar General could proceed to the establishment of a new and efficient ecclesiastical system. The antiquated diocesan framework of England could be renovated and some of the treasure and land taken from the monasteries could be used to establish schools and colleges – a completely revitalized system of education. Such dreams and plans were passing through Thomas Cromwell's mind as he prepared for the spring session of Parliament, 1539.

Parliament assembled on 28 April and Cromwell may well have received a shock on the very first day. Thomas Audley, the Lord Chancellor, read the King's Speech to the assembled nobles, gentlemen and burgesses in the Upper House. The royal exhortation had been prepared by the Lord Privy Seal and outlined the major matters to be dealt with in the coming session. But when he came to the end of it, Audley laid the parchment aside and continued, in words that Cromwell certainly had not devised:

His Majesty desires above all things that diversity of religious opinions should be banished from his dominions; and since this is a thing too arduous to be determined in the midst of so many various judgements, it seems good to him to order a committee of the Upper House to examine opinions, and to report their decisions to the whole Parliament.[54]

Cromwell was annoyed. This looked like a challenge to the carefully planned settlement he had arranged for the English Church. New formularies of faith had been set forth, old superstitions swept away, injunctions had obliged bishops and clergy to attend to the religious education of the people, and, above all, Cromwell had now given the people the English Bible. His policies only needed time to work themselves out and King Henry's realm would be able to boast a purified and revitalized Church, filled with Christian people who knew at least the rudiments of their faith. Here Cromwell showed a serious lack of understanding of his master's mind.

Henry was genuinely worried about the religious dissensions, which were much more widespread than ever before in England. He knew that in every town and village Christian doctrines were debated with heat by clergy and laymen of every degree. Men reviled each other as 'heretic' and 'papist'. Neighbour reported neighbour to the magistrates. Anabaptists, Zwinglians, Lutherans and the Pope's agents bombarded the realm with their propaganda. Neither in the King's court nor in the tiniest hamlet of England was religious harmony to be found. The King did well to be worried, for, not only did such a state of affairs disrupt the internal administration of the realm but it bedevilled the government's relations with other powers. European ambassadors – and particularly that king of gossips and troublemakers, Eustace Chapuys, the Emperor's representative – reported back to their courts that England was a divided nation. Such despatches made Henry look foolish and served to encourage his enemies.

It was not until this time that the opposition to Cromwell in the Council and at court began organizing itself into a recognizable faction. The leaders of the group were men who had their own reasons for opposing the King's Secretary. Thomas Howard, Duke of Norfolk, Britain's premier peer and one of the few surviving representatives of the old nobility, hated all upstarts and new men. He could not rid his mind of the conviction that the King should choose his chief advisers from the old landed families. The Tudor meritocracy which exalted base fellows like Wolsey and Cromwell to the most influential positions in the realm was not at all to his taste. A finer edge was put upon his hatred by the fundamental insecurity of his own position. The two Tudors, father and son, had slowly whittled down the ancient baronial families and Norfolk could never be sure that Henry VIII would not suddenly decide that the Howards were a danger to the throne. Insecurity and pride combined to turn the Duke of Norfolk against the now-powerful son of a Putney brewer.

Trouble between the two men had flared out in 1536. For insulting Cromwell across the Council table, Norfolk had been banished to his country estates and remained there until the King needed his services to help quell the Pilgrimage of Grace. Even his activity in the north during the following months had not brought a return of royal favour. Henry repeatedly criticized Norfolk's handling of the rebels and their supporters, sometimes in terms of the most biting sarcasm.[55] Matters between the two men had not improved in the summer of 1537 when Howard returned to the Council board and he was soon despatched to the north once more. Was there a barbed hint in the instructions the King sent to Norfolk on 18 September? The Duke was instructed to gather all the men of substance to him and inform them, among other things,

> . . . if there be any one amongst them, of what degree soever he be, who will not serve as humbly and readily, under the lowest-born person we can put in authority, as under the greatest duke in our realm, we will neither repute him for our good subject, nor, upon knowledge of his contumacy and pride therein, leave him unpunished, to the example of others.[56]

Norfolk's anger smouldered and he bided his time.

It was Stephen Gardiner, Bishop of Winchester, who was the brains behind the organized opposition to Cromwell. He opposed the Secretary for other reasons. Like Longland he had been a supporter of the divorce and of the breach with Rome but – again, like Longland – he did not like the trend that religious affairs had taken since. He opposed every move away from traditional Catholic doctrines and was the leader of the conservative bishops against heretical influences. Cromwell he viewed as the fount of the ills now plaguing the English Church and he worked industriously to undermine the Secretary's policies. In 1538 Cromwell had

had him recalled from his embassy in Paris because he mistrusted the line the Bishop was taking with foreign diplomats. From that point the struggle between the two men had become a personal conflict for influence with the King, and Gardiner, knowing that he could not by himself prevail against the mighty minister, began to enlist the support of Norfolk and other disgruntled members of the Council and the court. It was the King's growing alarm at the religious situation in his realm that encouraged them to hope for and contrive Cromwell's downfall. Henry's decision to appoint a commission on religious unity was the result of pressure on the part of Norfolk (well primed by the Bishop of Winchester), who further hoped that the outcome of such a commission would be a reaffirmation of Catholic doctrines.

The conservatives had laid their plans well. The committee appointed consisted of the Vicegerent and eight ecclesiastics – four reformers and four conservatives. Cromwell recognized the arrangement for what it was – a skilful Catholic plot. Political realist that he was, he did not try to oppose his enemies and never took his seat on the commission. The result was an inevitable deadlock which gave Henry the opportunity to send the Duke of Norfolk down to the Parliament House on 16 May with six ready-made articles for 'discussion'. The articles defended the Catholic doctrines and practices of transubstantiation, clerical celibacy, communion in one kind, auricular confession and the efficacy of masses for the dead. The Duke 'suggested' that if Parliament accepted these articles, they should be enforced on the people on pain of death by burning and confiscation of property. The bill was vigorously opposed in both houses and eventually Henry, himself, had to put in an appearance in the upper chamber. As Archbishop Cranmer later recorded, 'if the King's Majesty himself had not come personally into the Parliament house, those laws had never passed'.[57] The bill moved slowly through its various stages and became law on 10 June. Bishops Latimer and Shaxton resigned their sees, and for the first time England witnessed something of a religious emigration. Many men and women, particularly educated sons of well-to-do families who could afford to be led by their conscience, left to take up residence in the Protestant towns of Germany and Switzerland.

It was not in Cromwell's nature to panic and, besides, there was still work to do. On 12 May he had introduced into Parliament his bill for the suppression of the greater monasteries. The proposed legislation regularized the confiscations and surrenders of property not catered for in the 1536 Act and allowed the King to take to his own use the goods and lands of such monasteries 'which hereafter shall happen to be dissolved, suppressed, renounced, relinquished, forfeited, given up, or by any other means come to his Highness'. With this Act, passed on 23 May, Cromwell could now complete the vanishing trick. Within ten months English monasticism had disappeared. The Act mentioned many of the schemes that Cromwell had afoot for the constructive use of the monasteries' confiscated wealth, and during the following months Cromwell gave considerable thought to the creation of new dioceses and centres of learning. He lived to see only a fraction of these ideas implemented. It was easier to fill Henry's coffers with gold than to induce him to spend any of it in a good cause.

Another personal triumph which did much to offset the disappointment Cromwell felt over the 'bloody whip with six strings' (as the Six Articles Act was soon referred to in Protestant circles) was the completion in April of the first edition of the Great Bible. The creation and dissemination of the first authorized translation of the whole body of Scripture was Thomas Cromwell's greatest single contribution to the English Reformation. As a biographer has said, 'no book ever played a more creative part in moulding the virtues and cloaking the sins of a nation which soon begat likeminded offspring across the oceans'.[58] The minister had been interested in Bible translations since before 1534, when he had enthusiastically encouraged Queen Anne Boleyn's similar concern. In his injunctions of 1536 he had instructed every parish priest to set up a Latin and English translation of the Scriptures in his church (this directive was widely ignored). In 1537 Cromwell personally obtained the King's permission for two rival versions of the Bible to be sold in England. Early in 1538 he decided to bring into being a single authorized and authoritative translation. With this in view, he set Miles Coverdale to revise the Matthew Bible – a translation made in Antwerp by John Rogers, who leaned heavily on the work of Tyndale. When the work was finished, Cromwell received royal permission for the new translation to be printed in Paris and imported into England. He was extremely enthusiastic about the project, frequently sending messengers across to France to discover how the work was progressing. He even sank £400 of his own money in the venture.[59] Then, in December 1538, came a bitter disappointment; the Inquisitor General of France stopped the printing, confiscated the plates and ordered all pages already printed to be burned. Cromwell remonstrated at the highest diplomatic levels, but it was only after several weeks of argument and bargaining that he obtained permission for the precious plates to be shipped across the Channel. Thus it was that only in 1539 the Great Bible was born after a long and arduous period of pre-natal care and a particularly critical confinement. The midwife was Thomas Cromwell.[60]

Throughout 1539 Cromwell spent much time on plans for a complete overhaul of the royal household. The day-to-day administration of Henry's squalidly luxurious court required the services of a vast hierarchy of officials from the Great Master down to the meanest scullion. The whole organization was extremely costly and cumbersome. To Cromwell's tidy mind it was simply ripe for reform. But the great noblemen and gentlemen who held the leading positions at court, who had a vested interest in preserving its traditions and privileges, were not going to permit their functions to be 'rationalized' by a mere commoner. In 1537 the Secretary had drawn up a proposed list of reforms and his scheme received encouragement from the King. But some skilful behind-the-scenes lobbying had swiftly crushed the plan and no more was heard of it for over a year. It speaks volumes for Cromwell's influence and tenacity that, only a few weeks after the reversal of his religious policy in May 1539, he should have been once more defying powerful opposition and planning the re-organization of the King's personal household.[61]

The reform which made most impression on contemporaries was the creation of the band of Gentlemen Pensioners. This was an armed guard of fifty splendidly equipped young men whose main function was decorative. They added lustre to the royal entourage and were designed to dazzle and impress alike the common people and foreign visitors. The creation of fifty new posts of prestige close to the King meant increased competition for positions on the part of younger sons of good family, supported by their sires and patrons. Cromwell, naturally, appointed a number of his own followers to the band of Kings 'spears' (as they were commonly called). One young man who succeeded in gaining a place among the honoured fifty was Sir William Ayscough's third son, Edward.

It seems that either the young man's father or his brother Christopher, who was still a gentleman of the Privy Chamber, had successfully sought the patronage of one of the great men about the court, for on 28 December Archbishop Cranmer sent Edward to the Lord Privy Seal with a note:

> In favour of Edward Ayscough, the bearer, my servant, son of Sir William Ayscough, who has been preferred by some nobleman, to the room of one of those new spears in the court, without his or my knowledge. He is very meet to furnish such a room.[62]

The provision of fifty extra places in the royal household for young gallants who could swagger around the court and its environs in the royal livery can hardly have been in Cromwell's mind when he embarked upon his reforming schemes. Probably it was the price exacted by a vain monarch who loved display, for permission to make economies elsewhere.

Nor was Cromwell able to cut down on the expenses of the royal chamber. This was the inner core of the household and the gentlemen who occupied positions in the Privy Chamber or Outer Chamber considered themselves very much a social elite. They were a haughty and lively group, the scions of ancient families, who, because of their closeness to the King, considered themselves quite above discipline and normal standards of behaviour. It was among these young bucks, the darlings of the court, that the reputation of Henry's household for loose morals largely originated. Their behaviour is clearly hinted at in an order from the Council dated 18 September 1540. Addressed to Robert Tyrrwhit, acting Vice Chamberlain on the King's side, and Sir Edward Brynton, the Queen's Vice Chamberlain, it gives instructions for the 'sober and temperate' order of their charges in the chambers of presence and particularly singles out for correction their behaviour towards members of the Privy Council and other notables.[63] The King, who smiled upon the gaming, drinking, wenching and haughty behaviour of his chamber staff, now protected them from Cromwell's bureaucratic pruning-hook. Indeed, the number of chamber officers was increased. In future the Privy Chamber and Outer Chamber were to be served by the following personnel:

## Privy Chamber

16 Gentlemen (who performed all the personal tasks about the

King such as making the royal bed – a task that included rolling on it to test it for concealed daggers – and dressing the royal person)

2 Gentlemen Ushers (who guarded the door of the Chamber)

4 Gentlemen Ushers' Daily Waiters (who were employed on various errands by the ushers and gentlemen)

3 Grooms

2 Barbers

## Outer Chamber

3 Cup Bearers

3 Carvers

3 Sewers

4 Squires of the Body (Personal attendants on the King about the court)

Additional chamber staff included two Officers of the Robes, five Officers of the Beds, one Groom Porter, eight Gentlemen Ushers' quarter waiters, four extra sewers, four pages and twelve grooms.

The new household ordinance came into being at Greenwich on Christmas Eve 1539[64] and Cromwell filled as many of the new posts as he could with his own nominees. He would have done this in any case but circumstances made it more important than ever to have friends and supporters in the King's Chamber. Norfolk and Gardiner were rallying courtiers and councillors to their party.

A few months before, Gardiner had risked an open argument with Cromwell at a Council meeting.[65] The subject of the dispute was Dr Robert Barnes, the Cambridge heretic. Barnes now enjoyed the patronage of the Vicar General and was employed as a preacher in support of the royal supremacy. Furthermore, he had been sent by the King as an ambassador to the German princes. This support for a known heretic with an unbridled tongue was an outrage in Gardiner's opinion. He had once been a friend and patron of Barnes and had attempted to wean the ex-friar from his false opinions but now friendship had soured to such an extent that Barnes was launching public attacks on the Bishop of Winchester. In September 1539 Gardiner had demanded action against this heretical troublemaker. As a result the Bishop had been dismissed from the Privy Council. He was still smarting under this indignity at the end of the year and was more ready than ever to stir other malcontents against the outrageous Thomas Cromwell.

Cromwell, by employing his 'new broom' throughout the household, had aroused many resentments and made the task of the conservatives easier. His provisions for financial reform and closer supervision of court officials were considered by many as unwonted interference with traditional privileges and procedures. Men of such importance as the Lord Great Master, the Treasurer of the Household and the Controller of the Household, who were also Privy Councillors and ministers of state, resented being told by Cromwell that they were to report every day to their court offices and check over the accounts of their underlings. Those underlings in their turn did not welcome the stricter control imposed on their income and expenditure. Cromwell's reforms undoubtedly put an end to many corrupt practices by which court officials had diverted money, goods and provisions to their own use; they certainly did not help him to win friends and influence people. So a few more faithful supporters among the close band of Chamber officers might provide a useful counterpoise. Among those who received promotion to the King's service at this time was John Lascelles. He was appointed a sewer of the Outer Chamber. In this important position he was responsible (working on a shift basis with his two colleagues) for supervising the arrangement of the King's table, for seating the King's guests, for serving the King's food and – perhaps most important of all in the household of a Renaissance monarch – for tasting every dish set before the King.

The position of a minister of the crown to King Henry VIII was always hazardous. The Sovereign allowed his representatives considerable scope in the formulation and execution of policies. He took the profits of and often the credit for his ministers' successes. The blame for failure fell entirely on the agent. Henry could be extremely generous in rewarding faithful service but once his minister had made a mistake or outlived his usefulness, previous years of devotion counted for nothing and the man's downfall could be swift and complete. On two matters Henry was particularly sensitive. Foreign affairs were, he believed, the preserve of princes. He might allow his ministers to initiate policies and begin to carry them into effect but he was quite capable of inaugurating contradictory policies of his own without the knowledge of his

Council. The other matter on which Henry felt strongly was his own matrimonial affairs. Other political failures he might occasionally tolerate but let a minister bungle the King's marriage or divorce arrangements and he was as good as dead. Wolsey had failed in his foreign policy and he failed to deliver Henry from an uncongenial marriage. He was fortunate enough to encounter death before he could meet his enraged King. Cromwell also failed in his foreign policy and succeeded all too well in forcing Henry into an uncongenial marriage. He did not share the good fortune of his predecessor.

The story of Cromwell's last months is quickly told. In December 1538 the Pope ordered the bull of excommunication against schismatic England (issued three years earlier) to be fully implemented. The Roman curia was, at long last, beginning to organize its Church to face up to the forces of Protestantism and nationalism. Europe's two great Catholic powers, France and the Empire, were temporarily united against the Turk, and the Pope hoped to turn their swords against the heretical English. There were two courses open to Henry's government. One was to try to break the Habsburg-Valois alliance and pursue once more the old policy of playing off the two continental powers against each other. The other was to form a counter-alliance with the Protestant states of northern Europe. Cromwell gave his full backing to the latter policy and German diplomats came to England to discuss the terms of a settlement. But they insisted on making theological unity the basis for political alliance. Henry VIII was no Lutheran and made his orthodoxy quite plain in the Six Articles. He wished to make clear to his brother sovereigns that his quarrel lay with the Pope and not with the Catholic Church. In the summer of 1539 England was on unfavourable terms with both the Lutheran and Catholic powers of Europe. This situation Cromwell found intolerable and hurried Henry with an uncharacteristic lack of caution towards an alliance with the House of Cleves. Duke William of Cleves was a Catholic but had close connections with the Schmalkaldic League. Because his territories were seriously threatened by the Emperor he was only too willing to sign a treaty with England – a treaty involving the marriage of Henry VIII with his sister Anne.

In backing the Cleves match for all he was worth Cromwell deliberately deceived his King as to the virtues and qualities of the Lady Anne. The services of Hans Holbein, the painter, were obtained to reproduce on canvas the plain, pock-marked features of the 'Flanders Mare' in such a way that they would captivate the heart of the English King. Not even the genius of the greatest portrait painter of the age could conjure beauty into a face completely devoid of that quality but his finished painting showed a comely enough lady and on the strength of it and the carefully-doctored reports of his ambassadors, Henry declared himself willing to end his two years' widowerhood. The treaty was signed on 4 October 1539.

When Henry came face to face with the reality of his espoused on New Year's Day 1540, the experience turned his stomach. He could not back out of the marriage, which was solemnized on 6 January, but beyond that (if we accept his testimony) he was quite unable to go. The sight of his new queen in naked bridal bed was utterly repugnant to him and he could not bring himself to consummate the union. Anne's plainness was probably her salvation. Her head may not have been a pretty one but, at least, she kept it on her shoulders. By this time Catherine Howard had already been introduced into the court and now she was dangled before the eyes of the frustrated and disappointed monarch by her scheming uncle, the Duke of Norfolk. In February the Franco-Imperial alliance broke down and an impending dispute between Charles V and Duke William of Cleves threatened to involve England in a quite unnecessary military adventure.

Cromwell's plans had completely misfired and his enemies did not hesitate to take full advantage of the fact. Gardiner succeeded in having three of Cromwell's protegés arrested on heresy charges and after their arrest the Secretary did not dare to intervene on their behalf. Instead he attempted to obtain a reconciliation with the Bishop of Winchester. Being invited to dinner and flattered by Cromwell must have delighted Gardiner, for he now saw that the all-powerful minister was beginning to feel insecure. On 12 April Cromwell attempted publicly to bring himself into line with the King's religious policy and rebut all suggestions of heresy. In a speech to Parliament on that day he made a plea for Christian unity, condemning, on the one hand, the 'inveterate corruption and superstitious obstinacy' of the papists and, on the other, 'the temerity and carnal liberty' of the heretics. He explained that the King inclined neither to one side nor the other 'but professed the true faith of Christ'. For the time being the King seemed satisfied

Henry VIII in triumph, trampling on Pope Clement VII. A woodcut from John Foxe's *Acts and Monuments*.

The Windsor Persecution. A woodcut from John Foxe's *Acts and Monuments.*

with his minister. Indeed, on 18 April he lavished on Cromwell the greatest honour the royal servant had yet received – the earldom of Essex. This placed him on socially equal terms with most of his enemies among the nobility and removed the stigma of his humble origins.

But Cromwell was not deceived by titles and honours. He had some idea of what his enemies were planning, though the details eluded him and the final blow came as a surprise. He laboured as never before to commend himself to the King. On 6 June, for instance, we find him writing to Dean Heneage at Lincoln with instructions for the demolition of the shrine of St Hugh – 'a centre of idolatry and superstition'. From Lincoln 2,621 ounces of gold and 4,285 ounces of silver were soon on their way to the vaults of the Tower of London.[66]

But the drama was moving inexorably towards its final scene. By now Henry was infatuated with Catherine Howard and was paying her nightly visits at Lambeth. Gardiner, now reinstated on the Council, was making Winchester House available to the King for meetings with his new mistress. At the beginning of June the vital decision was made – Henry vowed to marry Catherine, his 'rose without a thorn'. An ambassador was sent to assure the Emperor that the Cleves alliance was the work of a minister who had exceeded his instructions. Preparations were made for the annulment of Henry's marriage with Anne. Henry decided on an extravagant sacrifice which would reassure the Emperor, make him popular in the eyes of his people and assuage his own wrath over his marriage fiasco. On 10 June, as Cromwell was presiding over a Council meeting, the captain of the guard came in at a pre-arranged signal from Norfolk and arrested him. With unconcealed delight Norfolk and Southampton stripped his honours and decorations from him before he was marched away to a waiting barge, by which he was conveyed to the Tower.

The charges which formed the basis of his attainder were demonstrably false. There were eleven points to the accusation. Four concerned alleged abuses of power and official position. Four related to his supposed propagation of heresy and his encouragement and protection of heretics. One denounced him as a profiteer who had enriched himself at the expense of king and country. The other two referred to treasonable intentions and statements to which Cromwell had supposedly been driven by his overweening

I

ambition and his zeal to spread heresy. It mattered nothing that these charges could not be proved. What did matter was that Henry could be persuaded to believe them.

Henry, infatuated with Catherine Howard, needing a scapegoat for unpopular policies, extricating himself from the Protestant alliance and ever fearful of his own security, was prepared to be persuaded. He accepted the portrait of Cromwell painted by Gardiner and Norfolk which depicted the Lord Privy Seal as an over-mighty subject who would stop at nothing to force abominable heresies on England.[67]

And so Cromwell waited in vain for some sign of favour from his King. For forty-eight days he was able to reflect on his fate, and surely, with the anger, resentment and self-pity he must have felt, there was mingled a sense of frustration that he had been forced to leave so many tasks unfinished. For though he had accomplished more in six brief years of power than any of his predecessors in the whole history of royal government in England, he could never be content while anything still remained to be done. His judicial murder was attended to on 28 July 1540 by a bungling executioner who only succeeded after several attempts in severing the head from the body. Henry VIII celebrated the event by marrying Catherine Howard.

# 5

## *Check, Countercheck*

———❦❦❦———

T HE next few panels of the tapestry are crowded with
figures. No central personality engages our attention.
Between the years 1540 and 1543 rival groups in Church
and State struggled to control the destiny of England. When the
handle of the plough was no longer in Cromwell's firm grasp,
others groped and grappled for it. As a result the furrows of national
policy veered wildly from side to side. The uncertain course of
English life resulting from this struggle affected all the people of
the realm. Some who had before been insignificant pawns in the
game now found themselves in the centre of the board, making
moves which were to have momentous consequences for the
history of England.

The effects of a fresh, vivacious, teenage bride on England's
thrice-divorced and once-widowed royal egoist were magical.
Henry was besotted with Catherine's youthful gaiety. He lavished
jewels and clothes upon her[1] and his extravagance extended to the
whole court. It was almost like a return to the carefree early days
of the reign of Bluff King Hal, with frequent entertainments at
Westminster and Greenwich and public displays and pageants in
the streets of London. But if Englishmen felt a new age had
dawned, it was not only because a new queen had danced her way
into Henry's affections; it was also because a hated minister had
joined the sombre dance of death. After Cromwell's fall, the people
looked forward with more hope than reason to a brighter future.
Some wished to see a return to the good old pre-Reformation days.
Most longed only for years of peace, free from religious and

political tensions, in which they could adjust to the changes imposed during the preceding decade.

King and commoner alike were soon to be woken from their deep dream of peace. Henry was to suffer bitter disillusionment in the discovery that Catherine Howard was not the fresh, fragrant, unplucked rose he had thought her. Religious discord continued to divide his countrymen. Catholics were encouraged by the Act of Six Articles and the overthrow of Cromwell to denounce 'heretical' neighbours to the authorities. Protestants openly read their English Bibles and believed they found within its pages a higher sanction for their attacks on the 'papists'. This religious friction was to be found at all levels from the King's Council and court downwards.

John Lascelles felt very bitter about the downfall of his patron, nor was he without sympathizers among the close servants of the King. When they were free from their duties these courtiers would attend secret Bible-study meetings in London backrooms and listen to Protestant sermons preached from city pulpits. Perhaps they even organized their own meetings for Bible-reading and prayer within the court. Certainly they discussed the state of religion in the country and the beliefs and activities of their superiors.

On 15 September 1540 Lascelles, returning to court after a period of absence, walked into the Outer Chamber and found three of his colleagues there, Messrs Johnson, Moxey and Smythwick. Very soon the conversation turned to matters of religion.

'What news is there pertaining God's holy word, seeing we have lost so noble a man [i.e. Cromwell] which did love and favour it so well?' asked Lascelles. 'I know my Lords of Winchester and Norfolk are no lovers of the Bible.'

'No,' replied Moxey, 'I heard my Lord of Norfolk declare that he had never read the Scriptures in English and never will. Only yesterday I overheard him say, "It was merry in England before this new learning came up".'

All present agreed how intolerable the new 'cocks of the walk' had become. Norfolk and Gardiner had waged open war on the champions of the true faith and no one could prevail against them, so secure were they in the royal favour. Smythwick urged that, notwithstanding the undoubted power of their adversaries, faithful men about the court should stand firm as true soldiers of Christ against the agents of the papal Antichrist.

'Not so,' replied Lascelles. 'Let us not be too rash or quick in maintaining the Scriptures. If we wait quietly and do not oppose Norfolk and Winchester, but rather suffer a while in silence, they will overthrow *themselves*. For they stand so obviously against God and their Prince that they cannot long survive.'

Smythwick's zeal could not be so easily compromised. 'The Duke has spoken openly against the King's religious policy,' he said. 'Surely we can bring him to justice for that.' He described various occasions on which Norfolk had openly shown his contempt for the religious changes of recent years, opinions far from being reserved for private gatherings. Norfolk had spoken boldly in the King's Great Chamber, and but recently had quarrelled with a suitor in the Court of Exchequer.[2]

'How so?' enquired Lascelles.

'My Lord of Norfolk rebuked the man for marrying a nun. "Marry," says the man, "I know no nuns nor religious folk, nor no such bondage, seeing God and the King have made them free." At this the Duke waxes angry. "By God's body sacred," he swears, "that may be, but it will never be out of my heart as long as I live."'

Smythwick paused, while his friends pondered his words. Surely here was verbal treason, within the scope of the 1534 Act.

After a few moments John Lascelles said quietly, 'Best report this to Mr Hare.'[3]

Then the group split up, each going quietly – and thoughtfully – about his work.

The 'Mr Hare', to whom Smythwick did, indeed, report on the following day, was Sir Nicholas Hare, member of the Council, ex-Master of the Court of Requests, Speaker of the House of Commons and, until recently, a close colleague of Thomas Cromwell. Hare was no friend of the Howards but he was far too circumspect to allow himself to be drawn into open conflict with the Duke of Norfolk. He was one of a small band of adroit and quietly ambitious Tudor administrators, who served in various capacities under successive sovereigns and survived all the changes of policy which took place in the middle decades of the century.[4] Sir Nicholas listened carefully to the earnest Smythwick and advised him to repeat the story in person before the King's Council. This the zealous courtier eventually did, only to learn that it would take more than the truth to dislodge a man secure in the royal favour.[5] Henry knew Thomas Howard for the proud, blustering rather stupid man he was. He knew when any of his mightier subjects were likely to prove dangerous. For the moment he was prepared to allow Norfolk to bask in his niece's reflected warmth. Besides, the man had his uses. The King, therefore, took no action and Smythwick learned a lesson in court politics. He and his colleagues were disappointed but they remained vigilant. If they were faithful God might still choose to use them as his agents against the powers of darkness.

For the time being the powers of darkness seemed to be only too well established. On 30 July three leading Lutherans, who had long troubled the ecclesiastical authorities, were burned at Smithfield. They were Thomas Garrett, William Jerome and Robert Barnes.

Garrett we have met already as an active disseminator of Lutheran books at Oxford and as a licensed preacher who proved to be a thorn in the flesh of Bishop Longland. As an advocate of the royal supremacy Cromwell found him very useful and it was largely because of the patronage of the Lord Privy Seal and the Archbishop of Canterbury that he had kept out of trouble for so long. In 1537 he became one of Cranmer's chaplains and Cromwell appointed him to the living of All Hallows, Honey Lane in London. There he continued, unmolested, to preach advanced doctrines until Bishop Bonner, to please Cromwell, put Garrett's name on the list of Lent preachers at St Paul's Cross in 1540. The sermons were an important feature of the liturgical year in London and always attracted a crowd. Heretical doctrines or subversive opinions expressed under these conditions could hardly go unmarked by the authorities. This Stephen Gardiner knew well. In his opening sermon of the series, the Bishop of Winchester went out of his way to make a deliberately provocative attack on reformed doctrines. Garrett rose to the bait, and, when his turn came, he answered with an attack on Gardiner.

William Jerome was another of the Lenten preachers to exceed the bounds of fair comment in the opinion of his superiors. An ex-Benedictine monk of Canterbury, he had become notorious, especially in the north of England, for his Lutheran views. For a while he was associated with the fascinating Sir Francis Bigod.[6] In 1537, through Cromwell's patronage, he was presented to

Stepney Church (the parish in which Cromwell lived), where he lived peacefully until the troubles of 1540.

Dr Robert Barnes was the most prominent of the three. His vigorous activities as Protestant propagandist were notorious. As preacher, writer and diplomat he had done all in his power to draw England closer to the Continental Reformation. He had only been allowed to continue unmolested because of Cromwell's patronage and he was one of the men marked for destruction as soon as the minister's position became insecure. Gardiner, of course, had personal motives for desiring Barnes's downfall.

The sermons of Barnes, Jerome and Garrett were considered heretical and inflammatory and the three men were committed for examination by learned divines. This time (as Gardiner well knew) Cromwell was in no position to come to their aid and the preachers were forced to make a public recantation of their heretical opinions in sermons from the pulpit of St Mary Spital during Easter week. When the time came, the three Lutherans tried to have their cake and eat it. Their recantations were half-hearted affairs designed to save their skins without outraging their consciences. This prevarication exasperated Gardiner and even Henry, who had personally taken part in Barnes's examination. By order of the Council the heretical trio were imprisoned in the Tower. Their enemies then proceeded against them by Act of Attainder and not by prosecution under the Six Articles – presumably to prevent them appearing in their own defence and possibly wriggling out of the extreme penalty. On 30 July 1540, two days after the execution of Thomas Cromwell, Barnes, Jerome and Garrett were taken to Smithfield to be burned.

If Gardiner and the conservatives hoped that this would be the beginning of a Catholic reaction, they were soon disappointed. Henry would not be pushed to religious extremes by anybody. This he demonstrated in a lucid if macabre way on 30 July. On that day the three heretics were conveyed through the streets of London, each one lashed to a hurdle. But each one was not the sole occupant of his hurdle; by his side lay a papist, convicted of treason for refusing the oath of supremacy. In Smithfield the three Protestants were burned and the three Catholics were hung, drawn and quartered *simultaneously*: Henry VIII's enacted parable to teach his people to keep to the *media via*.

Another reason why Gardiner and Norfolk did not have everything their own way was that they still had opponents on the Council. Of the great men of the realm, no one was closer to the King than Charles Brandon, Duke of Suffolk. The son of Henry VII's standard bearer at Bosworth, Brandon was raised to high honours and wealth because of his family's loyalty to the Lancastrian cause. But he became much more than a devoted servant of the Tudor regime. He became a close companion of the young Henry VIII. 'In personal qualities, indeed, he was not unlike his sovereign; tall, sturdy and valiant, with rather a tendency to corpulence, and also with a strong animal nature, not very much restrained at any time by considerations of morality, delicacy or gratitude.'[7] Like Henry, also, his matrimonial entanglements were many and complex. He had already been twice married when, in 1515, he had the audacity to win the heart of the King's sister Mary. After eighteen years of married life his royal wife died and Brandon married his young ward, Catherine Willoughby d'Eresby, a wealthy Lincolnshire heiress. This fourteen-year-old girl was to grow into one of the most formidable grand ladies of her age and a heroine of the Reformation (see below p. 237). It is doubtful whether Suffolk shared his young wife's religious ardour but he was certainly sympathetic towards the reformed faith. Two of his personal chaplains were at one time or another in trouble for their advanced religious opinions[8] and he raised no objections when Catherine read her Bible and taught members of her household from it. He rarely conflicted with the conservative councillors on matters of religion; though he did not like Gardiner, his differences were mainly with Thomas Howard and they were personal. Brandon was one of those whom Norfolk looked down on as 'upstarts'. Before he had found favour with the King he had been nothing. Now he was Duke of Suffolk, Great Master of the Household and stood higher in the King's favour than members of the ancient Howard family. Furthermore, Suffolk had on occasions outshone Norfolk as a military commander – and martial valour was a quality the King set a great price on.

Yet, if Suffolk was considered something of an upstart by the Howards, what did they make of Edward Seymour? This son of a Wiltshire landowner had made a career for himself as courtier and soldier in the '20s and had been knighted on campaign by the Duke of Suffolk in 1523. He had quickly found favour with the King.

Lands and honours had come to him in abundance. But it was when the royal fancy lighted upon Edward's sister, Jane, that the Seymours' ship finally came home. Jane supplanted Anne Boleyn, the Howard protégée, as Queen of England in May 1536. In June, Sir Edward Seymour became Viscount Beauchamp of Hache, with large grants of lands in Wiltshire. In July he was appointed Governor and Captain of Jersey. In August he became Chancellor of North Wales. In the following January he succeeded to his father's estates and received fresh grants of land in Somerset. In May 1537 he became a member of the King's Council. In October he was created Earl of Hertford. How the Howards – and particularly Norfolk's hot-headed son, the Earl of Surrey – hated him.

In religious matters Hertford was a follower of the New Learning – a rational humanist, strongly inclined to Protestantism. He warmly supported Cromwell's policies between 1537 and 1540 and was particularly enthusiastic about the Cleves match. In a letter to Cromwell dated 17 July 1539 he declared himself as delighted about the forthcoming marriage 'as ever I was of anything since the birth of the Prince; for I think the King's Highness should not in Christendom marry in no place meet for his Grace's honour that should be less prejudicial to his majesty's succession'.[9] In August he entertained the King and Cromwell at his Wiltshire home and a few days later he received the Sheen Charterhouse as a result of Cromwell's intercession. In December he escorted Anne of Cleves from Calais to London.[10] It is an indication of Hertford's high standing with Henry and of his political acumen that Cromwell's fall (and, indeed, the death of Queen Jane in 1537) did not affect his steady rise to power and fortune.

In 1540 the split in the Privy Council, which had begun with the conservative reaction against Cromwell, widened. A division was growing between the 'new men', of liberal outlook, who were sympathetic towards the movement for further reform, and the reactionaries, mistrustful of change, who wanted to stamp out heresy and other insidious new influences. In April of that year the Council ceased to be under the domination of one man, the Secretary. From that time onwards there were two secretaries[11] who had important administrative functions but who could not be said to *dominate* meetings. The situation was thus a fluid one which readily permitted personality clashes and group rivalries to develop. There is, moreover, every indication that the King, realizing that no body of nineteen men[12] lacking forceful leadership could avoid splitting into factions, made a point of keeping the rival groups evenly balanced. The Privy Council as it had emerged by 1540 was a new national institution. Gone was the medieval body of royal advisers. The new organization was a permanent instrument of government with well-defined procedures and functions. It was also an organization unsure of its exact powers. In theory it could do nothing without royal sanction. In practice many day-to-day matters were conducted on the authority of conciliar decisions, and the King allowed his Privy Council considerable latitude. During the last six years of the reign the Council was groping for authority, just as groups within the Council were groping for supremacy. This was a tense, and potentially dangerous, state of affairs.

After their initial failure to wield the 'six-stringed whip' with full ferocity, the Catholic leaders changed their tactics. Clearly any attempt to instigate mass prosecutions would not be permitted by the King. The conservative bishops, therefore, proceeded cautiously, indicting only those heretics who were really troublesome. Yet it was quite obvious that selective, sporadic persecution would not stop a virulent Protestantism which was spreading with a truly alarming rapidity. It was probably the conservative councillors who devised a daring scheme which, if successful, would prove an effective check to the growth of this religious cancer. They proposed to strike at prominent Protestants in Church and State. Nothing had more encouraged the spread of reformed doctrines in recent years than noble patronage or royal favour extended to known 'heretics'. So, reasoned Gardiner and his supporters, if these powerful patrons could be removed or frightened into outward orthodoxy, the Protestant flood might be stemmed until the end of Henry's reign. For it now began to be obvious that the obese and prematurely aged monarch could have few years left to him and that, in all probability, he would be succeeded by a son who was still a minor. There seemed little reason to doubt that any regency council would be dominated by Norfolk – and that, under him, a Catholic reaction could be set in motion.

The conservative leaders began cautiously with attacks on London preachers patronized by members of the court. Of all the city churches, St Mary Aldermary was something of a Mecca for Protestants. There was the pulpit of the eloquent Dr Edward Crome. Crome had learned his new faith during his days at

Cambridge, where had had been a member of the White Horse Inn group. He had proved very useful to Henry at the time of the divorce and enjoyed the patronage of Anne Boleyn and Thomas Cranmer. It was Queen Anne who had procured for him the living of St Mary Aldermary, where, despite occasional clashes with higher ecclesiastical authority, he had preached unmolested against cardinal Catholic doctrines and openly advocated biblical religion since 1534. His sermons attracted large congregations which included lawyers, wealthy merchants[13] and courtiers. John Lascelles and his colleagues were well acquainted with Crome, as were the King's doctors (Dr Butts and Dr Huick) and many others about the court. During the Bishop of London's attempted persecution of 1539 Crome was protected by the King himself and the Vicar of Aldermary continued to preach in his usual vein. He had as curate an equally formidable Protestant champion in the person of Dr Robert Wisdom, who had already fallen foul of Bishop Longland in Oxford and Bishop Stokesley in London.

It was against Wisdom that the authorities struck first. Shortly after the downfall of Cromwell, Bonner, the new Bishop of London (who had been an enthusiastic supporter of Cromwell's policies but now found it convenient to turn his coat), arrested the curate of St Mary Aldermary and had him brought before the Privy Council. The Council consigned him to a spell of imprisonment in the Lollard's Tower, where he spent some time writing a reply to the accusations brought against him.

The conservative councillors allowed little time to elapse before proceeding against Wisdom's vicar. Crome and an adversary, named Dr Wilson, spent part of the autumn of 1540 engaged in a contest of pulpit oratory, which created a considerable stir throughout the city. Both contestants were ordered to stop preaching until they had been examined by the Council. The examination took place on Christmas day. Gardiner did all in his power to make a charge of heresy stick but Crome was protected by Henry, in the highest of spirits during that first Yuletide with his young Queen. Crome's preaching licence was taken away for a spell but otherwise he was not further molested.

The spring and summer of 1541 saw a fresh burst of examinations under the Statute of Six Articles. Among those now troubled was Alexander Seton, chaplain to the Duke of Suffolk. Seton was an ex-friar from Scotland. Accepting reformed doctrines, he became a violent critic of the Scottish bishops and soon stirred up so much powerful opposition that he had to flee southwards. The Brandons took him under their protection and he received a licence to preach in England. Here, his sermons were as uncongenial to the Church authorities as they were in his own country. He was examined by the Council and ordered to make a public recantation of his errors. This he did at St Paul's Cross. Apparently he behaved himself for the short remainder of his life. He died at Suffolk's town house in 1542.

At about the same time, the conservatives struck at one of the King's courtiers. Sir George Blagge was a great favourite of Henry's, who used to call him his 'little pig'. Blagge also was a Lutheran. In the summer of 1541 the conservatives did not dare to bring a charge of heresy against one so close to the King but they did call Blagge to account for failing to attend his parish church, and the reluctant courtier was forced to resume attendance at a mass he found repulsive.

All in all, things were going well for the forces of reaction. Henry was very worried about increasing religious discord in the country. Proceedings against heretics had resulted in many recantations and only a few stubborn individuals had persisted in error unto death. Some, like the notorious John Bale (now in Germany), had fled the country. The Howards were still triumphant and in June Norfolk and many of his supporters were chosen to accompany the King and Queen on a triumphal progress into Lincolnshire and Yorkshire. Gardiner was away in Germany on a diplomatic mission but his colleagues were confident in the royal favour and were planning their next moves against the protagonists of reformation. They had reckoned without the insignificant sewer of the King's Chamber – John Lascelles.

Master Lascelles was an embittered young man. A year before, he had confidently forecast the downfall of Norfolk and his supporters, yet the Howard clan now seemed unshakably secure. The temperamental young Queen was feted and fawned on by all at court, her moods and tantrums indulged by everyone from the King downwards. More and more Howard protégés were introduced into court offices and, as the Catholic campaign intensified, John Lascelles and his co-religionists felt increasingly insecure. The examination of his friend, Sir George Blagge, had come as a nasty shock and there were other Protestant sympathizers at court who were becoming the subjects of gossip and intrigue. It was rumoured that all who had frequented the sermons of Dr Crome would be sought out and brought to trial under the Act of Six Articles. John was particularly angry about the silencing of Crome, whom he considered a fearless prophet of God. Though there were still other preachers to hear in London, none had the fiery zeal or the persuasive ardour of the Vicar of St Mary Aldermary. On every side the armies of Satan were prevailing in the battle. That champion of the faith, Cromwell, had been overthrown. Would not God raise up another to smite the hosts of Mideon? Or could it be that the Lord was calling him, John Lascelles, to wield the sword to the destruction of the foe? For John Lascelles was beginning to believe there might be a way to break the power of the mighty Howards. Of late, as he watched the plump, dark-haired Queen, whose smile never failed to charm her dotard husband, snatches of stories and old gossip had flitted through his mind – tales told by his sister Mary. Could it be . . . ?[14]

In June the royal entourage left London for the north, and, as John Lascelles had not been selected to accompany the royal party, he rode into Sussex. There lived his newly-married sister, wife to Mr Hall, a gentleman of the county. During the following weeks John probed Mistress Hall's memory of her stay in the Duchess of Norfolk's household.

Piece by piece John assembled the chronicle of Catherine Howard's love affairs. At the age of fourteen she had held evening assignations in the Duchess's chamber with Henry Manox, her music teacher. This first sally into the excitements of love-play had not gone beyond intimate caresses. Of a different nature was the affair with Francis Dereham. Dereham, a gentleman attendant upon the Duke of Norfolk, took to visiting the girls' dormitory at night in company with other young gallants. They would bring with them 'wine, strawberries, apples and other things to make good cheer' – prepared for nocturnal entertainment and the satisfying of more than one kind of appetite. The relationship between Catherine and Dereham soon developed into something more than amorous dalliance – certainly as far as the gentleman was concerned. He repeatedly asked his mistress to marry him but eventually had to accept the fact that no Howard girl was her own to give. At length Catherine was placed at court and Master Dereham's visits had to cease. So much and more did John Lascelles learn from his sister.[15]

His next problem was to decide whether he dared use the information. To blurt the story out and be disbelieved would be to court certain imprisonment and probable death. Even if the story were proved true to the King's satisfaction the storyteller might well feel the backlash of the royal displeasure. Whichever way we look at this sordid episode it is clear that Lascelles had nothing to gain personally from informing on the Queen. He acted out of religious zeal tinged by hatred for the men who had brought about Cromwell's fall and had declared themselves the enemies of reformed Christianity. He did not need to convince himself that it was his plain duty to God and the King to reveal what he knew.

Once action had been resolved on, the opportunity for executing it was not difficult to find. In fact, the time was hardly more propitious. All the members of the Howard faction were in the north with the King. Only a remnant of the Privy Council had been left behind to attend to affairs in the capital. The prominent members of this 'rump' were the Lord Chancellor, Sir Thomas Audley, Archbishop Cranmer and the Earl of Hertford. Of the three, there was only one (perhaps, indeed, he was the only one in all England) who would dare to confront the King with the humiliating and heart-breaking news – Cranmer. Lascelles returned to Westminster and sought out the Archbishop.

The story that Lascelles told Cranmer must have been, to say the least, a greatly simplified version of the truth. He related his recent visit to Sussex and declared that he had urged his sister to seek service with the Queen, who would surely remember her kindly after their days in the Duchess's household. Mary had, according to her brother, declined to accept his advice, declaring that she was very sorry for the Queen. 'Why so?' Lascelles had demanded. 'Marry, for she is light both in living and conditions.' The brother had been, he assured Cranmer, astonished to hear this and had incredulously demanded what Mistress Hall could possibly mean. Whereupon Mary had *reluctantly* told the story of Catherine Howard's fornication.

The responsibility now lay with Cranmer and the burden weighed heavily upon him. He brooded long over the matter and then discussed it with his two colleagues on the King's Council in London. It must have been with some sense of satisfaction that they decided that it was their painful duty to inform the King. On 29 October the court returned from its northern tour and took up residence at Hampton Court. Cranmer joined the royal party there and waited, with extreme nervousness, for a suitable opportunity to confront his master. It was not until 2 November that the Archbishop could bring himself to approach Henry. Even then he dared not speak damning words against the Queen. Instead he drew the King on one side as he was leaving a mass celebrated by Bishop Longland and handed him a letter containing a full account of Lascelles' confession. He urged the King to read it privately and then hurried away before the storm broke.

But there was no thundering of royal wrath, for the simple reason that Henry did not believe a word of it. He was convinced that the whole story was a malicious fabrication, and sent William Fitzwilliam, Earl of Southampton to Westminster to examine John Lascelles and to shake a confession out of him. Southampton took the young informer into a quiet room of the palace and went over every point of the story. Nowhere could he find a discrepancy. Lascelles, nervous but resolute, would neither change nor retract one word of his evidence. This Fitzwilliam had to report when he had at last let Lascelles go and ridden back to the King at Hampton Court.

If Henry's confidence in his Queen's purity was beginning to waver, he certainly did not show it. So, if John Lascelles remained obdurate then Fitzwilliam should ride into Sussex to examine sister Mary. It should be an easier task to crack open the story of a weak woman. Southampton left Hampton Court on 4 November for a 'hunting trip' while Manox and Dereham were secretly apprehended by the King's officers, taken to Lambeth and examined by Wriothesley and Cranmer. The poison was working inexorably and before the Earl could return to relate Mary Hall's confirmation of every detail of her brother's story, Catherine's two admirers had broken down under examination. Manox confessed frequent intimacy with young Mistress Howard and Dereham acknowledged that 'he had known her carnally many times, both in his doublet and hose between the sheets and in naked bed'.[16]

On the morning of the sixth the King attended in person a full Privy Council meeting. There all the evidence concerning the Queen and her former lovers was laid before him. How Henry must have felt his years suddenly heavy upon him. He wept tears of

anger and self-pity. Why had God cursed every one of his marriages? Was there no one he could trust? Was he surrounded only by
men and women who flattered and deceived him for their own
selfish ends? Wearily he left his councillors to do what they had to
do, while he made his way secretly back to Westminster. That
afternoon a body of Council members visited Catherine to confront
her with her crimes and inform her that she was to be confined to
Hampton Court until further notice.

From 12 November, when the scandal was made public, it
seemed that the entire Howard family would fall under the royal
displeasure. The Duke of Norfolk threw himself into a frenzy of
activity directed against his niece and her lovers, hoping thereby
to dissociate himself from their crimes. When he had done all he
could, he prudently retired to his East Anglian estates. He was
alone among the leading members of the family not to be arrested.
Everyone connected with Catherine and her days at Horsham and
Lambeth was sought out. All the ladies of the Duchess's household
were questioned and some detained. The only exception made was
for Mary Hall. The 'Council with the King' at Greenwich specifically informed the 'Council in London' that Mistress Hall was, 'as
an encouragement to others to reveal like cases, not to be troubled'
– an instruction which the recipients considered 'most graciously
determined'.[17] The Dowager Duchess, herself, was conveyed to the
Tower on 10 December whither Lord William and other members
of the family had already preceded her.

Meanwhile, intent on finding an excuse for the execution of the
Queen and Dereham (for pre-marital intercourse, even in a queen,
was scarcely sufficient to justify the death penalty even in Tudor
times), the Council was busy fabricating a charge of adultery.
Dereham was accused of continuing a carnal relationship with
Catherine after her marriage to the King. Then the bloodhounds
got on to a new and genuine scent. The Queen had been carrying
on an adulterous love affair – but not with Francis Dereham. For
months she had been having clandestine meetings with Thomas
Culpepper, a gentleman of the King's Privy Chamber. News of
this rash and stupid liaison must have leaked out sooner or later.
By indulging it the fickle Queen was erecting her own gallows. It is,
indeed, ironical that the Privy Council should have stumbled on
the truth accidentally, while attempting to create a falsehood.

The wheels of Henrician 'justice' ground slowly, but they ground

GARDINER BISHOP of WINCHESTER.

*From an original Picture in the Possession of*
EDMUND TURNOR ESQ? FR. & ASS.

*ab. July 1.1790. by E.Harding N°132. Fleet Street.* HENRY VIII.

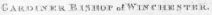

Chancelor

Members of the Conservative
Faction.

*Above left:* Stephen Gardiner,
Bishop of Winchester.

*Above:* Thomas Howard, Duke of
Norfolk, *by Holbein.*

*Left:* Sir Richard Rich, Chancellor
of the Court of Augmentations, *by
Holbein.*

Members of the Reforming Faction.

*Above left :* Thomas Cranmer, Archbishop of Canterbury, *by G. Flicke.*

*Above :* Edward Seymour, Earl of Hertford, *by Nicholas Hilliard.*

*Left :* John Dudley, Lord Lisle, *artist unknown.*

exceeding small. On 1 December Dereham and Culpepper were tried and convicted of treason and on the tenth they died at Tyburn. Both had appealed to the royal clemency, asking that the normal barbarous traitor's death might be commuted to execution under the axe. The boon of a painless death was granted to Culpepper, the adulterous courtier: but it was refused to Dereham, who could confess to nothing more than that he had had intercourse with a woman to whom he was lawfully married* before there had been any suggestion that she might marry the King.[18] Catherine had to wait until Parliament reassembled in January before official proceedings were begun against her. Then a bill of attainder for high treason was presented to and passed by both Houses. It was on the morning of 13 February 1542 that Catherine Howard – a foolish and frightened girl, but a Queen – stepped out on to Tower Green to meet her executioner.

Was John Lascelles present among the small group of spectators who had come to witness the passing of their Sovereign's fifth queen? Did he feel impelled to be present at the last act of a drama to which he had spoken such a powerful prologue? Whether or not he was there to witness Catherine Howard's last breath hang on the winter air, he must have been feeling a deep sense of satisfaction. With the Duke of Norfolk skulking in the country in fear of some manifestation of the royal displeasure and other members of the hated family behind bars and stone walls, Lascelles could at last feel that Cromwell's death had been avenged. Now that the Catholics' most powerful champion was removed from court and Council the work of reformation might, he hoped, be resumed under the leadership of Cranmer and Hertford. Truly 'the whirligig of time brings in his revenges'. But, unfortunately for John Lascelles, the whirligig had not stopped turning. For the Howards, the loyal sewer of the King's Chamber was now a marked man. If, somehow, they were able to swing back into Henry's favour, Lascelles must needs look to his own safety.

For a while the Catholic councillors were silenced – but not the Catholic bishops. As they had feared, the open English Bible had provided ammunition for the growing throng of critics, who were challenging the very foundations of English Christianity. As we have seen, their concern was shared by the King, who disliked the

---

* Verbal pre-contract followed by intercourse constituted one recognized form of marriage in the sixteenth century.

K

way in which religious issues had become one of the most frequent subjects of alehouse disputation. Now the Catholic bishops (who, since the resignation of Latimer and Shaxton in 1539, had had a large majority in Convocation) launched a vigorous campaign aimed at stopping or restricting the reading of the vernacular Scriptures.

Each diocesan did all he could in his own bishopric to bring pressure to bear on his clergy and laity. Bonner, for instance, early in 1542 issued *An admonition and advertisement given by the Bishop of London to all readers of this Bible in the English tongue*. In it he complained that 'the abuse, default and ill behaviour' of a few persons indiscreet and ill-advised in their understanding of Scripture was hindering, rather than helping, the spread of the Gospel.[19] What Bonner was trying to stop was the public Bible readings which many zealots were giving in churches and private houses for the benefit of their illiterate neighbours. The setting forth of the Great Bible had provided bold Protestant spirits with an ideal means of proselytizing. They would read from the chained Bible of their parish church to groups of eager listeners, while their priest stood angrily and powerlessly by. They would hold meetings for Bible-study in their houses. Wealthy householders would gather their servants around and teach them the Scriptures. In such groups exposition frequently led to interpretation and interpretation to exhortation. Thus Protestantism spread and no amount of episcopal injunctions could stop it as long as Englishmen were permitted and even (by royal injunction) encouraged to read the Bible in their native tongue.

In February 1542 the conservatives in Convocation decided that something must be done about the Great Bible. They demanded that it should be called in and a revised edition issued. What they had in mind was a revision carried out largely by themselves which should be made to support Catholic dogma, to contain no disputable interpretations and to leave no foothold for deliberate misinterpretation. Cranmer had no desire to see the Great Bible for which he had fought and prayed bowdlerized by the conservatives, and used his influence with the King to sink Convocation's resolution. On 10 March he was able to inform the assembled divines that the King had decided to order a revision but that it would be carried out by the universities and not by the bishops. This, as Cranmer's opponents well knew, would entail months or years of delay while the learned doctors of Oxford and Cambridge pored over the texts. Probably the whole scheme would end up by being quietly shelved. They were angry but quite unable to do more than protest.

It was in the following year, 1543, that the Catholic leaders struck – repeatedly and hard. A move in foreign policy created a favourable atmosphere for fresh anti-Protestant activity. On 11 February Henry VIII ratified a treaty with Catholic Spain. The alliance which Gardiner had advocated for so long had thus come into being. Its effects in England were felt almost immediately.

Gardiner's faction now made an all-out attack on influential Protestants. In this work the Bishop used the services of a very able spy – none other than Dr John London, the quondam Warden of New College, Oxford.

Since his persecuting career at the University had come to an end, he had been one of the leading commissioners involved in the dissolution of the monasteries and had shown as great a zeal in dispossessing the religious as he had done in hunting down heretics. After the death of Cromwell, he attached himself to Stephen Gardiner, and received preferment from him. The Bishop found a use for London's odious talents in ferreting out offenders against the Statute of Six Articles. In 1543 the inquisitor found himself hot on the scent of a group of heretics in Windsor.[20] The central figure in the group was Anthony Parsons, an active preacher and dispenser of banned books. Other local men such as Henry Filmer were implicated in his heresy but London (and his master) was much more interested in the more important figures who had encouraged and supported the priest. These included Robert Testwood and John Marbeck, singing-men from the Chapel Royal, and a number of courtiers: Sir Thomas Caradine, Sir Thomas Weldon and Edmund Harman. But the most important members of the 'catch' were Sir Philip Hoby, one of the King's gentlemen ushers, and Dr Simon Heynes, Dean of Exeter, a leading ecclesiastic and staunch supporter of Archbishop Cranmer. Armed with all London's evidence, Gardiner unburdened himself to the King at the beginning of March about his concern at the spread of heresy at all levels of society. Henry agreed that it was very disturbing and gave the Bishop licence to take action against the offenders.

Gardiner went straight for the most prominent members of the sect. Hoby and Heynes were arrested and examined by the Council on 18 March.[21] They failed to satisfy their examiners and were sent to the Fleet prison. Gardiner would doubtless have liked the affair to go further, but Henry was not disposed to allow prominent members of the establishment to be put on public trial as heretics. The two men were allowed to cool their heels in prison for six weeks and were then released. Meanwhile Parsons, Filmer, Testwood and Marbeck were also imprisoned. While in custody they were examined by the Privy Council and Marbeck particularly was interrogated repeatedly by Winchester and his agents in an attempt to get him to implicate his superiors.

But while all this was taking place another net was being cast to trap the biggest fish of all, Archbishop Cranmer.[22] Many of his prebendaries at Canterbury had long resented Cranmer's reforming activities. In April, with Winchester's encouragement some of them, led by Germaine Gardiner (Stephen's nephew and secretary) and the ubiquitous Dr London, formally protested to the King, presenting him with a list of Cranmer's heresies. Henry received the complaints without comment, and after a few days licensed the Council to take proceedings against the Archbishop. But he had no intention of allowing himself to be robbed of a faithful and pliant servant. He had already lived to regret having given the Howard-Gardiner party its head in the campaign against Cromwell. On the same day that he received the prebendaries' accusations, Henry took the opportunity of a chance meeting with his Archbishop to warn him of what was afoot. Summoning Cranmer aboard the royal barge in the damp April evening the King is reported to have greeted him jovially: 'Ah, my chaplain, I have news for you. I know now who is the greatest heretic in Kent,' and he held out the prebendaries' articles. The crestfallen Archbishop had no alternative but to submit himself humbly to the King's justice but Henry was having none of that. He declared that these were serious charges brought by the prebendaries. They must therefore be examined by a wise and experienced commissioner. Who better for the task, he suggested, than Cranmer himself? In vain did the royal chaplain protest that he could scarcely be considered impartial in a case so closely touching himself. We have already seen just how much store Henry VIII set by judicial impartiality.

Cranmer was thus left to deal with affairs at Canterbury in his own way but the threat of action by the Privy Council remained. Henry had not mentioned this to the Archbishop and he now consented to Cranmer's arrest during a meeting of the Privy Council. Gardiner who was, of course, behind this manoeuvre was delighted and reported to his colleagues. Some of the Councillors had misgivings about the whole business. They could not believe that the King would give up his Archbishop to certain death. But Gardiner and Norfolk were convinced that they had triumphed. They envisaged a repeat performance of Cromwell's denunciation and arrest. With both the architects of the Reformation out of the way, there would be no one of any consequence left to uphold their policies.

On the night before the Council Chamber drama was scheduled to take place, Henry sent one of his court favourites, Sir Anthony Denny,[23] to fetch Cranmer across the river to Westminster. The Archbishop arose from his bed and hurried to obey the summons. In a quiet corner of the gallery at Whitehall, the two lonely figures, their servants dismissed, stood talking in the dim, guttering torchlight. Two ageing and lonely men discussing matters of life and death. The King told Cranmer of the Council's complaint and concluded:

'Therefore, I have granted their request.' He looked hard at the Archbishop, whose features remained impassive. 'But whether I have done well or no, what say you?'

What could poor Thomas Cranmer say, but thank the King for this forewarning and declare himself content to be subject to the royal justice. Such naïve other-worldliness was too much for Henry, the realist.

'Oh Lord God!' he cried out. 'What fond simplicity you have, to let yourself be imprisoned, so that every enemy of yours may take advantage against you. Do you not know, that when they have you once in prison, three or four false knaves will soon be procured to witness against you, and condemn you, which otherwise, you being at liberty, dare not once open their lips or appear before your face. No, not so, my Lord, I have better regard unto you, than to permit your enemies so to overthrow you.'

Henry paused and took one of the many rings from his fingers.

'I will have you come to the Council tomorrow. And when they break this matter unto you, require of them that you may have your accusers brought before you. And if they will, under no circumstances, condescend unto your request, but are determined to send you to the Tower, then appeal from them to our Person, and give them this my ring, by which they will understand that I have taken your cause into my hand and away from them.'

Henry was thinking, perhaps, of other occasions when his ministers had overreached themselves. 'They well know this ring, and that I use it for no other purpose but to call matters from the Council into my own hands, to be ordered and determined.'

Cranmer took the token with profuse thanks and left the palace, stumbling down to the quayside behind his torchbearer, and so was rowed home.

The following day events fell out as the King had foreseen. Cranmer was summoned to the Council meeting but on arrival found the Chamber door locked against him – a calculated snub by his enemies who were relishing every insult they could heap upon the Archbishop. For over an hour he was kept waiting in the antechamber with lackeys and suitors before his colleagues deigned to receive him into the room where he had sat at the Council board for the last ten years. At last he stood before his fellow councillors, some of whom made no attempt to conceal their malice, while others tried to avoid looking at the accused; none dared support the Archbishop either by word or gesture. Their spokesman – probably Gardiner – read the indictment: 'That he, and others by his permission, has infected the whole realm with heresy', and informed Cranmer that he was to be taken forthwith to the Tower. Might not he meet his accusers and have an opportunity to answer their charges, the prisoner asked. But the conservative faction had no intention of allowing the Archbishop to defend himself either in the Council Chamber or anywhere else. Their plan was to proceed by Act of Attainder – as had been done in the case of Cromwell – which allowed the accused no defence, nor even the right to be present at his own trial.

Cranmer's enemies had doubtless expected to see some signs of nervousness or fear in their quarry by this time, but the Archbishop was as unruffled as ever.

'I am sorry, my Lords,' he said, 'that you would drive me unto this exigent, to appeal from you to the King's Majesty.' Cranmer opened his right hand to reveal what had lain concealed in his palm as he continued: 'who, by this token hath resumed this matter into his own hand, and dischargeth you thereof.'

The King's ring now lay before them on the table.

Had it been a coiled snake instead of a circlet of gold, its effect could not have been more dramatic. Some stared open-mouthed. Others leapt to their feet. John Russell swore loudly, glaring round with his one eye,[24] 'Did I not tell you, my Lords,' he thundered, 'what would come of this matter? I know right well that the King would never permit my Lord of Canterbury to have such a blemish, as to be imprisoned, unless it were for high treason.' Gardiner and his supporters had blundered and they knew it. The only thing to be done now was to repair to the King with all haste and hope to salvage something from the wreck of their fortunes. The whole Council, therefore, went straight away to the royal apartments, for all the world like a band of dejected schoolboy offenders on their way to the headmaster's study.

And, in fact, Henry's handling of the matter smacks somewhat of the Victorian public school pedagogue.

'Ah, my Lords, I thought that I had a discreet and wise Council, but now I perceive that I am deceived. How have ye handled here my Lord of Canterbury? What make ye of him? A slave? Shutting him out of the Council Chamber among serving men?' And he proceeded in this vein for several minutes before ordering them all to shake hands with the Archbishop and to avoid all malice in future. Then he instructed Cranmer to entertain each of the councillors to dinner in the near future as a sign that they were all friends again. So the affair ended with nothing worse than sharp words to be endured. But no more attempts to disgrace Cranmer were made during the reign of Henry VIII.

If the King was prepared to spare individuals whom he liked or who were useful to him, that did not mean that his concern about the spread of heresy was feigned. While Gardiner and his colleagues were failing to bring down the Archbishop, they were scoring two notable successes in the sphere of official Christian doctrine in the Church of England.

On 29 May there was published the latest official statement of faith of Henry's Catholic Church – the *Necessary Doctrine and Erudition for any Christian Man*. This doctrinal code, better known as *The King's Book*, was a revised edition of the earlier *Bishop's Book*. It was set out more clearly, was more precise in its definitions and more Catholic in tone than any earlier formulary of the reign. In its support of such medieval doctrines as sacramental penance, transubstantiation, prayers for the dead and salvation by works as well as faith, it clearly reflected the opinions of the reactionary bishops, led by Gardiner.

The second triumph of the conservatives was the passing through Parliament of the Act for the Advancement of True Religion. It condemned anew all unauthorized translations of the Old and New Testaments and then went on severely to restrict the numbers of people who might read the Great Bible. All women, artificers, apprentices, and others under the rank of yeomen were utterly forbidden to read the Scriptures either privately or publicly. Noblemen, gentlemen and merchants were permitted to study the Bible with their households at home. But apart from these wealthy – and, therefore, presumably discreet – members of society, all Englishmen were to lose a privilege they had enjoyed for barely four years.

A liberty bestowed and then snatched away is worse than no liberty at all. Throughout the country, men – by no means all of them Protestants – bitterly resented the new restrictions. Reformers, most of them safely lodged in Dutch, German or Swiss towns, poured forth a stream of tracts condemning the new legislation.

> ... it was told me that the bishops had made an Act that none but gentlemen and gentlewomen might read the Scriptures, and certain rich men. But I will ask the authors of that Act whether they suffer the gentle and the rich to read the Scriptures for their souls' health, or for their pastime. If they suffer them to read it for their souls' health, died not Christ as well for craftsmen and poor men as for gentlemen and rich men and would not Christ that the poor labouring men should have wherewith they might comfort their souls as well as rich men and gentlemen? ... But some politic man perchance will say: 'The rich men and the nobles are wiser than the poor people, and can order it well and so can not the ignorant poor people'. Well, in answer I say besides that there are more gentle fools than yeoman fools, number compared to number ... whoever thou art that for any cause would keep poor men from the Scriptures, I say that thou art one of the Pharisees' fools.[25]

So wrote William Turner from Basle in his *The Man of Sin – With His Disclosing*. There were others who expressed themselves more rationally and some who expressed themselves more vehemently. All pointed out the fallacy of the equation wealth = wisdom.

This fallacy must have been obvious to the leaders of reaction themselves, yet they were unable to act immediately against the spread of heresy among the upper classes. For one thing, they were still blinkered by old-fashioned ideas about heretics. Despite the clear evidence of new ideas gaining ground in influential circles at court and in the shires, the Catholic bishops still thought of heresy as an essentially lower-class phenomenon. With one or two insignificant exceptions, no one above the rank of yeoman had been punished for erroneous opinions in England since the Conquest. The official ecclesiastical mind revolted against the notion that the new learning and the English Bible were rapidly creating a middle class of educated, Protestant laymen – a class, moreover, which, since the dissolution of the monasteries, had a financial as well as an ideological stake in the continuance of the Reformation. There were, in addition, purely practical problems involved in proceedings against gentlemen and noblemen on matters of religion. These were the men who were the government's representatives and agents throughout the country and their solid support was essential to the smooth running of the administration. In particular the King and his Council needed a group of men with a stake in the political Reformation to act as a bulwark against a revival of papalism – still a very real possibility in Henry's tiny, schismatic 'empire'. The realization only dawned slowly on the government[26] that political Reformation and religious Reformation could not be separated. Thus the educated gentleman might reason within himself that if the King and not the Pope was supreme in the Church, then the individual conscience was a surer guide to the soul's health than the parish priest, and the Bible was a greater authority than centuries of tradition. That Bible was as potent a force among the frequenters of the corridors of power as it was among the denizens of the gutters of obscurity.

The attack on lesser heretics was continued. In May, notwithstanding the failure of the plot on Cranmer, the Privy Council sent special commissioners to examine the religious situation in Kent.[27] At the same time Robert Wisdom was sent for again. Since 1541 he had been in the Midlands with another priest of similar opinions, John Becon. They were now both brought back to London, examined and forced to recant publicly at St Paul's Cross on 14 July.[28]

Throughout the spring and early summer, the Windsor heretics had remained in prison. The end of their ordeal was now at hand. On 20 July they were returned to Windsor for trial by the local Six Articles commissioners. Their examination and condemnation occurred on 25 July. The result of the trial was immediately communicated to Gardiner, who was with the court at Woking. The Bishop immediately did something which at first sight seems strange: he appealed to the King for Marbeck's pardon. The request was granted and when, two days later (Saturday, 27 July), the three remaining heretics (Parsons, Testwood and Filmer) were burned at Windsor, Marbeck remained in prison.

The reason for Winchester's clemency towards Marbeck was that he hoped to get more information out of him. The Bishop had still not relinquished his hopes of dragging down prominent men and women of the court. Dr London and his colleagues were still hard at work gathering evidence, but this time they were to be thwarted. On 29 July word reached some of the gentlemen of the Privy Chamber that Gardiner's bloodhounds were on to their scent and accumulating information which their master hoped to use to persuade the King into a full-scale purge of heretics at court. They discovered that a certain Robert Ockham was that very day hastening to court with written evidence to lay before the Bishop of Winchester.

The gentlemen, led by Sir Thomas Caradine, had to act quickly, if they were to prevent Ockham completing his mission. King and court were due to move next day to Guildford but there was still plenty of time for Gardiner's messenger to reach his master. Caradine's first delaying tactics were crude in the extreme. He sent a few of his men, armed with cudgels, to lie in wait for Ockham. They encountered the unfortunate messenger outside Woking and so handled him that he was unable to continue his errand that day. Meanwhile Caradine and his colleagues hurriedly sought out one of their friends on the Privy Council, Lord Russell. Russell promised to do all he could to help them.

Meanwhile the indefatigable Ockham recovered from his bruises and continued his journey. Very early on the following morning (Tuesday, 30 July) he was waiting for admittance to the court. Caradine, who had been kept informed of Ockham's movements, went down to the gate, gave Ockham cordial greeting, and kept him talking for over an hour. When he saw that Gardiner's messenger was growing impatient over the delay, he casually informed him that it would be quite impossible to see the Bishop of Winchester that day as the whole court was moving on to Guildford. Disgruntled, Ockham had no choice but to depart and make his own arrangements for following the court.

Clearly this game of snakes and ladders could not go on indefinitely and at Guildford the Protestant group made plans to possess themselves of Ockham's papers. By this time, the King himself had sanctioned certain members of the Privy Council to make discreet enquiries into Ockham's business. The manner of Ockham's arrest is neatly related by Foxe. Early on the Wednesday morning the determined messenger set off to deliver his papers to Gardiner. He was accompanied by a serving man, also bound for the court on business for his master, Robert Bennet.

> And as they were going in the street together, and coming by the Earl of Bedford's lodging [i.e. Lord Russell] Ockham was pulled in by the sleeve, and no more seen of Bennet's man, till he saw him in the Marshalsea.[29]

Sir Thomas Caradine and Sir William Paget (the King's Secretary) visited Ockham's lodging to make sure there were no other incriminating papers there and to examine Bennet's serving man to see if he was on a similar errand. Once they were convinced that they had all the evidence gathered by Gardiner's men, the Protestant councillors began to sift it carefully.

> ... among the which they found certain of the Privy Chamber indicted, with other the King's officers, with their wives; that is to say, Sir Thomas Caradine, Sir Philip Hoby,[30] with both their ladies, Master Edmund Harman, Master Thomas Weldon, with Snowball and his wife. All these they had indicted by the force of the Six Articles, as aiders, helpers and maintainers of Anthony Parsons. And besides them, they had indicted for heresy (some for one thing and some for another) a great number more of the King's true and faithful subjects.[31]

The councillors reported to the King while both accusers and accused waited nervously to know the royal pleasure. Henry so ardently desired religious unity in his realm – a unity which would silence the foreign critics who were claiming that the breach with

Rome had plunged England into religious anarchy. Yet neither the open Bible nor the attempt to enforce non-papal Catholicism by statute and injunction had prevented the spread of heterodoxy. Now here were members of his own household being indicted for heresy by the agents of his own bishops. It was almost impossible for an autocrat like Henry to admit that any aspect of national life lay outside his control but the beliefs and activities of English Catholics and Protestants were rapidly getting out of hand. However shocked he was at the spread of heresy, the Supreme Head of the English Church was not going to permit a full-scale purge in his own court. He readily pardoned Caradine and the other indictees and instructed the Council to arrest and examine Ockham's accomplices (Ockham was still detained in the Lord Privy Seal's house).

Accordingly Dr London and another inquisitor, William Symons, were conveyed to Guildford and examined along with Ockham. Gardiner did not dare come to their aid and they were left alone to pay the price of angering some of the country's most influential men. It was an easy matter for the gentlemen of the Council to entangle the bewildered prisoners in their own words. They were tricked into denying some of the activities they had undoubtedly carried out. The Council then charged them with having lied while under oath.

> Hereupon they were adjudged perjured persons and appointed to ride through Windsor, Reading and Newbury, where they had done most mischief, with their faces towards their horses' tails, and a paper upon their heads setting forth their crime. Also they were to stand upon the pillory in each of those towns. And that punishment they underwent, and then were sent to the Fleet.[32]

It was in the Fleet prison that Dr London died a short while afterwards. It was perhaps a fitting end for one whose obnoxious activities had resulted in the incarceration and execution of so many unfortunate victims. Strype attributed his death to 'shame and sorrow'[33] but the damp and pestilential air of a sixteenth-century prison may, perhaps, have had something to do with his passing.

John Foxe, another Protestant moralist, provides an affecting postscript to this episode.

> And as God would have the matter further known unto his Majesty, as he rode one day a hunting in Guildford Park and saw the sheriff

with Sir Humphrey Foster sitting on horseback together, he called them unto him, and asked of them how his laws were executed at Windsor. Then they, beseeching his Grace of pardon, told him plainly that in all their lives they never sat on matters under his Grace's authority, that went so much against their consciences as the deaths of Testwood, Parsons and Filmer. They up and told his Grace so pitiful a tale of the casting away of these poor men, that the King, turning his horse's head to depart from them, said, 'Alas, poor innocents'.[34]

By the autumn of 1543 the conservative faction's chance had gone. Not only had their plots misfired; their influence with the King had begun to decline. Henry, who, for all his faults, was a shrewd judge of character, noted the persistent intrigues of Gardiner and Norfolk and knew them as men who could be used but not trusted. In April the advanced group on the Council had been strengthened by the appointment of John Dudley, Viscount Lisle, the Lord Admiral, another man, like Hertford, whose martial vigour put him high in the royal favour.

But what advanced the Protestant cause more than anything else was, undoubtedly, the King's sixth marriage. On 12 July 1543 Henry took to wife the devout, patient, well-read Catherine Parr. Catherine had already married – and buried – two elderly husbands and was an ideal comforter for Henry VIII's declining years. As a sympathizer with the new learning she became the centre of the reforming group at court and a strong counter-influence to the Howard-Gardiner faction. Her close companions, the Duchess of Suffolk, Lady Hertford and Lady Denny were all convinced Protestants. Thus strengthened, the reforming faction were ready to take the offensive.

Their opportunity came at the end of the year. The Bishop of Winchester's companion and nephew, Germaine Gardiner, was a zealous and argumentative Catholic with none of his uncle's circumspection. In a particularly unguarded moment he laid himself open to the charge of denying the royal supremacy. The details of the case are lost. We only know that he was brought to trial along with three other clerics. He was found guilty and suffered the full rigours of death by hanging, drawing and quartering, in the following March.[35]

Naturally the event cast a shadow of suspicion over the Bishop of Winchester himself – a shadow which his enemies did all in their power to lengthen. It was Charles Brandon, Duke of Suffolk, who took the lead. With a deputation from the Council, the Duke attended the King and laid charges against Gardiner of being a secret supporter of papal supremacy. Henry was persuaded by the arguments of his old friend and gave his consent for Winchester to be despatched to the Tower to await trial. The Council planned to execute the royal warrant the following day. The delay was their undoing. Word reached Gardiner of what was afoot and he hastened to Westminster to abase himself before the King. Abject humility rarely failed to work with Henry and the Bishop left with a stern warning and the royal pardon.[36] But his power was – for the time being – broken.

In three brief years the whirligig of time had spun the Protestant and Catholic factions in and out of power and individuals in and out of danger. At the end of 1543 the reforming party seemed to be well established both in court and Council. But the whirligig was still revolving.

# 6

## *Rival Knights*

NOW we leave the claustrophobic atmosphere of the court to discover what had been happening in the open fields and fens of Lincolnshire during the years 1536–44. To the casual observer all was calm there after the Rising. But that calm was on the surface only. It cloaked religious tensions, territorial rivalries and family feuds which had been aggravated by the rebellion and its aftermath. The Rising of 1536 had been a cataclysmic event as far as the gentlemen of Lincolnshire were concerned. It had cut through society like a knife, dividing people into rival groups which were far more sharply distinguished than they would ever have been if the work of reformation had proceeded steadily without evoking a major crisis. The knights and esquires had been forced to decide where their sympathies lay, and though, in order to preserve their lives and lands, they had all ended up on the King's side – and therefore on the side of reformation – it was expediency and not conviction that made them 'comrades'.

Another cause of jealousy and friction among the leading landowners was the distribution of confiscated Lincolnshire estates. Because of the rebellion, most of the gentlemen were under a cloud in the vital years 1537–40 when the monastic lands came on to the market. The King was angry with them for not doing more to stop a rising which had cost him a great deal of money to suppress, and which had come near to toppling his throne. He was thus not favourably disposed to make grants or sales of land to Lincolnshire gentlemen. Yet some landed families in the county did benefit considerably from the land speculations of the period.

They were families such as the Tyrrwhits, Heneages and Skip-worths, who either wielded considerable influence at court or were able to persuade the government that they had not been implicated in the 'commotion'. Their neighbours, not unjustifiably, felt aggrieved at this discrimination. If the Heneages, Tyrrwhits and Skipworths had avoided trouble in 1536, it was only because they had been lucky enough to escape capture by the commons; they had certainly not been to the fore in raising forces for the King to suppress the rebellion. Thus, in addition to the gulf already existing between Catholic and Protestant sympathizers, there now appeared the chasm between the 'haves' and the 'have-nots'.

Yet the frictions in Lincolnshire society did not only arise from religious differences and rivalry over land. Particularly in the period immediately after the suppression of the rebellion, the important issue for many gentlemen was one of survival.

Just how important it was to curtain the events of October 1536 with actions of zealous and conspicuous loyalty is illustrated by the sad history of Sir Christopher Ayscough of Ashby. He belonged to a branch of the family only distantly related to the Ayscoughs of South Kelsey. He and his father, Sir William Ayscough of Louth, were men of some influence in the north-eastern corner of the county. They were popular with the people of those parts and to a large extent shared with them a conservative outlook and a mis-trust of religious and social change. When the commons rose in November 1536, Sir Christopher waited just long enough to see that the rebels had successfully taken the initiative before throwing in his lot with them. He raised and armed a body of men from the towns and villages of the north-east and marched them on Lincoln to join the main body of the insurgents. It took him little time to discover that he had backed the wrong horse. He joined the other gentry and hastily made his submission with them.

The only concern of the men of substance after peace had returned to the county was to clear themselves – a process which largely involved mutual recriminations and drawing the attention of the King's officers to other offenders. In this atmosphere of accusation and suspicion, Sir Christopher became a useful scape-goat. Ostracized by the other gentlemen, he sat nervously at Ashby waiting to be summoned to give an account of his part in the Rising, afraid that he might well lose everything.

His only hope of avoiding this catastrophe seemed to be to find some way of proving both his loyalty and his usefulness to the regime. Fortunately for him the continued disturbances further north provided the opportunity he sought. In January there was trouble around Hull[1] and Sir Ralph Ellerker sent to some of the Lincolnshire gentlemen for support. On 19 January Sir Christopher set off with some of his own men to join Ellerker. It was not, however, enough for acts of loyalty to be done, they must be seen to be done. So at seven o'clock the previous night a messenger had been despatched with a hurried note for Cromwell informing him of all that was happening across the Humber, and that Sir Christopher and his father were going to Hull with all the men they could collect to help Sir Ralph Ellerker, for 'no gentlemen as yet resort to him'.[2] In fact Sir Christopher only took a handful of men with him as he had received word that the trouble was over before he set out.

He wrote from Hull on the 20th to his uncle, Sir John Aleyn in London, reporting on events in the north, asking for money and arms for his men and begging Aleyn to use his good offices with Cromwell on his behalf:

> I . . . was ready to help the town of Hull with 100 men, or 200 or 300 if need were at an hour's warning, and also with victuals enough both for my men and the town. I am now in the town with Sir Ralph with 20 of my own household servants, and my father is ready with 200 or 300 to send to me if needed, and also to victual the town. My father is ready to serve the King where it pleases him and my Lord Privy Seal. And, Sir, the country about my father's house at Louth – Louthesk, Ludburgh and Haverstow – these three wapentakes have made request to me to sue for a commission that my father and I may have the rule of them, for they love not the rest of the gentlemen of the shire. The honest men are desirous to serve the King and especially to be under the rule of my Lord Privy Seal. Sir, Bellow was with me at Louth, which is my lord's [i.e. Cromwell's] servant and he can show my lord the truth.[3]

Sir John Aleyn received this letter on 27 January and immediately sent it on to Cromwell, commending the writer's 'good heart'. He refers to Ayscough's leadership of the commons and hopes that he will not be blamed for this because he was 'ill intreated' by the people to become their leader and has subsequently proved his loyalty to the King. Cromwell paid no attention to these representations. He would not authorize any payment for Sir

L

Christopher's men, and he certainly would not countenance the bestowal of any favour on a man he still thought of as a rebel.

Sir Christopher's funds were draining away, maintaining twenty men in idleness at Hull. Nevertheless when a fresh opportunity for service presented itself, he seized it. Early in February he marched his men over the snowy Pennines and up into the bitter mountains and lakes of the north-west. Here, the last survivors of the Pilgrimage of Grace were holding out under the leadership of a certain 'Captain Poverty'. It was to help the Duke of Norfolk in rounding up these miserable peasants that Ayscough set off from Hull.

He was back again in his county in the spring when the indictments against the rebels were being drawn up. Finding the opinion of local gentry and royal officers still against him, he wrote to the Duke of Norfolk for letters of recommendation. Howard replied on 16 April with a letter addressed to Cromwell asking him to be good lord to Christopher Ayscough 'who repaired to me like a true man during the rebellion in Westmorland and Cumberland, and continued with me till it was suppressed'.[4] Ayscough sped with this letter to London and as a result he was not among those who were punished for their part in the Rising; he shared in the general pardon issued to the majority of the rebels.

Life and limb and property had been secured – but only at immense cost. The last we hear of Sir Christopher Ayscough is a heartfelt appeal to Cromwell written some months later:

> Since I was last with your lordship . . . I have been in such case that I could not, according to your Lordship's command, come up to you to know your pleasure in the poor suit I have to you. Try me to the uttermost, and if I have ever done anything contrary to you, let me die for it. I served the King with 24 men, mounted and armed, both at London, Hull and with the Duke of Norfolk in the North, without wages. It has cost me all I had. I desire of the King's Grace but £15 a year and the house to dwell in, which is a farm I have off his Grace, a little cell for the term of my life, whereby I might be able to serve his Grace.[5]

Nothing worse appears to have befallen Sir Christopher, who continued to live at Ashby until well into the reign of Elizabeth,[6] but he never regained that royal favour, without which advancement was impossible in the Tudor century.

To avoid a similar fate, the leading Lincolnshire men threw themselves into the execution of Cromwell's policies. The grand jury, as we have seen, was compliant in sanctioning the predetermined condemnation of those singled out for punishment in 1537. The arrangements for the dissolution of the smaller monasteries were completed together with the seizure of those larger houses whose superiors had been implicated in the revolt. The attainted lands of Hussey, Darcy, Moigne and others were taken over by the King's agents and plans were made for their division and disposal. The Lincolnshire leaders enthusiastically enforced the various Reformation statutes and injunctions poured forth by the government during the years of Cromwell's domination. They also took particular care to keep under control the defeated rebels, among whom anxiety and discontent still lingered. Well might the men of Louth, Louthesk, Ludburgh and Haverstow make suit to the Ayscoughs of Louth because 'they love not the rest of the gentlemen of the shire'. They knew how their landlords and justices would repay them for having put their homes, families, estates, reputations and lives in jeopardy. Nor were their fears unfounded: the gentlemen still smarting under royal disfavour vented their feelings on those who were in their power. Yeomen awoke in the night to find their barns ablaze; tenants applying for renewal of leases found their rents astronomically increased; clergy were hauled before the justices and accused of offences against the royal supremacy; in a hundred and one different ways the gentlemen of Lincolnshire settled scores with the commons after the rebellion.

At South Kelsey the last four years of Sir William Ayscough's life were painful and troubled ones. The withdrawal of royal favour seriously affected his family's fortunes. Infirmity of body grew steadily upon him, so that throughout his last two years he was virtually an invalid. Two of his children died. He had serious arguments with his neighbours, which eventually resulted in complaints being made about him to the Privy Council. To crown all, the liberal education he had given his children was having repercussions: the advanced religious opinions of one of his daughters were creating disciplinary problems in the home and were even beginning to give rise to scandal in the locality.

Anne was the most impressionable of Sir William's children. In a family where the Bible was read and loved by all (with the possible exception of Dame Elizabeth), Anne was the one who took its precepts most to heart. She had begun to study Tyndale's New Testament almost as soon as she could read and it made a deep and lasting impression upon her during her early teens. As with many adolescent converts, assurance and strength of faith made her dogmatic and argumentative. How galling it must have been for the mistress of the household when her scoldings and threats were countered by quotations from St Paul and when birchings were received in a spirit of martyred innocence and aggressive forgiveness. If the mistress of the household reacted by forbidding Anne access to the Bible, this can only have increased the girl's determination to commit more of the sacred text to memory when once she was allowed to read in its precious pages. Anne's abhorrence of 'papistry' was enhanced by her experiences in October 1536. When the champions of the monasteries surrounded South Kelsey Hall, brandishing swords, pikes and scythes, threatening the household with violence if Francis and Thomas were not yielded up to them, Anne thought she could see the forces of Antichrist quite clearly at work. Through her fear there shone a determination to resist the forces of false religion. As she grew older she began to read the Bible to the servants and, perhaps, even to some of the villagers. Her behaviour did not contribute much to domestic harmony, and, though Sir William sympathized with most of Anne's beliefs, he frequently had to discipline her when his wife complained of the girl's pertness.

In the county Sir William Ayscough threw himself into the work of furthering Cromwell's religious policies with a fervour equalled by few of his colleagues. This only served to widen the gulf between him and other gentlemen such as Sir Robert Tyrrwhit and Sir Thomas Dymock. They considered Sir William Ayscough to be over-zealous in his persecution of Catholics and accused him, on the other hand, of harbouring and supporting heretics. Though this charge was undoubtedly exaggerated, it seems that Protestant preachers and anti-clerical elements knew Sir William as a lenient justice.

In the summer of 1538 matters came to a head between Sir William Ayscough and his colleagues on the commission for the peace in Lindsey. The constable of Barrow, one James Clarke, as the man responsible for the preservation of law and order in the town from day to day, was particularly sensitive to potential troublemakers who showed scant respect for authority – including ecclesiastical authority. When, therefore, he received a complaint from no less a person than the abbot of Thornton Abbey that a certain Thomas Bawmborough of Barrow had used 'proud words' against him, he took action.[7] Bawmborough was apprehended and brought before the justices at the next sessions. He was quite unrepentant and had only himself to blame that he was not dismissed, for when Thomas Dymock, from the bench, said to him, 'Get thee hence, there is over many such busy fellows in the county as thou art,' Bawmborough retorted 'with a proud stomach', 'By God's blood, there will be more before there be fewer.' Bawmborough was marked out for reference to a higher court.

There the matter might have ended had not the offender's father, Laurence Bawmborough, taken up the cudgels on his son's behalf. He had visions of Thomas being burned as a heretic. He bitterly resented the action of the officious constable and the judgement of the commission of the peace. 'This doing is appalling,' he complained to Clarke, 'and I trust this world will amend it.' The constable quickly tired of the aggrieved father's complaints, as also of the whispering and finger-pointing of citizens who took the Bawmboroughs' part. When he could stand it no longer he took Laurence Bawmborough before the nearest justice, without waiting for the next sessions. That justice happened to be Sir William Ayscough who was staying at the time at Stallingborough. Under existing law it was a criminal offence to criticize the workings of the King's courts and Clarke now applied to have Bawmborough arrested for uttering heinous words. He had not allowed for Sir William's complete lack of patience with pompous abbots, heresy hunters, self-important minor officials or commotions over petty matters. The elderly knight listened with increasing ill-temper as the two men stood before him accusing, excusing, alleging and denying. At length he cut them short with an oath and sent them packing: 'Get you home and agree together, for you will never let till one of you undo another.'

Laurence Bawmborough was jubilant but Clarke was a tenacious enemy and moreover he knew who to go to next – a man who would listen to him sympathetically for no other reason than that Sir William Ayscough had turned him down. The constable was quite within his rights to appeal from one justice of the peace to another. He, therefore, presented his case and his man to Sir Robert Tyrrwhit, who found that Laurence Bawmborough *had* spoken heinous words and, in defiance of Ayscough, committed the man to Lincoln Castle.

Sir William Ayscough and Sir Robert Tyrrwhit were more at loggerheads than ever before and Clarke was triumphant. He resolved to strike while the iron was hot and, at the next meeting of the quarter sessions at Caistor in August, he brought forward more suspected heretics, including Robert Hanschey (alias Smith) and one Teynby. One look at the document was sufficient to convince Ayscough that the constable of Barrow was making unnecessary trouble. He resolved on a rather naïve method to try to stop the accused coming to trial: he put the charge sheet in his purse, doubtless hoping that this case would be overlooked in the press of other business. When Clarke appeared to press his charge, Sir William claimed that he had heard nothing about these two men and that certainly the constable had not formally presented written accusation against them. This subterfuge failed when the other justices, Sir Robert Tyrrwhit, Sir Thomas Dymock, Sir John Heneage, William Dalyson and Robert Dighton, insisted on hearing the case. When the details were presented, Sir William did his best to persuade his colleagues of the utter futility of the case but again found himself up against Tyrrwhit who swayed the other justices with the result that Hanschey, Teynby and others were sentenced to the pillory. The indignant Sir William restrained himself until the hearings were over and the members of the commission had retired to private chambers, then he told his fellows just what he thought of the day's proceedings. The punishment meted out to the offenders was excessive and wholly without precedent. On the contrary, retorted Tyrrwhit, express orders had come from the King for the punishment of such offenders. At this point Sir William lost his temper, vehemently accusing his enemies on the commission of partiality: 'You were only severe with these men because I tried to help them.' 'That was foolishly spoken,' Heneage retorted. If Ayscough's blood was up now, so was Tyrrwhit's. 'It is you who are to blame for maintaining such lewd fellows. Barrow has never been quiet ever since you have borne any rule there.' At this point the two men would have come to blows had the others not intervened. As it was, the meeting broke up with Ayscough and Tyrrwhit mouthing threats and counterthreats. In the event it was Sir Robert who took further action, sending a full – though one-sided – report to Cromwell.[8] The Council do not appear to have taken action immediately, but these events can hardly have failed (as, indeed, they were intended) to discredit Sir William Ayscough further in the eyes of the government.

A year after the Caistor incident he was again in trouble, not this time for being lax but (in the eyes of his opponents) over-zealous. The priest of the chantry of St Helen's at Croft, a fenland village near Wainfleet, was reported to him for offences under the Act of Supremacy. Sir William sent for the man, examined him and committed him to prison. As soon as his enemies heard of this they wrote protesting at his over-zealousness to Cromwell. The Vicar General had received a string of complaints about Sir William, stretching over several months, and had already written to South Kelsey urging the knight to appear before the Council to answer charges against him. Cromwell was no friend of papists but he had no intention of putting the weight of the government behind a Midland justice who was, apparently, causing considerable trouble in the locality. He ordered Sir William to set the chantry priest free. Furious, Ayscough obeyed, pointing out to Cromwell that he did so 'notwithstanding good reason for expulsion, as thou shalt know hereafter'.[9]

During these years Sir William Ayscough took thought for the marriages of his children. A suitable wife was found for Edward in Margaret Skipworth, the young widow of George Skipworth. From her husband and her father (Thomas Gibson) Margaret inherited considerable lands at Keelby and Nun Cotham, close by the Ayscough estates in north Lincolnshire. Francis, the eldest son and heir, celebrated his marriage to Elizabeth Hansard in 1540 or 1541 and thus, at long last, confirmed the Ayscough family in possession of the ancient Hansard estates. The next child to be provided for was the eldest daughter, Martha. The choice of a husband for her indicates quite clearly just how far financial considerations dominated Tudor matrimonial arrangements. In seeking a wealthy spouse for Martha, Sir William chose, not the son of a close friend or acquaintance of his family, but a young fenland farmer, a scantily-educated man, knowledgeable in little save husbandry and market dealing. The evidence is sparse but judging by his later history, we are probably justified in visualizing the husband as a rural boor whose contempt for sophisticated modern ideas and fashions was as profound as his respect for the simple faith of his fathers. He was Thomas Kyme; his father owned extensive lands at Wrangle, Friskney and Stickford;[10]

he was closely related to Guy Kyme who had been executed
for the part he played in the Lincolnshire Rising. Unfortunately
for the ambitions of both families, Martha died before the wed-
ding could be celebrated. Loth to lose the dowry and to waste
all the months of negotiations spent arranging the match, the
Kymes asked whether Sir William would substitute his second
daughter. This arrangement was readily agreed to and so, in due
course, Anne, the fiery Protestant zealot, was wedded to Thomas
Kyme, the fiery, unimaginative Catholic. Perhaps Sir William
thought that such a match would tame the wild spirits of his
daughter. Whatever he hoped, it was fortunate for him that he did
not live to see the tragic consequences of the arrangements he had
made.

Thomas and Jane were also married between 1537 and 1541.
Thomas's bride Elizabeth was the daughter and co-heiress of John
Strelley, a member of a wealthy Nottinghamshire family. Both
parties were very young and presumably there can only have been
a formal contract of marriage between them. In any case, their union
was of a short duration, for Thomas was dead before 1540.[11] Thus
perished the only child of Sir William Ayscough by his second wife.
Jane was the only one of the Ayscough girls destined to find
happiness in marriage. She became the wife of George St Paul of
Snarford, the head of a prominent and ancient Lincolnshire family
and a man of Protestant convictions. He was a close friend of the
Duke and Duchess of Suffolk and was the steward of their extensive
estates in the county. Jane lived happily at Snarford with this
cultivated and accomplished man and bore him many children
before his death in 1558.[12] Jane's second husband, Richard Disney
of Norton Disney, Lincs, was also an advocate of biblical Christianity as we might easily infer from the names he gave some of his
children (by his first wife): William, Daniel, Zachary, Sirach,
Sarah, Judith, Humphrey and Susan. In Norton Disney Church
there still stands an attractive brass depicting members of the
family, including Richard and Jane. The inscription reads as
follows:

> The life, conversation and service of the first above named William
> Disney and of Richard Disney, his son, were commendable amongst
> their neighbours, true and faithful to their prince and country, and
> acceptable to the Almighty, of whom we trust they are received to
> salvation according to the steadfast faith which they had in and

through the mercy and merits of Christ our Saviour. These truths are thus set forth that in all ages God may be thankfully praised for these and such like his gracious benefits.[13]

Richard Disney was, indeed, true and faithful to his prince and country. He sat in Parliament for Grantham in 1554 and was sheriff in 1557. Besides this he was steward of the lands belonging to the Earl of Rutland.

Declining health was one of the reasons why Sir William hastened to settle his children's marriages. From the autumn of 1539 he was largely incapacitated; his legs would no longer support his large frame and this atrophy spread throughout his body. Yet he would not be bed-ridden. He carried on his work, refusing to be restricted by pain and weakness. He described his distressing symptoms in a letter to Cromwell the following year:

> ... I have not been able to go out except I am borne on two men's shoulders, and even in bed I require two men to turn me. As all the country knows, my flesh is clean decayed and wasted.[14]

It may be that Sir William was exaggerating a little in this letter for fear of being compelled to ride to London to present himself to the Council. The complaints of his enemies had succeeded in casting doubts on Sir William Ayscough's loyalty and wisdom. At the end of 1539 Cromwell summoned him in the King's name to repair in person to the Privy Council to answer 'certain questions' which would there be put to him. On 25 January 1540 Ayscough replied, excusing himself from attendance at the Council because of his illness and beseeching Cromwell to give him a respite until his health returned. The Lord Privy Seal was not pleased with this prevarication and wrote further letters marvelling 'that you have not at the King's command repaired unto his Majesty and the Council'. Within a few weeks of writing thus to Sir William, Cromwell had fallen from power and thereafter the old man seems to have been no further molested by the government.

By the summer of 1540 Sir William had been forced to take to his bed. On 6 August he made his will and prepared for his end. But death made no merciful haste to come to him. He had to linger on for months, an alert, healthy mind in a wasted and useless body. It was not until March of the following year that his soul at last found release and peace. His wasted corpse was buried, as he wished, 'in our lady's choir within the parish church of St Peter before the image of our lady in Stallingborough'.[15]

Sir William's last years had not been years of unrelieved gloom. He had seen his two younger sons making excellent progress. Edward was preferred to the royal service in 1539. Christopher had already begun to profit from his position at court: in 1538 he received from the Court of Augmentations the land of Humberstone Monastery, near Stallingborough.[16] His step-daughter, unfortunate widow of the 'traitor' Thomas Moigne, had made a much more suitable second marriage with Vincent Grantham, a merchant of Lincoln who had recently bought land and was establishing himself as a wealthy gentleman of the shire. Francis, the son and heir, was making excellent progress and had the making of a fine landlord and local administrator. In 1537 his name had begun to appear on royal commissions in the county. As soon as his marriage to Elizabeth Hansard had been solemnized, he had begun to expand his estates. In June 1540 he obtained from the Duke of Suffolk 'the manors of Owersby and Thornton, Lincs, and the rectory of Owersby'.[17] To all intents and purposes Francis Ayscough had already taken over his duties as head of the family in the summer of 1540, when his father had finally yielded to illness.

The master of the enormously increased Ayscough lands in Lincolnshire and Nottinghamshire was able to settle peacefully into his new role now that he was left alone at South Kelsey with only his wife and step-mother to look after. Yet, before many months had passed, the household was overwhelmed by all the excitement of the royal visit to Lincolnshire and Yorkshire. The court stayed at the newly restored bishop's palace in Lincoln in mid-August and then moved on to South Carlton, where the King and Queen were the guests of Sir John Monson. Sir Francis had a considerable amount of planning to do in connection with the royal progress and all his household was excited at the prospect of actually seeing the King and his young Queen.

If Anne Kyme travelled up from Friskney to be presented to the King it must have been an opportunity doubly welcome to her. Not only was it an exciting adventure in itself to see some of the almost godlike people Christopher and Edward had gossiped about on their visits home, it was also an escape from the hostility of her household and her neighbours.

Everything about her new home was uncongenial to Anne and a complete change from her earlier environment. Instead of the wooded slopes of the wolds and the meadows along the Ancholme, her window now looked out over a vast, unrelieved landscape of fen and dyke. Instead of friendly, familiar people, always ready to show her the respect due to her station, she was surrounded by unknown and unknowable, taciturn peasants, who regarded her as a stranger and would continue so to regard her if she lived in their midst to the age of ninety. Instead of educated conversation with well-bred relatives and friends, acquainted in some measure with a fashionable world, she had for companions neighbours whose book-learning was non-existent, whose knowledge (and interest) did not extend beyond the care of their fields and flocks. Above all, she found herself in the midst of a people who were horrified to know that she possessed and read an English Bible. There was a Great Bible chained up in the church. The church wardens had had to buy one because the King had said so, but no one ever opened it – not even the priest. Only heretics read the Bible – the Vicar, Thomas Jordan, said so. And everyone knew what happened to heretics. Round the walls of the parish church of All Saints there were paintings whose lurid colours and subjects had been there for a hundred years and more. One series set forth the praises of the consecrated elements – transformed by the priestly miracle into the body and blood of Christ. It depicted such elevating scenes as 'the King doing homage to the host', 'Jews stabbing the host' (and divine retribution falling upon them) and 'the irreverent woman despising the host'. Was this panel carefully pointed out to the new mistress Kyme when she boldly proclaimed the priestly miracle to be a fraud and transubstantiation a doctrine not founded on holy Scripture? In any case she cannot have failed to see it and nor to be sickened by it, as, indeed, she was by all the superstitious ritual which passed for religion among the people of Friskney. This place was for Anne 'the valley of the shadow'.

Her relations with Thomas Kyme can scarcely have been other than strained from the beginning. Anne doubtless conceived it her duty to convert her husband. He would not tolerate the idea of being tutored by a woman. As time went by Thomas found himself questioned by the clergy about his wife's beliefs and desperately tried to stop her talking about her faith–for her own sake and for the sake of avoiding scandal. Local legend says that Thomas and Anne had two children and that Anne neglected them in order to go 'gospelling' around the shire. The word 'gospeller' is one that was added to the English language in the 1530s to describe a new phenomenon for which no suitable terminology existed. A gospeller was a person who read in public to others from the English Bible and who frequently went beyond reading to exposition. Anne has thus been dubbed 'the fair gospeller'.

Is this a true description? She undoubtedly conceived it to be her Christian duty to make the Gospel message known to all who, by virtue of illiteracy, were strangers to it. In all probability she read from the Great Bible in Friskney Church, to any who would listen. Until the Act for the Advancement of True Religion in 1543 there was nothing to stop her. Doubtless, her husband tried, but he could not stand guard over her all day or keep her locked in her room. Apart from anything else, there was the influential Francis Ayscough to consider. If he heard that his sister was being ill-treated he could stir up all sorts of trouble for Thomas Kyme. However it is very doubtful that Anne's husband would let her travel very far afield on preaching tours.

After the passing of the 1543 Act the situation was changed. Word filtered through to the fenland Catholics that the King had forbidden some people – including women – to read the Bible. Master Kyme was delighted that he now had the weight of the law behind him in seeking to restrain his wife's gospelling activities. He took Anne's Bible away and forbade her to go near the chained Bible in the church. Anne bore it all with patience but her quiet suffering failed to bring down the promised rain of coals upon her adversary's head. For she had now come to look upon Thomas Kyme as an adversary of the truth and of the servants of the truth. All Anne could see was that she was being persecuted for her faithfulness to the Gospel by the man who was, by human law, her husband – and he was being egged on by papistical priests. For Anne the issues were quite clear: the papists were the agents of Antichrist and would always be opposed to the saints of God. She took comfort from the words of her Saviour: 'Blessed are you when men revile you and persecute you and utter all kinds of evil against you falsely on my account. Rejoice and be glad, for your reward is great in heaven, for so men persecuted the prophets who were before you.'[18] And shall we blame her if she interpreted her Christian warfare in terms of truth versus falsehood instead of in terms of love versus hate? In standing upon her own righteousness and excluding from her heart all love for her enemies, Anne Ayscough was very much a child of her age. The religious controversies which rent sixteenth-century Christendom engendered bitterness and hatred and almost completely excluded tolerance and charity from the arena. Each side strove to fight Christ's battle but used Satan's weapons.

By the end of 1543 the relations between husband and wife were so completely poisoned by bitterness that separation – for a time at least – was the only answer. Anne returned to South Kelsey and the protection of her brother. Francis was very fond of his sister and shared her beliefs, if not her zeal. He was quite willing to shelter her but there is no doubt that her presence under his roof was an embarrassment. Her case had achieved a certain notoriety. It was the subject of gossip throughout the shire. It provided a focus for the Protestant-Catholic debate: Catholics, taking the part of the aggrieved husband and arguing that the role of a wife was one of obedience in matters of religion as in all else, Protestants claiming that Anne was right in putting loyalty to Christ above everything. Francis tried to keep his sister at home, where she could play no active part in the controversy, but he, in common with every other man who came within Anne's orbit, was quite unable to force his will upon her.

Meanwhile Thomas Kyme was having second thoughts. As well as disgrace he was now having to face serious charges from the local priests and their supporters. Not only, they said, had he harboured a heretical wife and failed to tame her fanaticism, he had now suffered her to leave his house and as a result she was spreading her detestable opinions far and wide. It was his duty, they urged, either to take her back and beat her heresies out of her or to denounce her to the authorities. The second alternative was unthinkable. Ladies of leading Lincolnshire families could not be placed on trial for heresy. Heresy was associated with ignorant labourers and apprentices, not with gentlewomen. Certainly, no one in the county would be eager to become involved in proceedings against a close relative of the wealthy and powerful landowner, Francis Ayscough. Thomas Kyme therefore took the other – the only feasible – alternative. He asked his brother-in-law to send Anne back to Friskney.

But Anne had other ideas. Basing her arguments on the only

authority she recognized, she claimed that her marriage was no
longer valid in the sight of God. Had not St Paul written, 'If a
faithful woman have an unbelieving husband, which will not tarry
with her she may leave him. For a brother or sister is not in subjec-
tion to such.'?[19] She refused to go back to her husband and sought a
divorce from the bishop's court at Lincoln. The hearing took place
some time in 1544 and the case went against Anne. But, having
more faith in her understanding of the word of God than in the
laws of the Church, she would not accept this decision. Not only
did she refuse to return to her husband, she also challenged the
priests at Lincoln to prove their case against her from the Bible.

> '. . . my friends told me', she later wrote 'if I did come to Lincoln, the
> priests would assault me and put me to great trouble, as thereof they
> had made their boast. And when I heard it, I went thither indeed, not
> being afraid, because I knew my matter to be good. Moreover, I
> remained there nine days, to see what would be said unto me. And as
> I was in the Minster reading upon the Bible, they resorted unto me
> by two and by two, by five and by six, minding to have spoken unto
> me, yet went their ways again without words speaking . . . there was
> one of them at the last which did speak to me indeed . . . his words
> were of small effect. . . .'[20]

Such public defiance of ecclesiastical authority made Anne more
enemies and it was later rumoured that there were threescore
priests at Lincoln 'bent against' her.[21]

Soon after this, Anne decided to take her case to London to the
Court of Chancery. Her brother was no longer at home to act as
her protector, having departed for France to take part in the King's
new war (see chapter 7). At court she had relatives and friends.
Besides, she knew from Edward and Christopher that there were in
London many more people who sympathized with her religious
beliefs. Therefore, towards the end of 1544 Anne Ayscough left
the hostile atmosphere of Lincolnshire and took the long road which
led to the court and the capital, hoping to find there powerful
friends and supporters to help her to fight her case in the courts.

Not that she was without powerful friends and sympathizers in
her own country. In the East Midlands there was a rapid trend
among the landowning class towards acceptance of reformed
beliefs. Grimsthorpe, near Bourne, where the Duke and Duchess
of Suffolk were in residence for a substantial part of every year was
an active centre of Protestant influence. Thither came Hugh

Latimer and other reformers to preach to the Duke and his guests. There for a time Alexander Seton enjoyed Brandon's patronage. Seton's successor as chaplain was John Parkhurst, another thoroughgoing supporter of the Reformation and a close friend of Miles Coverdale.[22] The active and open support for the Reformation given by the leading family in the county must have been a considerable influence on other members of Lincolnshire's social elite. Little wonder that Anne Ayscough was not troubled with heresy charges in her native shire.

The Brandons were not the only influential family in the region to be affected by the new religious ideas. In the East Midlands as in other parts of the country, the years since 1536 had witnessed nothing short of an intellectual revolution among the educated classes. The steady flow of young men back from the universities and the inns of court, the influence of the English Bible, the spread of Lollard and Protestant literature, the impact of the continental reformers, and the demands made upon them by the political Reformation had combined to push many of the gentry beyond acquiescence into conviction. England's Protestant middle class had been born. The Markhams, Lascelles, Ayscoughs, Babingtons and Hercys had been among the first converts. By 1544 they had been joined by the Pierpoints, the Disneys, the St Pauls, the Meres, the Dightons, the Granthams, the Monsons, the Brocklesbys, the Girlingtons, the Hatcliffes, the Nevilles, and a great many more of the leading men of Lincolnshire and Nottinghamshire.[23]

But we must return with Anne Ayscough to London. The compact and squalid square mile of England's capital will be the background to the events and personalities crowded on to the remaining panels of our tapestry.

# 7

## *A Perilous Move*

---

LONDON in the closing weeks of 1544 was astir with rumours, fears and discontents. England was at war with France and on bad terms with the Empire. Traditional francophobia was at its height – intensified by apprehension of possible French raids along the south coast. At the same time the citizens of London (like their counterparts all over the country) were feeling the effects of their King's overseas adventures in the tenderest parts of their anatomy – their purses. In taverns and markets men and women grudgingly bought and sold with new light, debased coins. Over their ale they grumbled about the forced loans, benevolences (i.e. forced 'gifts') and subsidies levied over the past two years by a bankruptcy-haunted King. A few merchants and landowners managed to benefit from the government's diffi-culties by speculating in ex-monastic lands which now came on to the market in an unprecedented flood. Most of their colleagues, however, were puzzled and dismayed by the phenomenon of inflation which pushed prices and wages up while leaving rents fixed. The only solution they could find was to hoard family plate and undebased coinage and wait for better times.

Religious problems had not abated. The influence of Protestants in high places and the government preoccupation with foreign affairs had deflected attention from the growing problem of the spread of heresy. In 1544 there were very few prosecutions under the Act of Six Articles and, as a result, preachers and gospellers had become bolder and converts more numerous. As usual, this was particularly noticeable in the capital. Eighteen months later Bishop Bonner was complaining 'there are more heretics now than in the last three or four years'.[1] Church leaders were alarmed as never before at the spread of religious 'novelties', the more so as their hands were tied by a King who, partly because he did not want to upset potential allies on the Continent, refused to sanction an anti-heretical purge in his realm. In December Bonner did succeed in carrying out an attack on suspect books. On the fifteenth, bonfires were lit in various parts of London and thither the Bishop's officers brought armfuls of books and pamphlets 'against the sacrament of the altar and all other sacraments and sacramentals and naming divers times the Bishop of Winchester, with divers other bishops and learned men with great rebukes . . . of them'.[2] The pamphlet war was growing daily more intense and utterly scurrilous attacks on Gardiner and his colleagues were being made. One of the works burned in 1544 was William Turner's *Man of Sin With His Disclosing* which attacked the leader of the Catholic bishops thus: 'Do but mark the crafty deception of Winchester . . . how he patches up the old broken holes with patches of old papistry, sewing them together with new subtleties and wiles.'[3] One pamphleteer was even bold enough to send his brainchild to the Council, for there is a record in December of the councillors examining *A Supplication Touching the Church*, which appealed for further ecclesiastical reforms such as the abolition of chantries, complained about the ignorance of bishops and priests and their opposition to Bible-reading, and asked the government to refute the widespread rumour that the English Bible was about to be taken away from the laity altogether.[4] But the government took no sides. Its adamant neutrality was shown when, at the same time as the burning of heretical books, a Kentish priest was made to stand in the pillory at St Paul's Cross for cutting his finger and making it bleed on the host 'for a false sacrifice'.[5]

In the inner circles of power and influence, matters had gone well for the advanced group in 1544. Between March and May Hertford had covered himself in glory in a campaign against the Scots. Fearing that the French would employ their traditional tactics of encouraging and financing a Scottish raid across the border and also angered at the Scottish King's renunciation of a recent treaty, Henry had despatched Seymour to attack Edinburgh, Leith and St Andrews. The General's orders were to express his sovereign's anger in actions of the utmost ferocity. Man, woman nor child was to be spared. Hertford, though believing this policy to be

M

wrong, carried out his master's instructions to the letter.[6] Edinburgh and Leith were sacked and burned in a lightning raid and
Hertford returned triumphant. Henry was delighted with his
General, and Seymour's victories looked even more spectacular
than they were when contrasted with the unimaginative border
campaigns carried out in previous years under Norfolk's command.

Meanwhile preparations were well advanced for an English
invasion of France. This project was the fruit of that closer
relationship with the Emperor for which Gardiner and the Spanish
party had fought so long. The treaty which had been signed by
Henry and Charles in February 1543, among other items, pledged
the signatories to a joint campaign against the French. The prospect of a return to a more adventurous and martial foreign policy
had excited the King since the downfall of the cautious Cromwell.
He envisaged another magnificent French foray like the ones of his
youth, in which he, the successor of Henry V, would once more
take the field and lead his men to victory. The warrior monarch
was due to depart for the field of valour in March 1544 but a
recurrence of his leg ulcers delayed the expedition.

The King's bouts of pain were becoming more frequent and
those close to him were greatly concerned about his health. His
wife and his councillors cautiously but earnestly tried to persuade
him not to attend the French campaign in person. But Henry
angrily brushed aside all objections. Besides having set his heart
on another military expedition, he was the type of energetic man
who could never accept limitations caused by physical weakness.
He refused to rest except when pain forced him to take to his bed
and he imposed upon himself a rigorous daily programme which
included being up early and taking long rides. Through the spring
Henry recovered his health and his temper, and made it clear that
his plans to cross the Channel had been postponed, not cancelled.

At the same time the patient, cautious Cranmer was notching
up another victory for the cause of the Reformation in England.
Having achieved the authorization of an English Bible, the next
important step forward was the replacement of Latin by the
vernacular in church services. For some months the Archbishop
had been working on a translation of the Litany (a special service
of prayers and invocations chanted by priest and people in procession on certain holy days). This work was published in May and was
immediately seen to be not merely a translation but a considerable

modification of the medieval service.[7] Cranmer had obviously obtained the support of the King in this project, for on 11 June Henry ordered that the new vernacular service was henceforth to be used in all English churches.

By the time of Henry's departure for France on 14 July, the leading Protestants can hardly have been in a more favourable position. The warlords, Suffolk and Norfolk, had already crossed the Channel. Queen Catherine was left as Regent and Hertford was appointed Lieutenant of the realm. The Queen was provided with a small council: 'She shall in her proceedings use the advice and counsel of the Archbishop of Canterbury, of the Lord Wriothesley, Lord Chancellor of England, the Earl of Hertford, the Bishop of Westminster,[8] and Sir William Petre, Secretary.'[9] The Chancellor was later to prove himself a bitter enemy of the Queen but now he was a lone voice on a Council composed of obedient servants of the crown who shared a similar outlook on most matters.[10] Henry assumed personal command of his army for two and a half months. The campaign was a dismal and expensive one. Rain and supply problems hampered the progress of the troops. The Duke of Norfolk failed in the task assigned to him – the capture of Montreuil. Suffolk and Hertford (the latter summoned to the battle-front because the campaign was going badly) did succeed in capturing Boulogne, and the King hugely enjoyed making a triumphal entry into the town and organizing its defences. This was the one success the British had to show for eight weeks' fighting, and to mark the occasion Henry dubbed several new knights on his entry into Boulogne (18 September). Among them was Francis Ayscough, who was serving as a captain under the Duke of Suffolk. But on that same day Henry's ally, Charles V, angered at the English King's departure from their agreed strategy, signed a peace treaty with the French at Crépy. The full weight of the French army was now turned on the British force and Henry was left with no alternative but to order an undignified withdrawal. The King returned to England on 30 September, leaving the bulk of his army retreating ignominiously on Calais. Throughout October peace talks were held with French representatives, only to be broken off in the early days of November. Now England was diplomatically isolated as never before during the reign. A state of war existed with France and relations with the Empire had reached breaking point. Furthermore, the King who now had to attend personally to the problems of an empty treasury, a possible French invasion, a mounting religious tension and the creation of a suitable European alliance, was a failing man.

As Henry drove himself hard towards the grave and the succession of a minor became a certainty, positions closest to the King were sought more ardently than ever before. Henry's closest companion during his last three years was his Queen. In Catherine Parr he had at last found a patient, sympathetic woman, who adapted herself to his moods, was available when required but did not intrude herself when the King desired other company or no company at all. She was a good stepmother to his children and, in fact, did much to reconcile him with Mary. She was a sober and educated lady, accomplished in conversation, and, unlike some of her predecessors, she never let position or power go to her head. As the open sores on Henry's legs grew worse, Catherine alone was allowed to dress them and many times she suffered the King's outbursts of temper as spasms of pain shafted through his immense body. On occasions like this she would try to divert him from his suffering with absorbing conversation. Frequently religion formed the subject of these discussions, the Queen cautiously urging reformed doctrines on her Catholic spouse. At times she sought the royal favour for some preacher or Protestant sympathizer in trouble with the authorities and her influence in such cases was considerable. The Act of Six Articles was invoked very sparingly between 1543 and 1546 thanks largely to Queen Catherine.

The King's physicians were in daily attendance. They were Sir William Butts and Robert Huick. Both were highly respected and learned men and both were supporters of the Reformation. Butts, particularly, was a courtier who stood high in the King's favour and who never failed to use his influence on behalf of the Protestant faith. In 1543, when the Council proceedings against Cranmer were in hand and the dejected Archbishop was being carefully cold-shouldered by everyone who believed his downfall was imminent, it was Dr Butts who openly showed his continued friendship for the prelate and went in person to the King to protest at the humiliations being heaped on Cranmer by his fellow councillors. Later in the same year he sued to Henry on behalf of Richard Turner, an obscure priest of Kent, marked out by the Catholic leaders for destruction under the Act of Six Articles. Not even Cranmer, the man's diocesan bishop, dared to intercede for him. Butts, hearing of the matter from Cranmer's secretary, Ralph Morice, came to the King in his Privy Chamber, while he was being shaved by his barber. When Butts had explained the situation, Henry, without further enquiry, ordered the proceedings against Turner to be halted. Huick, a doctor equal to his colleague in learning and in boldness, was less admirable in other ways. Stubborn in all his opinions, of a biting wit and abusive in argument, he was not an easy man to get on with. It is not surprising that he was dismissed from his post of principal of St Alban Hall in 1535 for his outspoken rejection of traditional scholasticism. Nor is it very remarkable that his marriage proved a failure. By 1544 he was already estranged from his wife and, a few months later, he was suing for a divorce. Huick seems to have entered royal service as a result of the patronage of Catherine Parr, to whom many other humanist scholars owed their preferment. Huick's religious views went beyond humanism. He was a regular member of Dr Crome's congregation and an enthusiastic supporter of the opinions for which that cleric occasionally found himself in trouble. In religion, as in all matters, Huick was psychologically incapable of keeping his views to himself.

The King's court favourites included at least three men of advanced religious views. Sir Anthony Denny (knighted after the siege of Boulogne in September 1544), a scholar and soldier, was a man much after Henry's heart and was frequently seen in his company. He was a gentleman of the Privy Chamber and also a privy councillor. Thanks to the royal favour he was able to amass considerable estates in Hertfordshire at the dissolution. Like Butts, Denny was a convinced Protestant and ready to use his influence with the King to further the work of reformation. To the very last hours of Henry VIII's life Denny was a close friend and adviser.

Another known reformer was the King's 'little pig', George Blagge. Blagge's dislike of traditional religious forms has already been noted (p. 132). He, too, was a soldier and had for many years been a comrade-in-arms of the Earl of Surrey. Perhaps it was Blagge who tempted the Earl to flirt with Lutheranism in 1543.[11] Surrey quickly reverted to the more orthodox beliefs espoused by all the Howards, and religious differences caused a rift with his old friend George Blagge. This rift grew steadily wider until late 1546, when Blagge was one of those who brought about the Earl's downfall.

For the meantime the 'little pig' was one of the substantial group of Protestant gentlemen of the Privy Chamber.

The third gentleman who, in 1544, was but newly established in the royal favour but was clearly 'up-and-coming' was Sir William Herbert. At forty-two Herbert had put a headstrong youth behind him and, as a result of sterling military service, had already been advanced to the royal favour, before the great stroke of good fortune which befell him in 1543. He had earlier married Anne, daughter of Sir Thomas Parr. In July 1543 he therefore found himself brother-in-law to the King, when his wife's elder sister became Queen. Anne Herbert was appointed the Queen's chief lady-in-waiting, while lands and honours were showered on her husband. William Herbert and his wife were both followers of the new learning and perhaps already had a strong leaning towards the new trends in continental Protestantism represented by John Calvin. Herbert was a patron of one of the most ardent proselytizers in Henry VIII's retinue. This was Edward Underhill, one of the band of gentleman pensioners and already known as a 'hotgospeller'.[12]

Herbert, Denny, Butts, Huick, Blagge, Underhill, Lascelles, Edward and Christopher Ayscough, Caradine, Hoby – these were but a few members of the King's entourage known to be infected with the new religious opinions. There were many others among the lesser court officers and satellites. Above them were the leading councillors and men of state – Cranmer, who more than any other man permanently enjoyed the King's friendship and confidence, Russell, John Dudley Viscount Lisle,[13] and especially Hertford, whose star was still in the ascendant. The fact that the King was surrounded by so many men of the new persuasion is indicative not of a change in Henry's beliefs but of the incredibly rapid spread of a new, critical and inquisitive attitude to religion among the educated and influential classes. Henry tolerated 'heretics' at court because he liked to have around him bright young men capable of sustaining a lively, academic debate, but his own adherence to Catholicism was quite firm (even if contemporaries and later historians found it difficult to be certain exactly what he did believe).

But if Protestants of different kinds were only tolerated in the King's chambers, on the 'Queen's side' a different spirit prevailed. In the liberal atmosphere of the Queen's chambers the latest doctrinal novelties were freely discussed. Catherine Parr met frequently with her ladies and courtiers for Bible study and religious debate and to listen to sermons from her chaplains and visiting preachers. In 1543 John Parkhurst was preferred by his patroness, the Duchess of Suffolk, to the Queen's service. Parkhurst now became an important influence at court and never failed in his preaching to assert the importance of personal religion as against Catholic 'superstition'. Though Anne Herbert was the Queen's chief lady-in-waiting, it was Catherine Brandon, Duchess of Suffolk, who was the dominant personality in Catherine Parr's entourage. This vivacious twenty-five-year-old, half-Spanish,[14] *femme formidable* was quite irrepressible. She was lively and humorous in company but, as a contemporary remarked of her, 'It is a pity that so goodly a wit waiteth upon so froward a will.'[15] She was merciless in venting her sarcasm on people she disapproved of. For instance, she kept at court a pet dog, which she named 'Gardiner'. Nor had her 'victims' any redress. As wife of one of the most powerful men in the realm and as a firm favourite with the King and Queen, Catherine Brandon was hard to attack.

Most of Catherine Parr's other ladies were also Protestant sympathizers. Anne, Countess of Hertford, was a proud and quarrelsome beauty, who, as Seymour's wife and confidante of the Queen, gave herself airs and made many enemies – 'You your friends do threaten still with war,' as Surrey described her in a poem.[16] There were Lady Denny and Jane Fitzwilliam, third wife of Sir William Fitzwilliam, alderman of London, a close friend of Lord Russell. There was Anne, Countess of Sussex, whose differences of opinion with her husband, Henry Ratcliffe, on matters of religion were soon to lead to an estrangement. There were Jane Dudley, wife of the Lord Admiral and Maud Lane, widow of Sir Ralph Lane and the Queen's cousin. Also of interest, was the Lincolnshire lady, Elizabeth Tyrrwhit,[17] wife of Sir Robert of the Household and governess to the Princess Elizabeth.

The predominance of these Protestants at court decisively influenced the course of major events throughout the last two years of the reign. Its effect was felt both in domestic and foreign affairs. The Catholic bishops, and especially Bonner of London, were at their wits' end to know how to stop the transfusion of heretical blood into the body of the English Church when so many of the nation's leaders were deliberately encouraging preachers and gospellers. Gardiner and others, who like him were working for a *rapprochement* with the Emperor, found England's drift towards Protestantism a perpetual embarrassment. The imperial ambassador Vanderdelft reported:

> If the King favours these stirrers of heresy, the Earl of Hertford, and the Lord Admiral, which is to be feared both for the reasons that I have already given and because the Queen, instigated by the Duchess of Suffolk, the Countess of Hertford, and the Lord Admiral's wife, shows herself infected, words and exhortations, even in the name of your Majesty, would only make the King more obstinate to show his absolute power and independence and might engender a coolness towards your Majesty, which is at present undesirable.[18]

The new learning and the new religion had an even more assured place in the household of Prince Edward. In 1544 the formal education of the six-year-old prince was begun. In overall charge was the almoner, Richard Cox. Edward's principal tutor was John Cheke. Cox was a quiet scholar of moderate but firm Protestant persuasion. Adherence to his unorthodox beliefs had cost him his academic career at Oxford but influential friends gained for him the post of headmaster of Eton and, later, a position at court. Cheke was a brilliant humanist scholar who also had Protestant leanings.

There can be no doubt that Henry gave very careful thought to the choice of those men who were to shape the mind of his son. He must have known that in surrounding the heir to the throne with men of progressive opinions in matters of religion and education he was ensuring the continuance of doctrinal reformation. Yet with all the nation's scholars, not to mention foreign academics, to choose from, Henry made no attempt to balance the influences active upon Prince Edward. So the boy's opinions and ideals were moulded by Cox, Cheke, Roger Ascham, the great humanist and teacher, John Belmain, a French Calvinist brought over as language tutor to the young prince, and other progressives.[19]

If little concerted action was taken by the Catholic leaders to redress the balance in matters of religion throughout the whole of 1545, the reasons are not difficult to seek. England faced a threat greater than any she had known for generations[20] and the burdens of diplomatic negotiations, organizing national defence and raising money (while at the same time trying to preserve public morale) fell heavily on every member of the government. Under this pressure Council meetings frequently grew heated. Councillors disagreed on the desirability of an imperial or a German alliance, on the terms of a French treaty, on the means of raising money and on the levying and disposition of troops. Even when the Council, by unanimous or majority decision, made a recommendation to the King, there was no guarantee that he would act on it. He might lean instead unto his own opinion or trust to the advice of courtiers, ambassadors or generals. The atmosphere of panic, frustration and discord is clearly revealed in letters between members of the government, particularly during the autumn of 1545. Thus in September Norfolk wrote angrily to his son, the Earl of Surrey, who commanded the English army in France, 'Animate not the King too much for the keeping of Boulogne.' The Council had been urging on their Sovereign the importance of yielding the captured town in order to secure a peace treaty but what progress they had made in six days 'ye with your letters set back in six hours'.[21] In October Cranmer was frightened to take severe action against some of the King's troops, bound for France, who had been terrorizing the people of Canterbury.[22] In November Chancellor Wriothesley and Secretary Paget fell out because the former could not raise money that the King wanted and the latter had to report this failure to the King. Still smarting from Henry's reaction to the news Paget wrote to the Chancellor in great anger. Yet no amount of royal or secretarial wrath could stop the nation's bankruptcy, as Wriothesley pointed out:

> ... touching the Mint we be now so far out with that, if you take any penny more from it these three months ... you shall utterly destroy the trade of it ... as to the Augmentations it shall not be able to pay the £5,000 ... yet these six days ... And of the revenue ... there is yet to come in ... £15,000 or £16,000, but when we shall have it, God knoweth. As to the Tenth and Firstfruits, there remains not due above £10–12,000, which is not payable till after Christmas ... The Exchequer shall not be able to minister above £10,000 (and that at Candlemass) of the remainder of the subsidy. The Surveyors Court owes so much that when all shall be come in that is due to it ... they shall not be able to render up ... more than £5,000 or £6,000; and when that shall be, God knoweth. So that, if you tarry for more money to be sent to Boulogne at this time, you may perhaps tarry too long, before you have the sum desired ... I assure you, Master Secretary, I am at my wits' end how we shall possibly shift for three months following, and especially for the next two. For I see not any

great likelihood, that any good sum will come in till after Christmas. . . .[23]

The general despair in government circles was summed up by Bishop Gardiner in November:

> We are at war with France and Scotland, we have enmity with the bishop of Rome, we have no assured friendship . . . with the Emperor and we have received from the Landgrave [of Hesse], chief captain of the Protestants, such displeasure that he has cause to think us angry with him . . . Our war is noisome to our realm and to all our merchants that traffic through the Narrow Seas. . . . We are in a world where reason and learning prevail not and covenants are little regarded.[24]

The war certainly was 'noisome to our realm' and murmurings were particularly audible in the capital. Apart from the unprecedented amount of taxation (which, as we have seen, contributed but little to the Treasury's final war bill of over £2½ million) and the restrictions to trade 'through the Narrow Seas', the people had other grievances. Enormous numbers of the realm's able-bodied men were away on military service. In the summer of 1545, besides Surrey's army in France, there was another under Hertford on the Scottish border, the coasts were guarded by forces in Essex (under Norfolk), in Devon (under the Earl of Arundel), and in Kent (under Suffolk) and Dudley was at sea with twelve thousand troops. In all over sixty thousand men were under arms. In addition there was a special muster of another thousand men in London on 4 August for service in France. Food was another problem. Large quantities of grain and meat had to be commandeered for the army and this left the civilian populations to face short supplies and rising prices.[25] London even had to import grain from the Continent.

But more disturbing to the citizenry than all these privations was the threat of invasion. Throughout the early months of 1545 the southern coasts were put in a state of readiness and English agents kept a close watch on the French fleet. Throughout the spring and early summer wild rumours ranged the countryside. At the end of June, Francis I's battle fleet of two hundred ships set out. Throughout the latter part of July and all August the French harried the south coast and there were light skirmishes between the invading forces and the defenders. Occasionally Lisle's navy got to grips with French ships but all actions were inconclusive. In the southwest Lord Russell was having to fight rumour-mongers as well as Frenchmen, '. . . it was constantly affirmed here, that the Isle of

Wight was taken and burned, and divers other most false lies, the authors whereof I have punished in the pillory.'[26]

In the panic of those summer weeks of storms and gales (and the weather probably did more than anything else to prevent both the French invasion and any decisive naval engagement) religious strife broke out with fresh fury. There were not lacking preachers who saw in the invasion attempt the hand of divine retribution on a nation which had erred from Catholic truth. Nor were the voices silent of those who interpreted the signs as evidence of the machinations of papistical Antichrist. If anything it was the latter who were listened to more attentively. A new wave of anti-clericalism swept the country and particularly the southern counties, already keyed-up to breaking-point. Several priests were attacked on suspicion of being in league with Catholic France while in Dorset and Somerset a well-organized campaign was set afoot against the clergy. On 18 August Russell reported:

> This morning I received a letter from Sir John Horsey [Sheriff of Dorset and Somerset] signifying that in divers places about Sherborne and in the town of Sherborne also commandment was brought from place to place by men of honesty, as is supposed, to the constables and tithingmen in the said parishes, that the houses of priests should be diligently searched, and all kinds of weapons, books, letters and spits (wherewith they roast their meat) should be put in safe keeping. Because this was obviously done without the commandment of the King or Council I thought it good and necessary immediately to address my letters to Sir John Horsey . . . desiring him . . . to use all diligence for the . . . finding out of those which are the beginners and setters on of the said search.[27]

In London Protestantism thrived and spread as never before. The universal anxiety and discontent, the particular dissatisfaction of the merchants and the patriotic hatred of the leading Catholic nations disposed many, who in normal times would have disdained 'heretics', to read banned books and attend the sermons of suspect preachers. When, in November, Wriothesley got to hear that heretical literature was being circulated, and instigated a search, he began to receive threatening letters:

> Master Secretary, I send unto you herewith a bill, which was let fall yesterday, as I was going to mass, in my dining chamber. I pray you show it to His Highness and discover his pleasure, what he would

should be done about it. You know that when those naughty books were brought unto me, I could do not less than send them to His Highness, and also labour, as much as I could, to find out the author; wherein, though I have not much prevailed, yet some people be angry with my doing. Upon your answer of His Majesty's pleasure, I shall do as the same shall command me. I pray you return the bill again to me.[28]

The city was in an ugly mood when ministers of the crown were threatened (albeit anonymously) for taking action against heretics.

Just how united the supporters of Protestantism were, was shown by the House of Commons in November. By mid-October Henry had decided, while not breaking off other negotiations, to go all out for a new alliance with Charles V. This doubtless represents a triumph for Gardiner who had for months been urging this policy on the King. Perhaps Gardiner was also responsible for drafting a new anti-heresy bill which (he might well argue) would make a good impression on the Emperor and show that England was no longer paying court to the German Protestant princes. In any event, such a bill was introduced into Parliament during November. By then, however, Gardiner had departed to lead the English delegation at the imperial court, and was not available to press the new legislation through. Furthermore the initial talks with Charles's representatives were going badly and it may be that Henry's enthusiasm for the alliance had temporarily waned. Certainly he made no attempt to influence the parliamentary debate. The result was that the bill was dutifully passed in the Lords but resoundingly defeated by the Commons.

Anne Ayscough found this surly, troubled but vibrant and lively London an exhilarating place. Anywhere would have been exciting after the isolation of the fen and the cramped atmosphere of Thomas Kyme's household. At last, after four dreary years, she had escaped all that. She had come to the capital of England, that her father and brothers had told her so much about. At twenty-four years of age this educated, but simple, country girl was prepared to find London the city of her dreams. Here were the King and his new, Protestant, Queen. Here was their glittering court. Here were scholars and preachers well-versed in Holy Scripture. Here were hundreds, perhaps thousands of Christian men and women who shared her love of the Gospel. Here she would find fellowship, encouragement and instruction in the faith. Here she would find also the King's impartial justices, who would untangle the cruel knots which bound her to her ignorant, papistical clod of a husband. Thus she thought and in many ways she was not disappointed.

From a religious point of view, much to the distraction of Bishop Bonner, London had never been more active. The ex-Bishops Latimer and Shaxton had returned[29] and were once more occupying City pulpits and were received among the Queen's circle at court. Edward Crome was again gathering fashionable congregations at St Mary Aldermary. At St Bride's in Fleet Street, the vicar, John Cardmaker (alias Taylor), was attracting eager listeners to his doctrine of the mass and his occasional attacks on Gardiner and Bonner. The curate of St Catherine Coleman was the fiery Scot, Sir William Whitehead. He was one of the many outspoken priests and friars who had been forced to flee across the border by persecution in his native land. But licensed preachers were not the only – and, indeed, not the main – exponents of religious novelties in London. Throughout the city there were many groups meeting, some in secret, others more openly, for Bible study and discussion. Many of these groups were socially very mixed and for this, government legislation was in part to blame. The Act for the Advancement of True Religion[30] had forbidden men below the rank of gentleman to read the English Bible. One result was that zealous students, courtiers, lawyers and merchants had turned 'gospellers', reading and expounding the Bible to eager listeners in tavern backrooms and church crypts from Newgate to the Tower.

Anne Ayscough soon found herself a member of one of these groups. On her arrival in the city she took lodgings near the Temple, where she was near friends at the inns of court and could easily reach Westminster. She soon sought out a man she knew to be both an influential courtier and a religious sympathizer – her country neighbour John Lascelles. Lascelles introduced her to an assembly of pious souls, of which he was, in fact, the leader. Here Anne met some of Lascelles's friends from the court, as well as merchants, students from the inns of court, weavers and artisans, drawn together by nothing else but their love of the Gospel. Here too Anne encountered subtle and sophisticated doctrines culled from English and Continental reformers, which went far beyond her own simple biblicism. Within a very short space of time Anne was fully accepted as a member of this circle. And, since these semi-clandestine assemblies were not mutually exclusive, members of one group attending the meetings of others, Anne found herself a well-known 'sister' in the large family of London Protestants.

She also gained entry with ease to the more exclusive society of the royal court. Through John Lascelles, through her brothers and through other friends, Anne found it easy to gain introductions to many of the leading personalities at Westminster. She certainly made the acquaintance of some of the Queen's ladies and may even have attended the Bible study meetings in Catherine Parr's chambers.[31] Anne had high hopes that the influence of powerful people at court would help her matrimonial case in the court of Chancery. Her suit had been lodged soon after her arrival in London. While she waited for the slow machinery of the law to revolve, she had time to cultivate her acquaintances in the court and the city and to do all in her power actively to forward the cause of the Gospel.

London in 1545 had its fair share of bold spirits, of colourful and eccentric characters, but Anne Ayscough in the space of a few weeks had become the talk of the town. She was loved and hated, respected and scorned, pitied and condemned, but by very few unknown or ignored. Dutch merchants as well as their English counterparts, serving men as well as their masters, learned doctors as well as illiterate artisans, all came to know Anne Ayscough before 1545 had run its course. The reasons lay in her personality. She was a lady, but one who did not scorn to enter the humblest riverside dwelling to read the Bible to the common people. For all her fine clothes, her education and her breeding, she was one who had 'suffered for righteousness' sake' and this made her something of a 'darling' among the Protestants. She earned the respect of many for her monumental knowledge of the Bible. There was scarcely a topic of conversation on which she could not quote some relevant proof text. She knew the articles of her faith backwards and was unassailable in argument. But she was not solemn and unsmiling with it all; she had a ready wit and her arguments were spiced with jokes and jibes – not always kind, but always lively. Nor was she frightened to confront anyone; priests, bishops, canon lawyers, doctors of theology, she would express her opinions before all of them, in complete assurance that the truth must prevail. Nor was she any respecter of persons: her pert answers to adversaries and her rude jibes about Catholic leaders were soon being joked about in the city taverns.

Anne's new way of life among her wide circle of friends and acquaintances passed uneventfully until June. But by then she had come to the attention of the authorities and made enemies who were prepared to accuse her of heresy. As a result she and two other members of her group, Joan Sawtry, wife of a London merchant, and Thomas Lukine, servant to Sir Humphrey Brown (a justice of the King's Bench), were arrested by the Six Articles commissioners and presented for preliminary trial by the 'quest' at the Guildhall on 13 June.[32] Since the modified legislation of 1544, all suspects of heresy were required to be condemned by a jury of twelve before they could be committed to prison to await further examination. Accordingly the three were presented at the Guildhall 'for certain words spoken by them against the sacrament'. But the trial turned out to be something of a farce. No witness appeared to testify against the two women and the evidence presented against Lukine was considered suspect. Thus the trio were found not guilty by 'twelve honest and substantial men of the city of London' and released.

Was Anne subdued by this brush with danger? Probably not. She had faced worse experiences in Lincoln. In any case, in the summer of 1545 the city authorities had more important things to worry about than heresy proceedings. So, while London was gripped by invasion fears, Anne continued to attend Crome's sermons, meet with her friends for Bible study and to try and push her matrimonial affair through the courts.

July and August brought many alarms and disturbing rumours. Every day fresh stories were spread about successful French landings in Kent, Sussex or Hampshire. Some were taken so seriously by the city fathers that from 4 August special watches were posted throughout London. Garbled reports reached the capital of events on the Scottish border, where Hertford's army was, reputedly, meeting with little success. The French, it was reported, had landed an army in Scotland and a joint invasion of England was imminent. In Rome the Pope was summoning a Catholic council which would declare a crusade against schismatic states. These were the rumours and there was an element of truth in all of them.

On 22 August Charles Brandon, Duke of Suffolk, died at

Guildford. His death was sudden, a great blow to England at this time of national crisis and a real grief to the King. Suffolk had, by 7 August, completed the defences of Portsmouth and then returned to court. He was due to depart for France to assume command of the army when he was taken suddenly ill. He died within a few days.[33] At any time Henry would have mourned the passing of his old friend but coming as it did when he was surrounded by a host of other worries, its effect was profound. The King put aside Suffolk's wish – declared in his will – to be buried quietly at Tattershall. Instead he saw his friend's remains laid to rest in the royal chapel at Windsor. Henry personally paid all the funeral expenses.[34]

But the King's cup was now filled. By the end of September the situation had eased. Hertford had rampaged through the Tweed valley destroying and plundering villages, towns, castles and abbeys. This, for the moment, reduced Scotland to a state of surly truce. The French at last withdrew their fleet from England's coastal waters and the southern counties breathed again. The French King also called back his army of twenty thousand men from before Boulogne without a serious encounter with his enemy. On 24 September London celebrated the deliverance with a procession; the Bishop, all the clergy carrying the parish crosses and the city companies in their livery promenaded from St Paul's up to Leadenhall and back to the Cathedral, chanting a litany of thanksgiving. But no agreement had been reached for a permanent end to hostilities and there now followed months of inconclusive bargaining with representatives of the leading continental powers. Nobody outside the small circle of councillors and ambassadors attendant upon the King's peripatetic court knew from day to day which alliance was currently in favour. This uncertainty had its effect on the religious affairs in England. Cranmer, for instance, had moved beyond the vernacular litany and was drafting, with royal approval, a revision of canon law and of some of the services of the Church. He proposed the abolition of certain 'superstitious' ceremonies such as creeping to the cross and veiling images and crucifixes in Lent. Cranmer's suggestions were submitted to the King in their final form at the end of 1545. Then the diplomatic scene changed and Henry shelved his Archbishop's proposals. However, attempts to introduce fresh legislation against heretics failed (as we have seen).

But Henry was not unconcerned about the turbulent state of

affairs in the English Church. Growing discord between Protestants and Catholics disturbed him greatly. On Christmas Eve 1545 he took the opportunity of the closing of the session of Parliament to declare his mind to the assembled leaders of the nation:

My loving subjects, study and take pains to amend one thing which surely is amiss and far out of order, to the which I most heartily require you, which is that charity and concord is not amongst you, but discord and dissensions beareth rule in every place ... what love and charity is amongst you when the one calleth the other heretic and anabaptist, and he calleth him again papist, hypocrite and pharisee? Be these tokens of charity amongst you? Are these the signs of fraternal love between you? No, no ... I must needs judge the fault and occasion of this discord to be partly by you the fathers and preachers of the spirituality. For if I know a man which liveth in adultery, I must judge him a lecherous and carnal person. If I see a man boast and brag himself, I cannot but deem him a proud man. I see and hear daily of you of the clergy who preach one against another, teach one contrary to another, inveigh one against another without charity or discretion ... all men almost be in variety and discord and few or more preach truly and sincerely the word of God, according as they ought to do. How can poor souls live in concord when you preachers sow amongst them in your sermons debate and discord. To you they look for light, and you bring them darkness. Amend these crimes I exhort you and set forth God's word both by true preaching and good example-giving, or else I, whom God hath appointed his Vicar and high minister here, will see those divisions removed and those enormities corrected, according to my very duty, or else I shall be accounted an unprofitable servant and untrue officer ... you of the temporality be not clean and unspotted of malice and envy, for you rail on bishops, speak slanderously of priests, and rebuke and taunt preachers, both contrary to good order and Christian fraternity. If you know surely that a bishop or preacher careth or teacheth perverse doctrine, come and declare it to some of our Council, or to us, to whom is committed by God the high authority to reform and order such causes and behaviour, and be not judges of your own fantastical opinions and vain expositions, for in such high cases you may lightly err. And although you be permitted to read Holy Scripture, and to have the word of God in your mother tongue, you must understand that you have this licence only to inform your own conscience, and to instruct your children and family, and not to dispute and make Scripture a railing and a taunting stock against priests and preachers as many light persons do. I am very sorry to know and hear how unreverently that most precious jewel, the word of God, is disputed,

N

rhymed, sung and jangled in every alehouse and tavern, contrary to the true meaning and doctrine of the same. And yet I am ever as much sorry that the readers of the same follow it doing so faintly and coldly. For of this I am sure: that charity was never so faint amongst you and virtuous and godly living was never less used, nor God himself amongst Christians never less reverenced, honoured or served. Therefore, as I said before, be in charity one with another, like brother and brother. Love, dread and serve God (to which I, as your Supreme Head and sovereign lord, exhort and require you) and then I doubt not the love and league ... shall never be dissolved or broken between us.[35]

According to the King's Secretary, William Petre, and others who were present, this speech moved the whole assembly to tears of joy.[36] But its effect on those whom the King was metaphorically rapping over the knuckles was shortlived. Certainly Bonner and his colleagues were soon more worried about the situation than ever before. In 1546 the Catholic leaders moved into the attack once more. They doubtless felt the time to be propitious for fresh activity. Not only had the King openly declared his concern but the position of the Protestants had been weakened by the deaths of Suffolk and Dr Butts (the latter died on 11 November 1545). Hertford and Lisle were still engaged on military affairs abroad and the conservative elements held the majority on the Privy Council for the first time in months. Even so, it is significant that fresh persecutions did not begin until Gardiner's return to England in March 1546.

Anne Ayscough had certainly been no more subdued by her Sovereign's homily than by her own trial by jury. She continued attending sermons and meetings, gospelling throughout London and speaking boldly at court about her faith. Her case came up in Chancery sometime in the Hilary term and the outcome of it afforded Anne little satisfaction. The judges dismissed her plea and told her to return to her husband. Anne did not have long to brood over her disappointment. She soon had more important worries.

In some way Anne had made an enemy of a very powerful man. Thomas Wriothesley, Lord Chancellor of England, was not only powerful; he was determined. One contemporary wrote of him: 'I knew he was an earnest follower of whatever he took in hand, and did very seldom miss where either wit or travail were able to bring his purpose to pass.'[37] Wriothesley's rise had been fairly recent. He had pursued the upward path of his ambition through the rocks and briars of conciliar intrigue with consummate skill. Trained and patronized by Cromwell he yet survived and even benefited from the minister's fall. A long-standing enemy of Gardiner's during the 'thirties, he changed sides with alacrity in 1540. A zealous reformer and iconoclast under the Cromwellian regime, he became a mainstay of the conservative group on the Council and resolved to follow the old religion 'until the times do alter'. Advanced by the Howards in 1540–41, he did not hesitate to take a leading part in the examination of members of the family which followed on the disgrace of Catherine Howard. Having gained the post of joint principal secretary in 1540, Wriothesley took pains to commend himself to the King whenever opportunity presented, and Henry took the thrusting young man (he was thirty-five in 1540) more and more into his confidence. Wriothesley had already gained a reputation and considerable unpopularity as a seeker-out of heretics and Anne's activities cannot have escaped his notice. He also knew all about her legal proceedings in his court.

He made it his business to find out more. One of his employees in the court of Chancery was a certain Master Wadloe. The well-educated[38] Wadloe was one of the twenty-four cursitors in Chancery (i.e. one of the clerks who drafted writs), and was only too anxious to serve his master in any way outside the normal course of his duties if it would lead to his own advancement. Wriothesley accordingly employed him as a spy. The young clerk followed Anne and discovered all he could about her opinions, her friends and her rendezvous with her co-religionists. He even took rooms near Anne's lodgings close by the Temple. From his window he was apparently able to keep so close a watch on his quarry that he could report, 'at midnight she beginneth to pray and ceaseth not for many hours after, when I and others apply ourselves to sleep or do worse'.[39] As information came in from Wadloe, Wriothesley compiled his dossier on Anne Ayscough. Doubtless he was doing the same for other suspected heretics; yet probably he had a special interest in Anne. Was there already a half-formed plan in his mind about Anne and her supporters at court? Did the ambitious Chancellor already have a glimmering of how he might use this over-talkative country lass to attack some of his rivals on the Council and at court?

On 10 March 1546 Anne Ayscough was arrested a second time[40] on suspicion of heresy and brought again before the quest,[41] meeting on this occasion in Sadlers' Hall under the chairmanship of Christopher Dare. It was the task of this court to discover, by taking evidence and by asking certain standard doctrinal questions, whether the accused's views were suspect or not. Its job was completed when the jury had decided whether or not to hand the accused over to higher authority for further examination. When news spread that Anne Ayscough was to be brought before the quest, a crowd of Londoners flocked to the hall, as many as possible squeezing inside to watch the contest between the fair gospeller and her examiners.

And a contest it was. Dare leaned forward with his list of questions – theological questions which he imperfectly understood – on the desk before him. The jurors peered intently at the slight but defiant young figure whose fate they held in their hands. They were very conscious that no London quest had ever before been called upon to give its verdict on a gentlewoman. The chairman began his questions.

DARE: Do you believe the sacrament hanging over the altar is the very body of Christ really?

ANNE (after a pause): Can you tell me why Stephen was stoned to death?

DARE: No, but that has nothing to do . . .

ANNE (triumphantly, looking around at the audience, where she recognized many friendly faces): Then, neither will I answer your vain question.

When Master Dare was able to make himself heard again above the guffaws and sniggers, he wisely decided not to rely on his own inquisitorial eloquence and called loudly for witnesses. A woman stepped forward who was prepared to swear that Mistress Ayscough had poured scorn on the sacrament, saying 'God dwelleth not in temples made with hands'.

DARE: Did you say that?

ANNE: For answer to that you must read in the book of Acts, chapters seven and seventeen, and see what Stephen and Paul said therein.

DARE: Oh, and how do you interpret what is written there?

ANNE (she had her audience with her now, enjoying the entertainment and hanging on her every word): Oh, I will not cast my pearls before swine: acorns be good enough.

It was some minutes before the chairman could get silence to proceed.

DARE: You are also accused of saying that you would rather read five lines from the Bible than hear five masses in the Temple Church. Is that true?

ANNE: It is; for the one edifies me and the other doesn't. For the Bible speaks plain, but as for the Church, 'tis as St Paul says in I Corinthians 9, 'If the trump give an uncertain sound who shall prepare for battle?'

Dare now reverted to his list of questions and asked her opinions on the priesthood and auricular confession. In each case the young lady referred her hearers to the relevant portions of Scripture without committing herself in any way. The examiner now moved on to more dangerous matters.

DARE: What do you think of the King's Book?

ANNE: I have never read it.

Dare's next question was suggested by the knowledge that the more extreme Protestants – the Anabaptists – claimed to be beyond the reach of human laws because their only guide was the prompting of the Holy Spirit within.

DARE: Do you have the Spirit of God within you?

ANNE: If I do not, I am but a reprobate or a castaway.

The unfortunate Christopher Dare was quite at home haggling with hard-faced Hanse merchants over the price of their wares, but trying to discover what this young gentlewoman believed was putting him quite out of countenance. He even tried calling on the assistance of a supposed specialist, a priest – but to no avail. Anne simply refused to be led into the deep theological waters of sacramental doctrine. Her own later comment on the priest's attempted interrogation was: 'None other answer would I make him, because I perceived him a papist.'

Dare looked round at the jury. They seemed as bemused as he. Had they heard enough yet to reach a verdict? He resolved to ask one more question on a known point of controversy between Protestants and Catholics.

DARE: Do you believe in the efficacy of private masses for departed souls?

ANNE: It is a great idolatry to believe more in private masses than in the death that Christ died for us.

The inquisitor was out of his depth. Had his examinee been a

weaver or serving-wench he would have known what to do and his
jury would have wasted no time in bringing in their verdict. As it
was they were far too cautious to commit a gentlewoman to prison
on evidence which they scarcely understood. Christopher Dare
decided that he could not take the responsibility either for detain-
ing or releasing so notable a person as Anne Ayscough. He therefore adjourned his court and had Anne conveyed to the House of
the Lord Mayor of London, Sir Martin Bowes.[42]

Bowes was no more of a theologian than Dare and made sure of
obtaining the aid of a scholarly colleague in the person of the
Bishop's Chancellor, Dr John Standish.[43] The Lord Mayor must
have been most anxious to see for himself this eminent heretic who
had appeared within his jurisdiction. He was undoubtedly equally
anxious to please Bishop Bonner and relieve himself of an embarrassment by obtaining from Anne a statement of orthodox belief.
All that Bowes and Standish succeeded in doing, however, was
working themselves up into a rage. They went over the questions
that Anne had already been asked by the quest and she gave much
the same answers.

> Besides this, my Lord Mayor laid one thing to my charge which was
> never spoken of me, but of them, and that was: whether a mouse eating
> the host received God, or no. This question did I never ask; but,
> indeed, they asked it of me, whereunto I made them no answer, but
> smiled.[44]

This discussion of the mouse and the host was an old debating point
originating among the Lollards and used by them to expose the
foolishness of the grosser forms of transubstantiation. By the mid-
sixteenth century the use of this argument had become an accepted
mark of a heretic, though one which was not taken very seriously
by theologians.

Brushing aside such futile questions, Standish took Anne to task
for being so disrespectful in argument and in bandying Scripture
with her superiors. St Paul, he told her, had explicitly forbidden
women 'to speak or to talk of the work of God'. Anne's knowledge
of the Bible was proof against this argument:

> I answered him that I knew Paul's meaning so well as he, which is
> (1 Cor. XIV) that a woman ought not to speak in the congregation by
> way of teaching. And then I asked him how many women he had
> seen go into the pulpit and preach. He said he never saw any. Then

I said he ought to find no fault in poor women, unless they had offended against the law.[45]

At this point Bowes and Standish lost their patience and told Anne they were putting her in custody. Bowes utterly refused to release her on surety and she was sent to the Lord Mayor's prison, the Counter in Bread Street.

She stayed in the Counter with only a maid for company for seven days during which time none of her friends was allowed to visit her.[46] The only person who came to her was a priest sent by Bonner. He tried to gain Anne's confidence by making friendly conversation and sympathizing with her plight. He was met with suspicion, and when he moved on to the interrogation for which he had been sent, Anne completely refused to answer his questions. The priest had one more trick up his sleeve to make Anne talk; he asked her if she would make her confession. She replied, yes, as long as she could have Dr Crome, Sir William Whitehead or John Huntington to shrive her. Crome and Whitehead were city clergy, as we have seen. Huntington was apparently an unbeneficed preacher who had taken part in the examination of Alexander Seton in 1541 (see pp. 131-2 above) but had since experienced a conversion to the reformed faith and was now accounted by Anne a 'man of wisdom'.

The priest had not finished his questioning. He, too, brought up the question of the mouse eating the host. Again Anne was not to be caught out. 'Seeing ye have taken the pains to ask this question, I desire you also to take so much more pain as to answer it yourself. I will not do it, because I perceive ye come to tempt me.' The poor man was almost finished.

> Fifthly, he asked me if I intended to receive the sacrament at Easter, or no. I answered that, if I did not, I were no Christian woman, and that I did rejoice that the time was so near at hand. And then he departed thence with many fair words.[47]

He went straight away to report to Bonner.

All this time some of Anne's friends had been trying to see her and to find some way of helping her. On 23 March she had a visit from 'my cousin Britain'[48] who told her he was trying to obtain her release on bail. Britain went to see the Lord Mayor who sent him on to the Chancellor, explaining that Anne could only be released with the consent of a spiritual officer. But when Britain found Standish he was told that the Chancellor was not prepared to take responsibility for setting Anne at liberty because 'the matter was so heinous'. He was advised to come back the next day, by which time Standish would have had time to consult Bonner.

Bishop Edmund Bonner had been following the case closely through the reports of his subordinates. His overriding concern was to rid his diocese of heresy. By 1546 the problem was immeasurably greater than it had ever been before and Bonner was at his wits' end to know how to deal with it. As far as Anne Ayscough was concerned he had two objectives: one was to save her soul by persuading her to recant any erroneous opinions she held; and the other was to discredit her and her opinions by publishing her recantation. For if Anne Ayscough, one of the most celebrated London Protestants, could be broken, the shock to the entire movement would be considerable. What the Bishop did not want to do was to burn Anne. To have done that would either have resulted in the King's intervention or would have made a martyr of Anne Ayscough and thus have encouraged the growth of the movement. Thus, when Standish came and reported to him the latest moves in Anne's case, Bonner decided it was time to intervene personally. He arranged to interview Anne at 3.0 p.m. on 25 March. He encouraged her friends to ensure that she uttered 'even the very bottom of her heart' and promised that she would not be accused of anything she said during the interview. He even suggested that Crome, Huntington and Whitehead should be present to make sure that Anne 'was handled with no rigour'.

Here Bonner was not being open and honest. He wanted Anne to compromise herself quite unequivocally, instead of prevaricating as she had done in her previous examinations. Also he wanted to involve the three preachers mentioned, two of whom had been involved in heresy proceedings before and all three of whom were being closely watched. It is inconceivable that the Bishop would have kept his promise not to act on anything revealed during the interview. He was desperate to stamp out heresy from the city parishes and was prepared to justify any means to that end.

On the twenty-fifth Bonner had Anne brought before him at 1.0 p.m., two hours before the time appointed for the examination. When he began questioning her she asked permission to wait until her friends arrived. Bonner offered to send straight away for the three preachers, but Anne declared she would be satisfied with cousin Britain and Edward Hall, another friend from Gray's Inn.[49] Bonner went into his gallery and left his archdeacon to reason with her. But where others had failed this priest did not succeed and nothing was obtained from Anne until her friends arrived.

A little before three o'clock Britain and Hall arrived with several of their friends from the inns of court, including Edmund Butts, a younger son of Sir William, the King's Physician. They had decided to come in strength, the better to be able to support their friend in her hour of trial. The Bishop came down to his great chamber with Dr Standish and other clergy. All were seated and Anne Ayscough's next examination began.

Bonner began, benignly, urging her to speak anything that was on her mind:

BONNER: Now, if a man has a wound and goes to a surgeon with it he cannot receive treatment until the wound is uncovered. In just the same way, I cannot help you until I know what your conscience is burdened with.

ANNE: My lord, my conscience is clear on all things. It might appear odd if a surgeon were to lay a plaster on healthy skin.

BONNER: Very well, then you force me to lay to your charge your own reported words, which are these: you said that he that doth receive the sacrament from the hands of an evil priest, or a sinner, receiveth the devil and not God.

ANNE: I never spoke any such words. What I said to the quest and to my Lord Mayor, and what I now say again, was that the wickedness of the priest cannot hurt me, but in spirit and in faith, I receive nonetheless the body and blood of Christ.

(Here the Bishop detected a deviation from the Church's teaching on transubstantiation.)

BONNER: What a saying is this! In spirit?

ANNE: My lord, without faith and spirit I cannot receive him worthily.

BONNER: Did you say that after consecration the holy bread in the pyx is still only bread?

ANNE: No, my lord. When I was asked that question I gave no answer.

BONNER: But you quoted certain passages of Scripture in order to refute the doctrine of the mass.

ANNE: I only quoted St Paul's words to the Athenians in Acts 17: 'God liveth not in temples made with hands.'

BONNER: Oh, and how do you interpret these words?

ANNE: I believe as the Scripture tells me, my lord.

BONNER: Oh, then what if Scripture says the holy bread is the body of Christ?

ANNE: I believe as the Scripture teaches . . .

BONNER: And if Scripture says that it is not the body of Christ?

ANNE: I still believe as the Scripture . . .

BONNER: Well and what, in your opinion, does the Scripture teach?

ANNE: Whatever Christ and his apostles taught, that I believe.

BONNER: And what did they teach about the sacrament of the altar?

Silence.

BONNER: You have very few words. Why is that?

ANNE: My lord, Solomon saith, 'a woman of few words is a gift of God'.

Smiles flickered over the faces of the onlookers. The tension was momentarily relieved. But the Bishop was not smiling. He paced the floor for a few moments. Then paused to tower before Anne's chair.

BONNER: Did you or did you not say that the mass is idolatry?

ANNE: No, my lord. When the quest asked whether private masses relieved departed souls I answered: 'What idolatry is this, that we should believe more in private masses, than in the healthsome death of the dear Son of God.'

BONNER: What sort of an answer was that?

ANNE: A poor one, my lord, but good enough for the question.

The Bishop's patience was fast evaporating. This woman would do nothing but prevaricate. She denied having made any statements which might be considered heretical, yet she would not state clearly what she did believe. Obviously she was a heretic but how could he prove it? A long spell of imprisonment was the normal way of breaking down heretics but this woman had powerful friends. Very awkward questions might be asked if she were neither charged nor set at liberty. Bonner and Standish continued their interrogation for another hour until the shadows stretched themselves along the rushes on the floor, and lights had to be called for. They took her once more over all the questions the quest, the

Lord Mayor and the Bishop had already asked her. They brought up the matter of her conduct in Lincolnshire. They made accusations, some of which had only the slenderest connection with fact. And only when they were hoarse and exasperated from futile argument did they stop. Throughout the afternoon and early evening Anne Ayscough remained, though at times frightened, outwardly calm and self-confident while her inquisitors lost both face and temper. The last exchange between the Bishop and the young gospeller underlines this clearly:

BONNER: There are many that read and know the Scripture, and yet do not follow it nor live thereafter.

ANNE: My lord, I would that all men knew my conversation and living in all points; for I am so sure of myself this hour, that there are none able to prove any dishonesty by me. If you know any that can do it I pray you bring them forth.

At that Bonner flung out of the room and went to his own chamber. There he wrote out a document for Anne's signature. If he could not force her to recant, he would get her to confess her belief in the orthodox doctrine of the sacrament of the altar. That would serve just as well to discredit her with her sect. This was the confession he drew up.

> Be it known to all faithful people, that as touching the blessed sacrament of the altar, I do firmly and undoubtedly believe, that after the words of consecration be spoken by the priest, according to the common usage of this Church of England, there is present really the body and blood of our Saviour, Jesus Christ, whether the minister which doth consecrate be a good man or a bad man . . . Also, whensoever the said sacrament is received, whether the receiver be a good man or a bad man, he doth receive it really and corporally. And, moreover, I do believe that whether the said sacrament be then received of the minister or else reserved to be put into the pyx, or to be brought to any person that is impotent or sick, yet there is the very body and blood of our said Saviour. So that, whether the minister or the receiver be good or bad, yea whether the sacrament be received or reserved, always there is the blessed body of Christ really.
>
> And this thing with all other things touching the sacrament and other sacraments of the Church, and all things else touching the Christian belief, which are taught and declared in the King's Majesty's book, lately set forth for the erudition of the Christian people, I Anne Ayscough, otherwise called Anne Kyme, do truly and perfectly believe, and do here and now confess and acknowledge. And here I

do promise that henceforth I shall never say or do anything against
the premises, or against any of them. In witness whereof, I the said
Anne have subscribed my name unto these presents.[50]

Anne was now called into the Bishop's privy chamber, the
document was read to her and she was asked to sign it. Now she
really was in a corner. The choice was a clear one: sign or confess
to heresy and face the consequences. Still she tried to wriggle out
of the dilemma.

ANNE: I believe as much of this as the body of Scripture doth
agree to. Wherefore I desire you that you will add that thereto.

BONNER: Don't you try to teach me what to write, Mistress.

With that the Bishop went out to the great chamber and read
the document to the priests, lawyers and others who were still
waiting there. When they had heard the confession Anne's friends,
though they did not like the tenor of it, urged her to sign. She took
some persuading but, at length, agreed. The tension relaxed.
Everyone breathed a sigh of relief. The long ordeal was over.
Bonner sat down at the table, laid down the paper, drew up ink and
quill and showed Anne where to sign her name. All the other
gentlemen stood round the table to witness Anne's signature.[51]
She wrote: 'I Anne Ayscough do believe all manner of things contained in the faith of the Catholic Church' (i.e. the universal or
true, invisible Church as understood by Protestants. This Church
was not necessarily coextensive with the earthly institution).
Bonner leapt up from his chair in a rage. Was this woman incapable
of plain dealing? He strode back to his own chamber. Only after
Britain and Dr Weston (Professor of Divinity at Oxford and
Rector of St Botolph's, Bishopsgate) had been in to reason with
him did Bonner consent to accept Anne's signature and subscription.[52]

Anne's friends now believed that all that remained was for bail
to be arranged before Anne was released. They were mistaken. The
Bishop returned her to prison and caused her to appear next day in
the Guildhall, where her confession was publicly read out. Bonner
was determined to set well in hand the process of discrediting
Mistress Ayscough before he allowed her to wander through his
diocese disseminating her version of the trial. On 22 March the
Bishop's officers met Anne's sureties (Britain and Francis Spilman
of Gray's Inn) in St Paul's and there negotiated for her release.

Even now there were complications. According to Anne's account, Britain and Spilman were also required to stand surety for another woman they did not know.[53] Only after long argument was agreement reached and that afternoon the two men were able to proceed to the Counter, armed with the Bishop's warrant for Anne's release.

Anne wisely decided not to remain in London. The court of Chancery had ordered her to return to her husband. The Bishop had urged her to go back to her county. Her friends persuaded her of the great danger she would be in if she remained in London. Probably Anne herself, emotionally exhausted by the events of the past fortnight and depressed by the thought that she had signed a confession and, in some degree, compromised her faith, only wanted to get away to spend some time in quiet with her Bible and her God. So, at the end of March, attended by her few servants, she took the road northwards. It was, of course, to South Kelsey and not to Friskney that she went.

# 8

# *The Final Assault*

⸺ ❦❦❦❦❦ ❦❦❦❦❦ ⸺

HE final assault by conservative and Catholic forces on Protestants, men of the new learning, heretics and their patrons
began a few weeks after Anne's release. Bishop Gardiner
was its originator and sustainer. He returned from the Netherlands
in mid-March and was a regular attender at the Council until well
into the autumn (with the exception of the first two weeks of June,
when he was on embassy in France). During the spring and
summer Hertford and Dudley were on the Continent and did not
return until the end of July. It is highly significant that this last
persecution of Henry VIII's reign was concentrated into the
months of April and May and the period from mid-June to mid-
July.

By the beginning of April 1546 Gardiner had taken stock of the
current situation and decided the time was ripe for the overthrow
of his enemies. Time was not on his side. When he had reported
back from his mission he had been staggered to see how weak and
pain-racked the King was.[1] Henry could not be counted on to live
much longer. But while he lived he was as dominant as ever.
Gardiner knew the risk involved. If he overreached himself the
consequences might be disastrous. But it was a case of now or never
and the risk had to be taken. He immediately began forging a
chain of persecutions which should eventually reach to the highest
in the land.

It was Dr Crome who in April provided the first link in that
chain. The eloquent and fashionable preacher was quite unchasten-
ed by his earlier experiences, and the Catholic leaders, who kept a
careful watch on him, were only too anxious to attack him again.

In his Lent sermons in the Mercers' Chapel he repeated his earlier heresies, declared the sufficiency of Christ's once-for-all sacrifice and asserted that the Lord was not offered again in the Sacrament of the Altar. He continued to preach in this vein in his own church – St Mary Aldermary – unmolested through Passion Sunday (11 April) and during the five Easter sermons. Then Gardiner gave the signal for action and Crome was summoned to appear before the Council.

Even now the councillors had to proceed cautiously. They took little time to decide that Crome's views were objectionable, and that he was, in fact, a relapsed heretic. Any artisan in a similar situation would have been condemned to the flames out of hand. But Crome was a popular figure, an educated man, he had friends at court and he was in favour with the King. The Council, therefore, satisfied themselves by calling on the heretical Doctor for a public recantation at St Paul's Cross. This was fixed for 9 May, the Sunday after Low Sunday. This left Crome several days to reconsider his position and during this time several of his friends urged him to stand firm for evangelical truth. They argued that his position was secure and that Gardiner would not dare to take further action against him. Foremost among these bold counsellors was John Lascelles. Others were Robert Huick the King's Physician, John Taylor, Vicar of St Bride's, one of the Scottish exiled priests, a young court page by the name of Worley and 'Playne, the skinner'.[2]

It was one thing to give bold advice and quite another to stand up in public and follow it. However, Crome's resolve appears to have been strengthened by the promptings of his co-religionists and his declaration at Paul's Cross on 9 May was, from the Catholic point of view, quite inadequate. He read to the congregation the statement of orthodox doctrine prepared for him but afterwards added that 'he came not thither to recant nor to deny his words nor would not'.[3] The representatives of the Council who had attended the sermon to satisfy themselves that their wishes were carried out wasted no time. Crome was arrested again and re-examined by the Council the next day. A body of learned theologians was called in to assist the councillors. This group included Nicholas Ridley (Bishop of Rochester), Bonner, Heath (Bishop of Worcester), May (Dean of St Paul's), Redmayne (Master of Trinity, Cambridge), and Doctors Robinson and Cox (both prominent canon lawyers who assisted with most of the doctrinal formularies drawn up in Henry's reign and his son's).

Crome had played into the hands of his adversaries. His examiners not only reasoned with him; they threatened. The popular preacher was now in danger of the fire. Recantation was not now sufficient. If he wished to save himself he must provide the Council with the names of others who shared his beliefs. At first Crome stood firm but during a sleepless night in prison he was able to reflect on his situation and the next day (11 May) he broke down before the Council. Names were wrung from him and Gardiner's friends swung into action immediately. That same day the jubilant, but cautious, Bishop was able to report to Secretary Petre:

> As it appears that sundry persons have used themselves with Crome otherwise than is tolerable, the writers would know the King's pleasure (being loth to offend either by doing too much or too little), and have again the depositions and examinations. Crome notes that he was also comforted by one Lascelles, whom they are examining, not upon Crome's detection, but because he boasted a desire to be called to the Council. Dr Huick, the physician, appearing this day upon a complaint made against him, in the variance with his wife, the writers take the opportunity to examine him also, and will send his answers ... these cumbersome matters have consumed much time.[4]

This report was crucial. If the King sanctioned further action Gardiner and his colleagues would be able to make a rapid and sweeping purge. Henry's reply was favourable. The repercussions of Crome's confession were felt throughout the realm:

> This Doctor Crome, after his committing, while he was in the ward at Greenwich, in the court under my Lord Chancellor, accused divers persons as well of the court as of the city, with other persons in the country, which put many persons to great trouble, and some suffered death after.[5]

Quite how John Lascelles became involved is not clear. From Gardiner's account it would seem that he had boasted of his views, either because he felt sure of the King's support or because he really wished to court martyrdom. The Howards were, of course, delighted at Lascelles's arrest but probably had nothing to do with it. Norfolk was not involved in this last persecution. He was preparing in his own way for the next reign. Realistic dynast that he was, he had come to the conclusion that the position of the Seymours was unassailable. He therefore proposed an alliance between the two families. The scheme, for which the King's permission was obtained before the end of May, entailed the marriage of Thomas Seymour to the Duchess of Richmond, and the alliance of Surrey's two eldest sons and Lord Howard's son to three of Hertford's daughters. This delicate marital patchwork never came into being thanks, largely, to the intransigent pride of the headstrong Earl of Surrey. He hated the upstart Seymours with a hatred more passionate and open than that of his father. He loudly proclaimed the superiority of his noble birth and royal descent, and was already, illegally, quartering the royal arms with his own. He boldly asserted that when Henry died (a subject which it was treason even to refer to) Norfolk would be regent. These rash sentiments led to a quarrel between Surrey and the King's favourite, Sir George Blagge. At about the same time the Earl also ran foul of Sir Richard Southwell, a member of the Council. It was almost certainly as a result of Howard intrigue that both these gentlemen found themselves in prison before the summer was out.

Gardiner's closest colleagues in the new wave of persecutions were Richard Rich and Thomas Wriothesley. The Lord Chancellor was, as we have seen, an avowed enemy of heretics. Richard Rich was a man particularly suited to lead a heresy hunt. Ambitious and unscrupulous, he had climbed over the broken careers of friends and patrons whom he had helped to ruin, in his ascent to high office. A colleague of Sir Thomas More at the Middle Temple, he had been the chief prosecution witness at More's trial. Favoured and elevated to the important and lucrative post of Chancellor of the Court of Augmentations by Thomas Cromwell, he actively participated in Mr Secretary's downfall. Employed in the 1530s as visitor of the doomed monasteries, he changed sides in 1540 and became a mainstay of Gardiner's faction.[6] With these two powerful and determined men beside him Gardiner had little difficulty in dominating the Council.

The round-up of notable Protestants in the city continued. On 13 May the Council reported, 'This day we look for Latimer, the Vicar of St Bride's, John Taylor, and some others that have specially comforted Crome in his folly.'[7] Hugh Latimer had to submit to long and repeated examinations before the Council and angered his examiners by his prevarication. Having failed to discover his real opinions ('to fish out the bottom of his stomach', as

o

they described it), or to implicate him with Crome's heresy, they committed the ex-Bishop to the Tower.[8]

Gardiner was much too busy with the courtiers who had been arrested to bother about Hugh Latimer, whose influence had much diminished since his departure from London in 1539. On 14 May Dr Huick was examined. First of all the Council considered his matrimonial issue. They decided that he had been cruel and un-justified in turning his wife out of doors (despite the fact that he claimed to have the King's sanction for his action). Quickly leaving that matter behind they went on to consider the Doctor's religious opinions. Huick was as outspoken as usual about his beliefs and it is no surprise to learn that he was committed to ward to await further examination.[9]

Now it was the turn of John Lascelles. The Sewer of the King's Chamber refused to commit himself on matters of doctrine and claimed his master's protection. This drew forth a wry comment from Gardiner in his report.

> Lascelles will not answer that part of his conference with Crome which touches Scripture without the King's command and his protection, saying that it is neither wisdom nor equity to kill himself. Thus the King must pardon before he know, if Mr Lascelles may have his will.[10]

John Lascelles was apparently confident that the King would come to his aid (a confidence which Gardiner, obviously, did not share). His attitude throughout his examinations was obstinate. He never deviated from what he believed to be the truth and, when he saw that he could expect no help from the King, he willingly confessed his heresies and faced the consequences. Throughout these last weeks of his life he displayed a remarkable – even a fanatical – constancy. The next day, 15 May, Lascelles and his colleagues (Huick, Worley and 'Playne the skinner') were examined again and still proved obdurate. Two others appeared slightly more tract-able.

> The vicar of St Bride's shows himself of the same sort, but not so bold. The Scot is more meet for Dunbar than London . . . he will say whatever is required of him to get off.[11]

By 17 May the Council had had enough of examining heretics:

> Business – Doctor Huick, Lascelles, the Scottish priest, Worley and Playne, the skinner, for erroneous opinions and dissuading Crome

from his promise in the declaration of the articles, were committed to the Tower . . .[12]

John Taylor, presumably, recanted and was released.

The hunt for heretics was swiftly taken up beyond the capital. On 15 May Bonner, who had wasted no time in holding Six Articles commissions in his diocese, reported to the King that four men and one woman had been found guilty of heresy in Essex and wished to know if public example might be made of them. Henry's prompt reply revealed that he was still unprepared to instigate a large-scale persecution. He ordered that two men, who had repented, were to be released. The remainder were to be burned at Colchester and two other places – but, unless 'a general infection' was apparent or any others were 'notably detected', the commissioners were to dissolve their assembly 'until a more commodious time'.[13] It was on 15 May also that the justices of the peace in Suffolk arrested one John Kirby on suspicion of sacramental heresy.[14] On the same day a priest at Tenterden in Kent was sent up to the Council for uttering 'a lewd sermon'.[15]

Not content with prosecuting current troublemakers the Council dragged others out of rural obscurity back into the limelight. Ex-Bishop Shaxton was summoned from his parish at Hadleigh in Suffolk.[16] On 24 May two yeomen of the chamber were sent to fetch Robert Wisdom, who had been living in Staffordshire for the last three years.[17] As soon as he heard that the Council's interest in him had revived, Wisdom fled. Within days he was safely in Flanders. The two yeomen charged with apprehending Crome's ex-curate had another errand to perform; they 'had with them letters to one Kyme and his wife for their appearance within ten days after receipt'.[18]

Anne Ayscough's recall to London may have been part of the Council's new burst of activity against notable heretics but it seems more likely that the initiative now came from Thomas Kyme. Consider his position. The court of Chancery had ordered his wife to return to him but she had not done so. But Kyme did not really want her back – or, rather, he was in a dilemma. If he forced her to return to Friskney there would be a return to the bitter domestic situation which had prevailed between 1540 and 1544. On the other hand, with the situation as it was, he had no wife nor was he free to marry again. He must frequently have wished Anne dead. Furthermore, he was being goaded beyond endurance by the local priests. They had been disappointed and angry when Anne returned safely from London and they urged Kyme to take fresh action against her. She was a heretic and it was up to her husband to see that she was denounced as such. Whoever instigated the new proceedings, it is clear that both Thomas Kyme and Gardiner's party stood to gain from a fresh examination of Anne.

It was ostensibly because of the matrimonial issue that the Kymes had been called to London. It was up to Thomas to see that he reported with his wife within ten days of the receipt of the summons. He therefore sent an urgent message to Sir Francis Ayscough. Its tenor was respectful, but carried more than a hint of malice. Would Ayscough, Kyme asked, please see that his sister was ready to depart without delay. Should he be tempted to hide Anne, let him consider the results of incurring the royal displeasure. Furthermore if Anne persisted in evasion, then he (Kyme) was not without friends who would seek her out. When he received the letter, Francis was determined to do all he could to save his sister. He replied therefore that he did not know Anne's whereabouts.

Realizing that Sir Francis Ayscough was not to be easily persuaded to yield his sister up, Thomas Kyme (or perhaps his clerical friends) made contact with the Bishop's officers in Lincoln. Dean Heneage and his colleagues must have been reluctant to proceed against members of such a prominent Lincolnshire family, though there were many among them who shared Bishop Longland's fierce abhorrence of heresy. However with royal authority on his side Kyme held the winning card. Rather than be accused of hindering the processes of royal justice the Bishop's officers set off for South Kelsey.

Sir Francis, hoping his position would protect both him and his sister from interference, kept Anne at home until he received word that she was in danger. By that time, it was too late to send her very far for refuge and she was hidden in a cottage fairly close at hand. Sir Francis may well have reflected as the Bishop's men dismounted in his courtyard that it was almost exactly ten years since that other occasion when Catholic zeal had forced its way into South Kelsey Hall. In October 1536, he had been the quarry and it is impossible that he can have forgotten the fear and panic of being pursued by men full of a hatred inspired by religion. He knew not only how desperate was Anne's plight if she were captured; he knew just how she felt. So he and his wife submitted to the questions and threatenings of the searchers.

They might have succeeded in their subterfuge had the investigators not managed to intercept a note Anne had sent to her brother. Now the Bishop's officers realized that Squire Ayscough knew his sister's whereabouts. Francis was in a cruel dilemma, as the family chronicler pointed out when he wrote up the episode years afterwards:

Mine aunt Anne, after many threats and great search made for her by the prelates her persecutors, was by casual intercepting of her own letter discovered, and so unwillingly delivered into their bloody hands, by him, that both loved her and the religion which she professed, but was never the less overcome with fear (for he had much to lose) lest haply by concealing what was known he knew, he might so have brought himself into trouble. Thus much flesh and blood prevailed with him, which often had such power even over the most regenerate, that the Apostle Paul saith of himself, 'what I would that I do not: but what I hate even that I do'.[19]

Anne did have some warning that her enemies were on their way. According to the most colourful local story, she took the precaution of hiding any incriminating evidence she had with her before attempting to escape. She took her copy of Tyndale's New Testament, wrapped it in some bread dough she had been kneading and thrust it into the cottage's brick oven. Then she fled into Kelsey woods. Here it was that she was discovered. From the fact that she was never charged with being in possession of heretical literature it would seem that her New Testament escaped detection.

Having at last laid hands on her who was legally his wife, Thomas Kyme hastened to London with her. Sir Francis Ayscough was left behind, suffering, if the family historian is to be believed, terrible pangs of remorse – and worse:

From the time he had left her with them, till the hour wherein she suffered, a flame of fire presented itself in the day time to view such (as according to his own comparison) appeareth in a glass window over against a great fire in the same room. Doubtless this sign was given to him to some end, and I doubt not, but he made good use thereof.[20]

The ten-day time limit allowed to them had already elapsed before the Kymes reached the capital. Before the Council could arrange a convenient time to hear the case, June was already more than half spent. In the meantime Gardiner, Wriothesley, Rich and their agents had grown still more vigilant in their search for influential Protestants.

Latimer, Shaxton, Lascelles and others were still in prison and others were on the point of being detained. On 29 May William Huick's case came up for review again and he was bound over on recognizance until Michaelmas.[21] On 7 June more minor figures at court were apprehended: 'Weston the luteplayer for conferences with Barker, Latham, Lascelles and others "upon prophecies and other things stirring to commotion against the King's Majesty" committed to the Porter's Lodge.'[22] The depositions of these men, which were considered two days later, reveal Latham to have been more mad than heretical and Weston little more than rather foolish and unguarded in his speech. That the Council bothered with them at all, reveals the extent of their vigilance at this time.

At the same time (7 June) peace was made between France and England. At last the country was on friendly terms with both the great continental powers. On Whit Sunday a relieved London celebrated the event:

> Item: the 12th day of June after was Whit Sunday, and then was a general procession from St Paul's unto St Peter's in Cornhill with all the children of St Paul's School, and a cross of every parish church, with a banner . . . all the clerks, all the priests, with parsons and vicars of every church in copes, and the choir of St Paul's in the same manner, and the Bishop bearing the sacrament under a canopy with the mayor in a gown of crimson velvet, the aldermen in scarlet, with all the crafts in their best apparell. When the mayor came between the cross and the standard there was made a proclamation with all the heralds of arms and pursuivants in their coats of arms, with the trumpets, and there was proclaimed a universal peace for ever between the emperor, the king of England, the French king, and all Christian kings for ever.[23]

Yet it was not an easy peace and there was no way of knowing which way the diplomatic cat might jump next. Since the religious cat would have to jump in the same direction, the leading Protestants and Catholics remained in a state of uncertainty. Wriothesley and Rich became increasingly committed to a policy of pure party intrigue during these days. They now attempted by every means at their disposal to discredit or destroy influential court Protestants.

Rich had succeeded in enmeshing two leading courtiers in his coils who were now detained on suspicion of heresy. Probably in both cases personal malice played more than a small part. William Morice was a gentleman usher to the King and the father of Archbishop Cranmer's secretary, Ralph Morice. The latter held a key position among the group of nobles and gentlemen opposed to the Norfolk, Gardiner, Wriothesley, Rich faction. On more than one occasion he had used his influence to help those attacked on heresy charges. Clearly Morice's father was in a position to give valuable information to his accusers and as a hostage might prove valuable in a number of ways. Yet some contemporaries who well understood Baron Rich's devious mind, were not above suggesting another motive for his attack on Morice: that gentleman had valuable lands at Chipping Ongar, sufficiently near Rich's own Essex estates to make them particularly attractive to the Councillor.

The other courtier accused by Rich was Sir Richard Southwell. His religious beliefs cannot be considered as anything other than orthodox (indeed he later proved himself an enthusiastic persecutor of Protestants under Mary Tudor) but he was one of those men of comparatively humble origin who had been raised to positions of influence and usefulness by Cromwell. He was another member of the anti-Howard party and had but recently quarrelled with the Earl of Surrey. In the court of the ailing King, religious differences, political disputes and personal rivalries were mingling to create a 'dog eat dog' situation. Heresy was as good a charge as any other to bring against someone one wanted out of the way, and it was a good deal easier to prove than many other charges. In that intellectually exciting age, most educated men had bought or read banned books and listened to heretical sermons at some time or other.

It was 19 June before the Kymes appeared before the Council at Greenwich.

> Thomas Kyme of Lincolnshire who had married one Anne Ayscough called hither and likewise his wife, who refused him to be her husband, without any honest allegation, was appointed to return to his county till he should be eftsoons sent for, and for that she was very obstinate and heady in reasoning of matters of religion, wherein she avowed

herself to be of a naughty opinion, seeing no persuasions of good
reasons could take place, she was sent to Newgate to remain there to
answer to the law.[24]

So the matrimonial issue was quickly disposed of and, as all her
enemies wished, Anne was left to face renewed heresy charges.
From this point we can follow the sequence of events in some detail
from Anne's own account. From this we learn more of her examination before the Council, briefly referred to in the official
minutes.[25] Anne conducted herself differently during this second
series of interrogations. Her thinking seems to have been clearer,
her determination greater. She had not sought martyrdom. She
had avoided attracting attention to herself in previous months.
Nevertheless, she had been arrested and was once again on trial for
her faith. She was determined not to make a second recantation.
She was now familiar with the wiles and threats of her accusers and
vowed she would not succumb to them. If she had been arrested
against her will then it must be the Lord's doing and if He required
her to go to the stake then her last breath should cry 'Amen' to His
purposes. So, from the beginning she set her intentions steadfastly
on martyrdom.

Here was where her accusers made their great miscalculation. If
Anne could have been induced, for fear of the stake, to recant; if
her spirit could have been broken, then Wriothesley and Rich
could have pressed home their attack and forced her to reveal the
names of ladies and gentlemen at the court who were implicated
in her heresy. This technique had proved very effective in the case
of Dr Crome and was a very common method of getting information against members of heretical cells. Anne's martyrdom would
be of little value to the Catholic councillors and any forward-
looking ecclesiastic must have realized that its effect on London
Protestantism would be the opposite of dampening.

After Kyme's dismissal on 19 June, Anne was harangued by the
Council for over four hours. Wriothesley began by reopening the
matrimonial issue. Anne's reply was short; she had already said all
she had to say on that score and only to the King would she open
her mind again.

Leaving behind the question of her relationship with Kyme,
Wriothesley went straight to the heart of the matter which really
interested him: 'Then my lord chancellor asked of my opinion in

the sacrament,' Anne later recorded. She was expecting this and gave an answer which now reads like a prepared statement – which is almost certainly what it was: 'I believe that so oft as I, in a Christian congregation, do receive the bread, in remembrance of Christ's death, and with thanksgiving, according to his holy instruction, I receive therewith also the fruits of his most glorious passion.' This was a positive attempt to state a belief which agreed with the words of institution while avoiding the question of Christ's presence in the elements.

Not unnaturally Gardiner considered her reply mere prevarication. Did she or did she not accept the doctrine of transubstantiation? Anne refused to elaborate on her statement. The Bishop and other councillors plied her with questions and we can imagine from her conduct at her earlier trial how pert and disrespectful must have been her replies. Many of her interrogators grew heated as the afternoon dragged into evening and no progress was made with this obstinate heretic.

It would be wrong to think of all the members of the conservative group as sharing in the schemes of Wriothesley and Rich. There was a growing alarm at the spread of heresy in the realm and particularly among the influential classes. This appearance of high-class heresy made a nonsense of the normal well-established methods of dealing with erroneous belief. You could not humiliate the scions of noble houses by making them carry their faggot. You could not hustle gentlemen and gentlewomen to the stake. It was even undesirable to allow the ecclesiastical courts or the special Six Articles commissioners to try these people. And, anyway, had not the King, himself, recently decreed that the commissioners were not to be over-zealous in seeking out heretics? Under these circumstances the Council sought to talk high-born heretics out of their errors, usually with considerable success. The majority of the Councillors – and this was true even of 'Wily Winchester' – were appalled at the peril in which Anne was placing her immortal soul and of the influence she had over others in London and at the court. All they wanted from her was a recantation which would at once bring her back to the bosom of Mother Church and discountenance her in the eyes of her supporters.

At the end of four hours Anne was allowed to go, Gardiner angrily dismissing her as nothing but a parrot, repeating the heresies she had been taught by others. She was now lodged in reasonable comfort in Lady Garnish's house. Throughout the next week Anne remained in honourable confinement and was summoned almost every day before the Council.

June 20, the day after her arrest, was a Sunday and it was either then or the following day that she endured another lengthy examination. The Council immediately questioned her again about her understanding of the Lord's Supper, but she still refused to expand on her earlier statement. As the Council members were not disposed to spend another four hours reasoning with her, three of their number were deputed to carry on the interrogation in another room. They were William Parr, Earl of Essex, John Dudley, Lord Lisle, and Bishop Gardiner. So, in a small ante-chamber of Greenwich Palace, while the Council proceeded to more urgent business, Anne was urged to confess that the Sacrament was 'flesh, blood and bone'. Far from being cowed, Anne carried the attack into the enemy camp: 'Then said I to my Lord Parr and my Lord Lisle that it was a great shame for them to counsel contrary to their knowledge.' According to Anne they did get the opportunity to whisper a few hurried words to her: '. . . in few words they did say, that they would gladly all things were well.' Poor men. They would gladly have liked to help Anne, but under Gardiner's keen eye they were powerless.

Gardiner had already had some experience of what sort of a woman Anne was, and the abuse and disrespect he could expect from her. Nevertheless, he considered himself, experienced courtier and diplomat that he was, a better match for this obstinate female and resolved to try his charm on her. If only she would realize it, he explained, he was really her friend and sincerely desired nothing but her good. That, she retorted, was exactly the attitude taken by 'Judas, when he unfriendly betrayed Christ'.

Winchester's next step was to suggest that he be allowed to examine Anne alone. Quite what he hoped to achieve by this is not clear; perhaps he only desired to deny Parr and Dudley, who were far from being friends of his, the delight of seeing him discomfited by Anne's pert quips. However, Anne refused to be examined without witnesses and the Bishop was not disposed to press the point. He continued to question her about the Sacrament but again she turned the argument: 'Then, I asked him how long he would halt on both sides.' In Anne's opinion, Gardiner, in common with all the bishops, was trying to have his theological cake and eat it. He had rejected the temporal power of the papacy in England (indeed, he had been instrumental in overthrowing it), yet he clung to the papistical doctrine of the mass. The courtier Bishop was now getting angry. Where did she learn such disrespectful ideas? Back came Anne's answer: in the second book of Kings, chapter eighteen. Gardiner could stand no more of this Bible-punching slip of a girl. He left her with the warning that she would be burned if she remained obstinate. Anne, however, had not finished with Gardiner. 'God will laugh your threatenings to scorn!' she flung at the Bishop's departing back.

Now Secretary Paget tried his theology with her. How could she deny the plain words of Christ 'This is my body, which shall be broken for you'. 'I answered, that Christ's meaning was, as in other places of the Scriptures: "I am the door" (John 10), "I am the vine" (John 15), "Behold the Lamb of God" (John 1), "The rock-stone was Christ" (1 Corinthians 10) and such other like. Ye may not here, said I, take Christ for the material thing he is signified by; for then ye will make him a very door, a vine, a lamb, and a stone, clean contrary to the Holy Ghost's meaning. All these, indeed, do signify Christ, like as the bread doth his body in that place. And though he did say there, "Take, eat this in remembrance of me"; yet did he not bid them hang up that bread in a box, and make it a God, or bow to it.'

Paget tried to support the reverence of the Host by analogy. It was fitting that the King should be honoured in every possible way. God was with the Sacrament. Anne interrupted to rebuke the Secretary for tampering with Scripture. 'For other meaning requireth God therein, than man's idle wit can devise, whose doctrine is but lies without his heavenly verity.' Paget had tried his best and received only taunts for his pains. Well, if she would not listen to him, he asked, would she be prepared to discuss these matters with some wise man? She said she would. Paget hurried away to report this meagre triumph to the Council while Anne returned again to Lady Garnish's apartments.

To the other attempts to woo her back to Henrician Catholicism, Anne makes only slight reference in her abbreviated account. However, what she does say is very revealing about the methods and motives of the Council. The next visitation she received during the following few days was from Dr Richard Cox and Dr Thomas Robinson. Both were prominent canon lawyers and able theological disputants. They were at home among the subtleties and quibbles of scholastic debate and as such had been among the judges chosen to hear Dr Crome's case. That such eminent ecclesiastics should have been called in to examine a semi-educated, heretical gentlewoman shows what importance the Council attached to her conversion. These were obviously the scholars Paget had in mind when he extracted Anne's promise to listen to 'wise men'. It was, however, of no avail. Anne's only comment on their lengthy discussions was, 'In conclusion, we could not agree.' Undeterred, the reverend doctors paid her a second visit, bringing, this time, a paper for her to sign, setting forth the orthodox doctrine of the mass. But the days when Anne could be tempted into putting her name to such a document were gone. Her earlier 'confession' had been used as anti-Protestant propaganda by the Bishop of London, even though she had added the escape clause as a loophole for her conscience to crawl through. She now refused to sign anything that might be construed as a recantation.

Having now developed what might almost be called a morbid fascination for martyrdom, she had a very poor opinion of those who gave way under pressure. In the previous March when allowed spiritual counsellors she had asked to see Dr Crome, whose sermons she had often heard and for whom, as a leader of the London Protestants, she had a profound respect. By June, however, the unfortunate doctor had soiled his reputation by informing against others of like persuasion and Anne now asked, not for him, but for Latimer, who, refusing to be browbeaten, still languished in the Tower. The ex-Bishop was not allowed to come to her.

So, fatigued from repeated interrogation but not, if we can believe her report, shifting one inch from her ground, Anne remained for exactly a week in Lady Garnish's house at Greenwich. In all probability it was exhaustion which brought on an ailment of which she complained on Sunday, the 27th. What was the matter with her, she did not say but vowed 'In all my life afore was I never in such pain'. However, she was considered well enough to be taken to Newgate that same day.

It is very probable that this particular date for Anne's removal to prison was chosen for a very good reason – a reason too important to permit of postponement on such trivial grounds as the prisoner's illness. Newgate Prison, though outside the City Wall, was but a short step from St Paul's Cross. Thus Anne could conveniently be escorted from her cell to the open-air pulpit. Featuring there on Sunday 27 June was Dr Edward Crome, brought thither to make his final, considered recantation. The Council made sure that his public humiliation should receive a good hearing, especially by 'marked people' (i.e. those suspected of heretical tendencies). One member of the open-air congregation reported:

> Our news here of Doctor Crome's canting, recanting, decanting or rather double-canting, be these: that on Sunday last, before my Lord Chancellor, the Duke of Norfolk, my Lord Great Master, Mr Rich, Mr Chancellor of the Tenths, with the Southwells, Pope, and other nobles and knights; and on the other side the Bishops of London and Worcester, all principal doctors and deans, besides the city fathers and a rabble of other marked people. The reverent father first-named openly declared his true meaning and right understanding (as he said, according to his conscience) of the six or seven articles you heard of, as he should have done upon the second Sunday after Easter, but that he was kept from his said true intent by the persuasions of certain perverse-minded persons, and by the sight of lewd and ungodly books and writings, for the which he was very sorry, and desired the audience to beware of such books, for under the fair appearance of them was hid a dangerous encumbrance of Christian consciences . . . so he exhorted all men to embrace ancientness of Catholic doctrine and forsake newfangledness.[26]

Other activity continued behind the scenes. William Morice was bound over for a year on recognizances.[27] The Council records also note the examination of other, unspecified, persons of the court for heresy – all of whom were glad to be dismissed with a caution. Men of humbler origin fared worse. On 23 June Mr Lucas of Colchester, one of the commissioners for the Six Articles, hampered by the King's command not to be over-zealous in prosecuting offenders, sent up to be examined by the Council one John Hadlam, a tailor of Essex. He was interviewed at Greenwich the same day and was found to be obstinate. He was allowed time to consider his position and re-examined. Proving quite truculent, he was then sent to Newgate.[28] In Norwich, the Bishop acting, according to Foxe, in concert with the Duke of Norfolk had one Rogers arrested and sent to London and to the flames.[29]

Newgate and the Tower were housing more and more heretics every day. On 19 June, the day that Anne had been first brought before the Council, they also examined a London merchant: 'one White, who attempted to make an erroneous book, was sent to Newgate after we had debated with him on the matter. He showed himself of a wrong opinion concerning the Blessed Sacrament.'[30] It is interesting to note how little attention the Council paid to less important figures like White.

The time for Anne's formal trial had now come. 'On Monday following, quondam Bishop Shaxton, mistress Ayscough, Christopher White . . . and a tailor that came from Colchester or thereabouts [i.e. Hadlam], were arraigned at the Guildhall and received their judgement of the Lord Chancellor and the Council . . .' The picture of an ex-Bishop, a merchant, a tailor and a gentlewoman being tried together for heresy provides a graphic illustration of the extent to which the new ideas were spreading at all levels of society. Sometime during the previous week, Anne had written down and submitted to the Council her ideas concerning the Lord's Supper and it was on the basis of this that she was tried.

Anne and her three fellows stood before the members of the Council in the lofty Guildhall where Anne had first been put on trial just over a year before. The tailor, the merchant and the ex-Bishop were all found guilty and condemned to be burned. Anne's inquisition is best told in her own words:

> They said to me there, that I was a heretic, and condemned by the law, if I would stand in mine opinion. I answered, that I was no heretic, neither yet deserved I any death by the law of God. But as concerning the faith which I uttered and wrote to the Council, I would not, I said, deny it because I knew it true. Then would they needs to know if I would deny the Sacrament to be Christ's body and blood. I said, 'Yes,' for the same Son of God, who was born of the Virgin Mary, is now glorious in heaven, and will come again from thence at the latter day like as he went up. And as for that ye call your God, it is a piece of bread. For a more proof thereof, mark it when you list, let it but lie in the box three months, and it will be mouldy, and so turn to nothing that is good. Whereupon I am persuaded that it cannot be God.'

After such an outspoken declaration, there could be no question of an acquittal. Bent on doing all they could for her, Anne's judges suggested that she should receive a priest that she might make her confession. Anne gave no reply, but in the quiet, Gothic gloom of that vast hall she looked up at the assembled clerics and politicians on the bench and smiled enigmatically – infuriatingly. Did she object, then, to the ministrations of a priest, they wanted to know.

> I said I would confess my faults unto God, for I was sure that he would hear me with favour.

And so sentence was passed – death by burning. The court rose – the Catholic councillors withdrawing to continue their efforts to bring down their opponents, the prisoners being escorted to Newgate to meditate on the fiery ordeal before them. For two of them the prospect proved too terrifying; Shaxton and White recanted during the next few days and were assured of the King's pardon.

Henry was kept closely informed of the results of the anti-heretical purge and took a keen interest in it, even though he was preoccupied with other affairs during the summer months of 1546. Though the two-year war with France was over and peace had also been concluded with Scotland, other problems remained. The most notable achievement of the two conflicts was that they had emptied the royal treasury. Nor did the ending of hostilities with France mean that the international scene held no menaces for the England of Henry and the young Prince who would have to succeed him. For the Pope had set the wheels of Roman Catholic reaction firmly in motion by summoning the Council of Trent, which at that very time was considering how best to recapture the lands and souls of those countries which had been won over to the cause of reformation. Habsburg power was at its height and the Emperor Charles V was preparing for an all-out war on the Protestant princes of Germany. If the league of Pope and Emperor was successful in a holy war on the mainland of Europe, how long would it be before its zeal for conversion by conquest was turned upon England? Henry was sickened by the realization that the Catholic-Protestant conflict which threatened to engulf the Continent was all too apparent in his own realm, and, indeed, in his own court. His supreme egoism would not allow him to admit that his attempt, as Supreme Head of the Church, to enforce a reformed Catholic orthodoxy on his people was proving a failure. So, he continued to try to hold a balance between the forces of reformation and reaction. Distracted by pain though he was, little escaped his

attention and though he allowed Wriothesley and Rich to continue their campaign at court, he watched their progress carefully
and might at any time put a sudden halt to their activities.

The Catholic councillors knew, as a modern historian has put it,
that Henry's 'triumphant ride through life carried him unheeding
over the bodies of his broken servants'[31] and they proceeded with
caution in these delicate matters. Yet there was a definite need for
them to proceed also with some despatch. And so the 'troubling' of
Anne Ayscough entered a new and more gruesome phase.

The very next morning, 29 June, she was again fetched forth
from Newgate – not for another formal examination in the Council
chamber, not to the Guildhall to be re-tried, but to a private room
in one of the city inns, the Crown. The choice of venue was
probably governed by the psychology of interrogation. Away from
the dank prison cell, in the comparative comfort of the Crown,
Anne could enjoy at least the illusion of freedom and might be
ready to grasp at the opportunity of regaining the reality. There
she was confronted by the odious Richard Rich and the bellicose
Bishop Bonner. Perhaps the latter was called in because it was he
who had forced some sort of a recantation from her on an earlier
occasion. Now, he used every possible means to bring Anne to a
change of heart, while Rich stood by and interposed comments and
threats of his own. As Anne says, they 'with all their power went
about to persuade me from God'. They must have been hard put
to it by this stage to find any argument that had not been tried
before. They could, however, point to the fact that two of her
fellow culprits had already confessed the error of their ways and
been reprieved. Anne remained steadfast.

Exasperated by Anne's stubbornness, Rich was forced to play
one of the few good cards remaining in his hand. He summoned
the unfortunate Shaxton and left the ex-Bishop to urge the recalci-
trant heretic to follow his example. The once-proud Bishop of
Salisbury, who had been the scourge of his diocese and had, in
1539, boldly thrown up his position in protest against the passing
of the Act of Six Articles, was now, seven years later, utterly
broken by imprisonments. Anne had little regard for him and he
must have felt discountenanced and morally bankrupt as he confronted her. Lamely he tried to persuade her to recant as he had
done. He was not allowed to say very much before Anne launched
herself on a sermon for his benefit, the main purport of which was

Two of the King's closest friends.

Sir William Butts, Royal Physician, *after Holbein.*

*Below:* Charles Brandon, Duke of Suffolk, *artist unknown.*

Catherine Parr, *attributed to W. Scrots.*

Wriothesley Foiled. A Victorian artist's impression of the failure of the attack on Catherine Parr. *Painting by William Fisk, 1838.*

that Shaxton was an apostate and 'that it had been good for him never to have been born'. So humbled, ashamed and hugging to his soul the gift of life so dearly bought, Shaxton departed to confess his failure to Rich.

Was she now to be left to her prayers? Far from it; even worse was to follow. But to understand the next episode in Anne's story we need to know what had been happening at court during the latter half of June.

Throughout all their proceedings against leading Protestants there was one person above all whom Gardiner, Wriothesley and Rich hoped to destroy – Queen Catherine Parr. There seemed little prospect of encompassing this, until, one evening shortly after his return from France (about 13 June), an opportunity fell into Gardiner's lap.[32]

It was Catherine's custom to visit the King in his privy chamber 'either at after dinner or after supper'. On these occasions she would strive to divert him from his pain with lively or learned conversation. Frequently religion would be the matter of their talk. Sometimes Catherine had the temerity to disagree with her husband. Henry normally took this in good part. He was fond of his wife and pleased that she was an intelligent and well-read lady. He knew and approved of the sermons and discussions that took place in the Queen's apartments and probably even of the visits thither of 'marked' men to instruct Catherine and her ladies in the new faith. Henry was no hide-bound theorist either in matters of politics or religion. As long as he saw in them no danger to the peace of the realm or despite to his own person, the Monarch was disposed to let events run their own course. Yet his ever acute sensitivity to danger and insult and the apparent capriciousness arising therefrom were heightened by his physical anguish. His truculence and intolerance became more marked and were punctuated by periods of blind fury. Henry's patience with the Queen's religious lectures wore thin and she came very close to falling fatally foul of the royal passion.

On the evening in question the royal couple were together in the King's chambers and Bishop Gardiner was among the others present. The conversation turned once more to religious matters; the Queen spoke with firmness and conviction as usual. Abruptly Henry, 'contrary unto his manner', changed the subject. Although he gave no other sign of displeasure this action 'somewhat amazed

P

the Queen' and was well noted by Gardiner. Shortly afterwards
Catherine and her companions withdrew. When she was out of
earshot Henry muttered testily to his Bishop of Winchester, 'A
good hearing it is when women become such clerks, and a thing not
much to my comfort, to come in mine old days to be taught by
my wife.'

Gardiner seized his opportunity. He warmly agreed with the
King and went on to point out the dangers of the opinions
stubbornly maintained by the Queen and certain of her ladies.
Winchester inveighed against the disruptive elements of Protestantism:

> '... the religion by the Queen so stiffly maintained,' he said, 'did
> not only disallow and dissolve the policy and politic government of
> princes, but also taught the people that all things ought to be in
> common. So that what beliefs soever they pretended to hold, their
> opinions were indeed so odious, and for the Prince's estate so perilous
> that (saving the reverence they bear unto her for his Majesty's sake)
> the Council was bold to affirm that the greatest subject in this land,
> speaking those words that she did speak, and defending likewise those
> arguments that she did defend, had with impartial justice by law
> deserved death.'

The King was really disturbed. Had such rank heresies as these
really found a home within his palace? Had God, once again,
punished the sins of his youth by giving him a dissembling and
untrustworthy wife? Doubt and anxiety, for the time, clouded
Henry's mind. He was, in the words of Foxe (who recorded these
events), 'jealous and mistrustful of his own estate. For the assurance whereof princes use not to be scrupulous to do anything.'
Gardiner continued to play on Henry's vanity and apprehensions
until he had received permission to make enquiries into the conduct
and beliefs of the Queen, her ladies and certain others who had
care of the young prince. Gardiner hastened away to confer with
his colleagues and to draw up the necessary articles.

This interview marks the beginning of a new phase in the
activities of the conservative faction. Hitherto, as in their examination of Crome, they had only dared to obtain information about
and proceed against lesser persons connected with the court. This
persecution we have already traced from its cautious beginnings at
the end of April until mid-June. Gardiner's conversation with the
King must have taken place about the same time as Anne's exam-

inations (say between 15 June and 20 June). Now, with the King's
warrant, the Catholic faction could proceed uninhibited. They
were now at the height of their power. Wriothesley, Rich and
Gardiner held the initiative. They continued their inquisition at all
levels of society, from journeyman to courtier, from country priest
to the Queen of England herself. By 21 August, an English diplomat could report from Flanders:

> About 60 Englishmen have fled over here for fear of death . . . so that
> here are tales of persecution by the bishops, and the King is slandered
> for suffering it. These things are spoken by the best in the land . . .
> Also it is said that there are three temporal lords and one knight, with
> two bishops in England, which are so knit together that they have
> promised to burn all such as are known to be readers of the Word of
> God.[33]

In these June and July days, the conservative faction came within
an ace of overthrowing the seemingly impregnable position of the
Protestant group, of destroying the Queen, of disgracing Hertford
and other radical courtiers, of enforcing a de-papalized Catholicism, of maintaining the Henrician *status quo* into the next reign and
so of halting the progress of the Reformation.

They first attempted an oblique attack on the Queen, through
her ladies-in-waiting.

> . . . They thought it best, at first, to begin with some of those ladies,
> whom they knew to be great with her and of her blood. The chiefest
> whereof, as most of estimation, and privy to all her doings were these:
> the Lady Herbert, afterwards Countess of Pembroke, and sister to the
> Queen, and chief of her Privy Chamber; the Lady Lane, being of her
> Privy Chamber, and also her cousin germane; the Lady Tyrrwhit, of
> her Privy Chamber, and for her virtuous disposition in very great
> favour and credit with her.[34]

The object was to use whatever means presented themselves to
obtain information against these ladies. And not against these only,
but against anyone who was close to the Queen. 'During this time
of deliberation about this matter,' says Foxe, 'they failed not to use
all kinds of policies, and mischievous practices, as well as to
suborne accusers, as otherwise to betray her, in seeking to understand what books by law forbidden she had in her closet.'[35] The
extent of their 'mischievous practices' becomes quite clear in the

events in which Anne Ayscough became involved on Tuesday 29 June 1546.[36]

From the Crown she was sent, not to Newgate but to the Tower of London, where she waited until three o'clock before Rich arrived, in the company of another Councillor, Sir John Baker. Now the real motives of Rich and his colleagues throughout Anne's troublings appear. In the grim privacy of a Tower cell they tried to force Anne to reveal the names of others of her sect. Rich's position was now thoroughly weakened. Anne was condemned to death. She had refused to avoid it by recantation. There was nothing that he could threaten her with. It was, therefore, very unlikely that he would get anything out of her that he could use against the court Protestants. Anne was quite determined not to lay information against anyone:

> Then came Rich and one of the Council, Baker, charging me upon my obedience to shew unto them if I knew any man or woman of my sect. My answer was that I knew none.

Now Rich came out into the open:

> Then they asked me of my Lady of Suffolk, my Lady of Sussex, my Lady of Hertford, my Lady Denny, and my Lady Fitzwilliam.

Anne's reply was evasive: 'I answered, if I should pronounce anything against them, that I were not able to prove it.' The Councillors knew very well that she could provide them with a long list of names if she chose. Rich grew more menacing; they were under instructions from the King to discover all she could tell them about heretics at court. If the King really believed that she could provide him with any such information then he had been misled by mischievous advisers, she replied.

It may have been at this point that the Lord Chancellor arrived at the Tower to join his colleagues. Certainly the next questions that Anne was asked turned on information Wriothesley had obtained from his spies months before during Anne's earlier imprisonment.

'Who gave you money when you were in the Counter? Who visited you in prison and urged you to hold firm to your heresies?'

'No one visited me in prison. As to the scant help I received, it came only as a result of my maid's begging the charity of London apprentices in the streets.'

'Who were these mysterious and obliging apprentices?'

'I don't know.'

'Some of your supporters were not apprentices, but gentle-women of the court, were they not?'

'They may have been, but if they were I never knew their names.'

'We know that some of the ladies of the court sent you money. Who were they?'

'I only know what my maid told me.'

'What was that?'

'Once she was given ten shillings by a man in a blue coat. He said it came from Lady Hertford. Another time a servant in violet livery gave her eight shillings, saying that Lady Denny had sent it. That is what my maid told me. I will not swear to its truth.'

'Besides these ladies you had help from members of the King's Council, didn't you?'

'No.'

The interrogators were making little progress. Yet it was vitally important that they should obtain information against some of the Queen's ladies. In anger and desperation they decided to employ other methods to make Anne talk. The Lieutenant of the Tower, Sir Anthony Knyvett, was sent for and ordered to have the rack prepared.

The party descended to the Tower's slimy, Norman depths. There, in one of the dungeons, the Lieutenant ordered gaolers to strap Anne to the monstrous, creaking frame. It would be quite enough, he told the man, just to 'pinch' her – to give her a taste of this kind of torture.

But Knyvett was nervous. As guardian of England's principal gaol he was used to atrocities of physical torture, nor in his position could he afford to indulge the luxury of a squeamish conscience. Yet, here he was facing something that was not only an inhuman outrage; it was also illegal. In the interests of the state, the bounds of Tudor law were not infrequently overstepped within the stony secrecy of the Tower. The rack, however, was reserved for male felons and traitors, and they were for the most part persons of no social status. It was illegal to rack a woman and unthinkable so to torture a gentlewoman. Only some high cause of national security could possibly justify such a breach of law and human decency. Certainly it could not be excused in the interests of furthering a

faction struggle at court. So Knyvett had Anne lightly racked and
as she lay there Wriothesley, Rich and Baker fired more questions
at her. They did not realize that by this time Anne had reached
the stage of accepting each further torment as a proof of her own
constancy. Her tautened body might quiver with pain but her will
was stretched to a tense inflexibility. They might, and did, disjoint
her body; nothing could break her resolve. Anne looked up at the
frustrated courtiers in silence.

Knyvett had had enough. He signed to the gaoler to ease the
pressure and release her. Angrily Wriothesley turned on him. What
did the Lieutenant think he was doing? They were not finished
with Mistress Ayscough yet. She must be stretched again. Knyvett
anxiously pointed out that this was illegal. The Lord Chancellor's
voice was raised in anger. He ordered Sir Anthony to do as he was
bid. Knyvett refused. This, protested Wriothesley, was dis-
obedience against the King who should not fail to hear of it. Sir
Anthony was still not cowed. He had no authority to rack this
woman and he would not be responsible for giving any such order.
The gaoler had already been ordered from the room. The four
men stared at each other, ignoring for a moment the recumbent
form on the rack. After some moments, Wriothesley turned
contemptuously away to speak words with his colleagues. Then
Knyvett was astonished to see Wriothesley and Rich remove their
gowns, step across to the wheel of the rack, and personally apply
pressure to it.

> . . . And so quietly and patiently praying unto the Lord, she abode
> their tyranny, till her bones and joints were almost plucked asunder.[37]

And at the end of it all her torturers had learned nothing. Having
applied as much pressure as they dared, they, at length, on the
repeated protestations of the Lieutenant, released Anne, whereupon, overcome with physical agony, she fainted. It was probably
at this point that Knyvett slipped away from the dungeon, out of
the Fortress, to Tower wharf and there found a bargeman to row
him, with all speed, to Whitehall.

Still the inquisitors refused to admit failure. They brought Anne
round and remained in the dungeon arguing with her for a further
two hours while she sat, throbbing with pain, on the cold, damp,
stone floor, 'Where he the Lord Chancellor with many flattering

words tried to persuade me to leave my opinion. But my Lord God, I thank his everlasting goodness, gave me grace to persevere.'

The interrogation over, Anne was moved to yet another lodging. Keeping the matter secret was now more than Wriothesley could hope for. Apart from anything else, her racking had so much weakened her joints and muscles that she was quite unable to walk and had to be carried everywhere in a chair. He nevertheless arranged for her to stay privately in the house of a servant or friend where she would be away from the prying eyes and whispering lips of untrustworthy gaolers and curious fellow prisoners. Restored to comfortable surroundings again she went to bed 'with as weary and painful bones,' she wrote, 'as ever had patient Job'.

Meanwhile, learning that Sir Anthony Knyvett had gone, Rich and Wriothesley hurried to their horses and rode hard through the dusk to Westminster. The Lieutenant reached court long before them and managed to obtain an audience with the King. He explained the afternoon's episode to the Sovereign and asked pardon for refusing to obey the orders of the King's Chancellor, being careful to make clear why he had refused. Henry promptly pardoned the man and dismissed him. And that is the last we hear of the racking episode. Foxe attributes to the King a certain air of disapproval: 'He seemed not very well to like of their so extreme handling of the woman', but no record survives of the reception of the two councillors when they arrived at the court later that evening. What we do know is that the investigations of the conservative group continued. Henry, it seems, was still prepared to let them have their head.

Anne Ayscough had been of little use to the conservatives but she was still on their hands. The only thing Wriothesley wanted to do now was to get rid of her quietly, but she could only be set free if she would recant. She was too popular a figure to be released on any other terms. To set her free without a recantation would have been a positive encouragement to other members of her group. Within a very few days the story of her racking was common knowledge in the city and increased public sympathy for her. Such gossip was newsworthy and London merchants were even quoting it in their letters to the Continent:

> . . . the gentlewoman and the other men remain in steadfast mind, and yet she hath been racked since her condemnation (as men say)

which is a strange thing, in my understanding. (Ottwell Johnson to his brother, 2 July.)[38]

Wriothesley had no desire to make the situation worse by transforming her into a martyred heroine. Within the next few days he sent her a message again promising freedom if she would recant. Again she sent back her customary reply. Shortly after this she was returned to the Tower and there she remained until 12 July, when she was conveyed once more to Newgate – only a stone's throw from Smithfield. For the remaining few days of her life she was no more molested by her enemies. No more was she worried for information or pestered to recant. Only one more trial confronted her now, and of that she had no fear.

# 9

# 'One by One Back in the Closet Lays'

WHILE Anne was nursing her aching limbs in the Tower, a high drama was acting itself out on the other side of London at Westminster. Wriothesley, Gardiner and Rich were pursuing their campaign against the Queen and her attendants with more vigour than success. They had the King's support but they were finding it very difficult to gather evidence. From Anne they had obtained nothing. Their other hoped-for sources of information proved equally fruitless. They therefore changed their tactics. First they induced the King to issue a new proclamation. The wording of this document, in view of the situation at court, is particularly significant:

> From henceforth no man, woman or person of what estate condition or degree soever he or they be . . . shall have, take or keep in his or their possession the text of the New Testament of Tyndale's or Coverdale's translation in English, nor any other than is permitted by the Act of Parliament made in the session of Parliament held at Westminster in the four and thirtieth and five and thirtieth year of his Majesty's most noble reign; nor . . . any manner of books printed or written in the English tongue which be or shall be set forth in the names of Frith, Tyndale, Wycliffe, Joye, Roy, Basil, Bale, Barnes, Coverdale, Turner, Tracy . . .[1]

The proclamation was published on 8 July and possessors of the banned books were given until the end of August to surrender them. The next step by the Catholic conspirators was to obtain from the angry King a warrant for his wife's arrest. While she was conveyed to the Tower, search would be made in her rooms for the books known to be there and a charge of heresy would be brought against her.

Catherine remained ignorant of these designs for several days. In all probability she was not disturbed by the proclamation, believing that it would never be applied against her.[2] Then, a courtier who was privy to the plot let fall, perhaps on purpose, a paper containing details of the articles against the Queen. The document was brought to Catherine, 'who reading there the articles comprised against her, and perceiving the King's own hand unto the same, for the sudden fear thereof fell incontinent into a great melancholy and agony, bewailing and taking on in such sort as was lamentable to see . . .'[3] When Henry heard that the Queen was ill he sent one of his physicians, Dr Wendy, to her. It was Wendy who unfolded to Catherine all the details of the plot.

The Queen was not so distracted that she was unable to take action. She immediately ordered her ladies to get rid of all the banned books from her chambers. Then she awaited an opportunity to speak with the King. Late one evening it was reported to her that Henry was in his Privy Chamber talking with a few of his gentlemen and, being less pained with his leg than usual, was in a good mood. Immediately Catherine made her way through the draughty passages of Westminster Palace with Lady Herbert at her side and Lady Lane bearing a guttering candle before them. Henry received his wife courteously and Catherine wasted little time in unburdening herself. She declared herself completely obedient to her husband and king, who was 'so excellent in gifts and ornaments of wisdom' and avowed herself content to be guided by him in all matters of religion.

'Not so, by Saint Mary,' replied the King. 'You are become a doctor, Kate, to instruct us (as we take it) and not to be instructed or directed by us.'

'Kate' looked surprised and crestfallen.

'If your Majesty take it so, then hath your Majesty very much mistaken my intention. For I have ever been of the opinion to think it very unseemly and preposterous for the woman to take on her the office of an instructor or teacher to her lord and husband, but rather to learn of her husband and to be taught by him. And where I have . . . been bold to hold talk with your Majesty, wherein sometimes in opinions there hath seemed some difference, I have not done it so much to maintain opinion, but . . . rather to minister talk . . . to the end your Majesty might with less grief pass over this painful time of your infirmity, being attentive to our talk . . . and also that I, hearing your Majesty's learned discourse, might receive to myself some profit thereby.'

Henry, already tiring of the machinations of Gardiner and Wriothesley, was infinitely relieved to have the opportunity to forgive and forget his wife's indiscretions. He took her in his arms as she knelt by his couch and comforted her:

'And is it even so, sweetheart? And tended your arguments to no worse end? Then perfect friends we are now again, as ever at any time heretofore.'

King and Queen remained together until far into the night, murmuring endearments to each other while the atmosphere was charged with emotion. But when Catherine at last took her leave with her lord's blessing the final scene in this little drama had yet to be played.

That scene was enacted the following afternoon. Henry had experienced one of those complete changes of heart to which he was singularly prone and had now resolved, instead of degrading his Queen, to humiliate those who had plotted against her. He therefore said nothing to Gardiner or Wriothesley, but allowed them to proceed with their plan. He had promised to make sure that the Queen was present in the garden at an appointed time so that the Chancellor could arrest her. Accordingly, Henry sent for Catherine as he walked in the garden after dinner.

As they strolled between the flower beds and hedges in the drowsy afternoon, the King, leaning heavily on one of his gentlemen, chattered gaily. Henry's stentorian laugh was the only loud noise that punctuated the buzz of conversation, the birdsong, the trickle of fountains and the river noises drifting up from the nearby Thames. Suddenly, another sound was heard beyond the garden wall – marching feet on cobbles. A garden gate was flung open and Lord Chancellor Wriothesley strutted into the garden, followed by forty of the King's guard. He bowed to the King and held out the warrant for Catherine Parr's arrest. To his surprise, Henry scowled and drew him aside almost (but, apparently, not quite) out of earshot of the Queen. Wriothesley fell on his knees and reminded the King of the agreed arrangements for Catherine's apprehension. The King's harsh whisper cut across his words like the slash of a rapier.

'Knave! Arrant knave, beast and fool!'

Had the Chancellor and his friends, Henry wished to know, nothing better to do than ferret out information against a lady who surpassed them all in virtue? The King swiftly terminated the brief interview with the command, 'Avaunt my sight!' turned his back on the confused Wriothesley, and returned, all smiles, to the Queen. The Chancellor retreated quickly, doubtless to vent his ill-temper on others and to report to Gardiner that they had gone too far and could no longer look to the King for support in their persecution.[4]

The Queen was safe but she was clearly in no position to attract attention to herself by interceding on behalf of other court Protestants who now came under fire. Immediately after the publication of the new proclamation, the Catholic faction had sought out more enemies. Two of them, Sir Hugh Calverley and Edward Littleton, resolved on a new attempt to pluck from the King's bosom his old friend Sir George Blagge. The Lutheran courtier was accused of having spoken against the Sacrament of the altar at St Paul's Cathedral almost three months before. He was clapped into Newgate gaol. Two days later Blagge and Lascelles (who had been in the Tower since 17 May) were arraigned together at the Guildhall with a certain John Hemsley, who had been sent up to London by the zealous Six Articles commissioners of Essex.[5] During his detention many attempts had been made to get John Lascelles to recant. He had been visited by the Bishop of London and others but had only become more adamant in his opinions. And, indeed, his religious doctrines were extreme and totally irreconcilable with Henrician orthodoxy. While in prison he wrote a statement of his beliefs concerning the Holy Communion which marks him as a sacramentary, not prepared to acknowledge any kind of divine presence in the consecrated bread and wine of the mass.[6] In the Guildhall he readily acknowledged his heresies and was condemned to death. Hemsley did likewise but Blagge demanded a hearing before the quest. He was, accordingly, tried before a jury later that same day. He only gained a few hours: he was found guilty and soon re-joined the growing number of condemned and suspected heretics in Newgate prison.

Now that the intrigue at court had taken a turn in their favour with the disgrace of Wriothesley and Gardiner, Blagge's sympathizers decided to approach the King on Sir George's behalf. It was Lord Russell who told Henry what had befallen his 'little pig'. As soon as he heard the news the King flew into a rage and sent for the errant Wriothesley. The Chancellor was forced to make out, in person, the writ for Blagge's release and, within the hour, Blagge was in the King's chamber thanking his master for his deliverance.

There was to be no deliverance for Anne Ayscough and John Lascelles. They remained in Newgate and there occupied themselves not only in prayer, but also in writing messages for other members of their group. Anne wrote a long and detailed account of her two trials which was then smuggled out by her maid and delivered to Anne's friends in the city. Anne's main object in doing this was to counteract the official version of her trials which was being published by the Council and particularly the story of her recantation. She also had in mind a friend 'not yet thoroughly persuaded in the truth concerning the Lord's Supper', and hoped even from prison to convince him by her exhortation and her example. Neither of the prisoners was allowed to receive visitors but scores of their friends clamoured for news of them and managed by bribery and cunning to get messages into Newgate. Within the grim, dank walls Anne and John were even kept apart from each other, but their spirits never faltered. John had suffered less and carried himself throughout his troubles with a flamboyant defiance. Sir George Blagge described how after his condemnation he was in a relaxed and talkative mood. 'He mounted up into the window of the little parlour by Newgate and . . . was merry and cheerful in the Lord . . . and said these words, "My Lord Bishop would have me confess the Roman church to be the Catholic church, but that I cannot, for it is not true".'[7] While he waited for news of his impending execution John bethought himself of his sister in the Lord, wondering how she endured not only mental anguish but also her physical pain. He wrote a note of encouragement and managed to persuade a gaoler to convey it to her. Anne's reply showed how little she was in need of moral support:

O friend most dearly beloved in God, I marvel not a little what should move you to judge in me so slender a faith as to fear death, which is the end of all misery. In the Lord I desire you not believe of me such weakness. For I doubt it not but God will perform his work in me, like as he hath begun. I understand the Council is not a little displeased, that it should be reported abroad that I was racked in the Tower. They say now that what they did there was but to frighten me;

whereby I perceive they are ashamed of their uncomely doings and
fear much lest the King's majesty should have information thereof.
Wherefore they do not want any man to tell it abroad. Well, their
cruelty God forgive them.

Your heart in Christ Jesus,
Farewell and pray.[8]

Anne was certainly mistaken in believing that the King was
ignorant of the way she had been treated in the Tower but she
was right when she wrote that her persecutors were angry that the
news of her racking was all over London. Throughout the entire
sequence of her trials and sufferings the Catholic leaders' main aim
had been to discredit her. Already Anne Ayscough was an acclaimed
heroine.

Anne did make an appeal to the King for pardon but it was not
the grovelling, self-abasing plea for mercy which was normal
among Tudor prisoners. She sent it via the Lord Chancellor with
the following note to Wriothesley:

The Lord God, by whom all creatures have their being, bless you
with the light of his knowledge. Amen.
My duty to your Lordship remembered, etc. It might please you to
accept this my bold suit, as the suit of one which, upon due consideration, is moved to the same and hopeth to obtain. My request to your
Lordship is only that it may please the same to be an intermediary for
me to the King's Majesty, that his Grace may be certified of these few
lines which I have written concerning my belief which, when it shall
be truly compared with the hard judgement given me for the same,
I think his Grace shall well conceive me to be weighed in an uneven
pair of balances. But I remit my matter and cause to Almighty God,
who rightly judgeth all secrets. And thus I commend your Lordship
to the governance of him, and to the fellowship of all the saints.
Amen.

The letter to the King read:

I Anne Ayscough, of good memory, although God hath given me the
bread of adversity and the water of trouble (yet not so much as my
sins have deserved), desire this to be known unto your Grace. Foras-
much as I am by the law condemned for an evil-doer, here I take
heaven and earth to record that I shall die in my innocence. And
according to what I have said first and will say last, I utterly abhor
and detest all heresies. And as concerning the Supper of the Lord, I
believe so much as Christ hath said therein, which he confirmed with

his most blessed blood. I believe so much as he willed me to follow, and I believe so much as the Catholic church of him doth teach. For I will not forsake the commandment of his holy lips. But . . . what God hath charged me with by his mouth, that have I shut up in my heart. And thus briefly I end for lack of learning.[9, 10]

Did Anne's appeal ever reach the King? If so it is unlikely to have done her much good. Henry had but recently had cause to complain about one woman who, seemingly, did not know her place. He was unlikely to be sympathetic towards another who had not only forsaken her husband but proved quite intractable in religious matters. Did anyone speak to the King on behalf of Anne or John Lascelles? The Queen and her ladies were not in a position to do so. It would be pleasant to be able to picture Francis Ayscough rushing up to London and, together with his brothers, canvassing support at Westminster for their sister. But there is no evidence and, on the whole, it seems unlikely that Anne's family (or for that matter John Lascelles') were prepared to risk sharing the disgrace of a condemned heretic. If any moves were afoot in the court to liberate John Lascelles, we may be sure that Norfolk and his supporters would have done all in their power to scotch them. Thomas Howard remembered all too clearly the events of the autumn of 1541. John and Anne therefore remained in Newgate gaol while other more favoured prisoners were pardoned (another prominent courtier – Nicholas Throckmorton – seems to have languished there for a few days on a heresy charge before powerful friends secured his release).

Shortly before her death Anne wrote a prayer which may stand as a prelude to the account of her execution. These are the last words we have from her hand and show the spirit in which she faced death.

O Lord, I have more enemies now than there be hairs on my head. Yet, Lord, let them never overcome me with vain words, but fight thou, Lord, in my stead, for on thee cast I my care. With all the spite they can imagine they fall upon me, which am thy poor creature. Yet, sweet Lord, let me pay no heed to them which are against me, for in thee is my whole delight. And, Lord, I heartily desire of thee, that thou wilt of thy most merciful goodness forgive them that violence which they do and have done unto me. Open also thou their blind hearts, that they may hereafter do that thing in thy sight, which is only acceptable before thee, and to set forth thy verity aright, without all vain fantasy of sinful men. So be it, O Lord, so be it.[11]

Our eyes move inevitably to the last scene depicted in this tapestry. Its colours are harsh and garish, its subject matter grim. In the background the stained, grey stone of St Bartholomew's Church in Smithfield. Before it had been erected a temporary scaffolding covered by an awning. Seated in this prominent position were Sir Thomas Wriothesley, the Duke of Norfolk, Lord Russell, other members of the Council and Sir Martin Bowes the Lord Mayor. They needed to be in an elevated position for a large crowd had gathered and was with difficulty being kept outside the roped enclosure. Still more spectators had gained vantage points in nearby windows and even on roofs. Since the main entertainment had not begun, sections of the audience were being diverted by the antics of tumblers and jugglers. Others took advantage of the diversion to pick pockets and snaffle purses. The air was alive with the chatter of an expectant, holiday crowd. Mounted soldiers clattered about keeping order. Within the arena stood three solid, eight-foot wooden stakes. Bundles of sticks and straw were already being piled round the stakes.

Suddenly heads turned and fingers pointed. Mothers held their children aloft to see the prisoners making the journey of a few hundred yards from Newgate. A pathway opened through the jeering crowd, and the pitiful procession arrived. John Lascelles and John Hemsley walked with heads erect between their guards. With them came John Hadlam, the Essex tailor. Few members of the crowd had to strain their necks for a view of Anne Ayscough. She had been so weakened by her torture that she approached the stake carried on a chair, borne by four men. The crowd fell silent at the sight of her, even the hostile and the insensitive touched by pity. But it was not only the sight of the prisoners that silenced the mob. Much to everyone's surprise, the condemned heretics were accompanied by a band of sympathizers, fearlessly performing a last act of friendship by walking with them to the place of execution. There were Sir George Blagge and Nicholas Throckmorton with his two brothers, George and Kenelm, and the Reverend John Loud. Such open support for the heretics was tantamount to a defiance of the authorities which had condemned them. Someone in the crowd shouted out to warn the courtiers of the danger they

The burning of Anne Ayscough, John Lascelles, John Hadlam and John Hemsley. A woodcut from John Foxe's *Acts and Monuments*.

The monument of Sir Francis Ayscough in St Peter's Church, Stalling-borough.

Sir Francis Ayscough's Will, 1564.

were in, 'Ye are all marked that come to them. Take heed to your lives.'[12] But the gentlemen were not lacking in bravery[13] and stayed with the prisoners until the last possible moment. John Loud even went so far as to walk up to the Councillors' platform and shout out, 'I ask vengeance on you all that do thus burn a member of Christ!' He was lucky to escape with no more than a blow from a Councillor's fist.[14]

By now the condemned had been bound to the stakes. Anne's legs would not hold her and she could only be kept upright by a strong chain passed round her waist, which cut cruelly into her flesh as she sagged against it. There was to be no question even now of a speedy end. The whole prolonged ritual had to be enacted. First of all the sermon. A few paces away a pulpit had been erected. Poor Nicholas Shaxton had been singled out for the honour of preaching to the four heretics whose souls were in such imminent danger. This was the last act in his public humiliation and was designed to underline his own recantation. But the unfortunate man could hardly make himself heard. As well as the continuous bustle and murmur of the crowd he had the unquenchable Anne Ayscough to contend with. Anne paid close attention to every word of Shaxton's address and gave a running commentary on it, pointing out all the learned doctor's errors.

At last the ex-Bishop was done preaching and thankfully clambered down from the pulpit. The next piece of ritual to be performed was the final offer of pardon in return for a recantation. Wriothesley sent down a message but the condemned refused even to read it. Anne spoke for her companions when she called out, 'I came not hither to deny my Lord and Master.'

During the sermon men had been piling faggots around the stakes and all was now ready for the execution. John Russell as an act of mercy had ordered bags of gunpowder to be hung round the bodies of the four heretics. When the other Councillors saw this being done they became alarmed and Russell had to assure them that the bags had been most carefully filled and placed. There was no fear of a violent explosion. The moment had now arrived. The executioner stood ready with a flaming torch. The crowd fell silent. Sir Martin Bowes' simple command was clearly heard across Smithfield. 'Fiat Justitia!'

As the sticks smoked, crackled, hesitated, then flared, the four martyrs bade each other warm farewells, knowing that beyond the

Q

fire they would be reunited. The flames sprang up mercifully quickly. The stench of burning flesh had scarce begun to drift across the arena before the first of the muffled explosions was heard. The crowd silently counted the other three, which soon followed.

> Thus they confirming one another with mutual exhortations tarried looking for the tormentor and fire, which, at the last flaming round about them, consumed their blessed bodies in happy martyrdom, in the year of our salvation 1546.[15]

The account of the deaths of Anne Ayscough, John Lascelles and their companions on 16 July 1546 should, strictly speaking, end this book. But there were certain consequences and corollaries of that day which should be mentioned. They can perhaps be thought of as final flourishes around the border of our Tudor tapestry.

First, there was the impact of the suffering and death of Anne Ayscough. She became – and has remained – one of the most famous of English martyrs. Soon, not only London but all England was ablaze with stories of her heroism and constancy.

> At one of the sessions of the Six Articles by us held within your Majesty's city of York, were convicted two persons, sacramentaries, the one named Richard Burdone and the other John Grove, who repaired hither immediately after the execution of Anne Ayscough, Lascelles and others, and were present at the same. And we have spared for a time the execution of the said Burdone and Grove, until your Majesty's pleasure be further known therein. . . .[16]

Burdone and Grove were not the only Protestants who fled from London in the second half of July.

Rumours and reports passed on by word of mouth were soon supported by written testimony. The accounts that Anne had written of her trials had been smuggled out of prison and had reached some Dutch merchants who took them back with them to the Continent.[17] There they fell into the hands of John Bale who immediately set about preparing them for publication. Early in 1547 they were published at Marburg with Bale's own trenchant glosses throughout the text. Before the first anniversary of Anne's trial before Christopher Dare, Bale's pamphlets could be bought in London.

The widespread reaction against the burning of Anne Ayscough and John Lascelles undoubtedly helped to tilt the balance of royal policy once more in favour of further reformation. Henry and most of his subjects felt there was something wrong and unnatural about burning men and women of rank. When a courtier and a gentlewoman were prepared to go resolutely to the stake, when they were supported in their heresies by some of the highest in the land, when other gentlemen preferred to flee to the Continent rather than endure the threat of persecution in England, even Henry VIII had to realize that there was a force at work in his realm which he could not control. Once again the King realized he had made a mistake in allowing the Catholic Councillors to have their head.

Long before the patch of blackened earth in Smithfield had faded back to its proper hue, a reaction had set in. Within ten days of 16 July Hertford returned to England and to his place on the Council. He was followed a week later by Dudley. Not only did the two warriors return but they returned having successfully negotiated a peace with France and brought to an end England's long period of agonizing diplomatic isolation. Catholic ascendancy on the Council was now broken, never to return during Henry's reign. During August the King entertained the French ambassador, Admiral d'Annebault, at Hampton Court and there he is reported (by Foxe) to have suggested that England and France should harness the power of the new Protestantism against the Catholic countries now uniting behind the Pope and the Council of Trent. He proposed that, as a first step, both countries should abolish the mass and substitute a communion service. Cranmer was instructed to begin work on the new liturgy.

The closing months of 1546 saw the downfall of the two leaders of the conservative faction. Thomas Howard was at last brought low by the folly of his son and the industry of his enemies. The Earl of Surrey had been heard to comment that when Henry died, his (Surrey's) father would be regent. Under Tudor law it was treason even to refer to the death of the sovereign. But the Earl had also been quartering the royal arms with his own. These acts, embroidered upon by Surrey's enemies, prominent among whom was his erstwhile companion Sir George Blagge, were made to appear not as mere stupidity and pride but as evidence of treasonable intent. Surrey was arrested, found guilty and beheaded in

January 1547. At the same time his father, the Duke of Norfolk, was arrested. He, too, was condemned, imprisoned in the Tower, and his execution fixed for 28 January. But at 2.0 a.m. on that day Henry VIII, himself, died and Norfolk's life was preserved for another seven years.

Gardiner forfeited Henry's confidence during the autumn of 1546 and never regained it. He was frequently involved in arguments at the Council board and, on one occasion, Dudley was suspended from meetings for a month for striking the Bishop of Winchester across the face. By the end of November, Gardiner, himself, was in disgrace and forbidden to approach the court. When, on 26 December, an ailing Henry VIII appointed a council of regency to advise his son, he deliberately left Winchester's name off. His comment on this occasion shows how well he understood the 'old fox': 'I could myself use him and rule him to all manner of purposes, as seemed good to me, but so will never you do.'[18]

From there on the story of the firm establishment of the English Reformation during the brief reign of Edward VI is well known. By 1549 the Church of England had a completely new liturgy. The mass and its altar had been replaced by the Holy Communion and the table. The doctrines enshrined in Cranmer's first Prayer Book were not identical with those of Anne Ayscough and John Lascelles but there was some truth in the claim made by the heretic Joan Bocher at her trial in 1550: 'It was not so long ago that you burned Anne Ayscough for a piece of bread, yet came yourselves to believe the doctrine for which you burned her.'[19]

Anne and John were representatives of a new social phenomenon – the English Protestant middle class. That class was both created by and helped to create the Reformation. It appeared in the middle years of Henry VIII's reign and dominated almost every aspect of English life until its power was broken in the twentieth century by forces as potent as those of the Reformation. Most of the country gentry approved (for a variety of reasons) the official acts of the Henrician Reformation. They resented the spiritual power of the priests which, often vested as it was in unworthy hands, yet rivalled their own political and judicial authority. They read their English Bibles and found in them justification for rejecting sacerdotalism and asserting the standing of the individual before God.

Many came into contact with the new doctrines gaining ground at the universities and the inns of court, and became an extremist fringe of the movement. Leaving the separatist, purist element to one side, we can safely say that in this body of informed opinion, which embraced the open Bible of the new movement and rejected the mediating priesthood of the old, we have the deepest tap root of Anglicanism. Six months after the July fires of Smithfield, the martyrs who died there would not have been prosecuted. Three years later a new English Prayer Book brought official Church of England doctrine far closer to those opinions for which Anne and John had suffered.

And what of the others who have figured prominently in these scenes from English life at the time of the Reformation? The lives of the great are well enough known. Catherine Parr was able to marry Thomas Seymour, to whom her heart had been pledged before King Henry had demanded it. But she was to know little connubial bliss with the Lord Admiral[20] and her death in childbirth in 1548 was in many ways a merciful release. The colourful Dowager Duchess of Suffolk had an eventful career before her. In 1552 she remarried, choosing a Protestant courtier, Richard Bertie. When Mary Tudor came to the throne, the devout pair decided that life under a Catholic regime would be intolerable. Accordingly they 'fled' to the Continent. Their departure from England took five weeks and they were accompanied by a large train of servants. Queen Elizabeth restored them to their old honours and lands. Catherine's two sons by Charles Brandon died of the sweating sickness in 1551 and thus the main line of the Dukedom died. The title was however revived in favour of Henry Grey, Marquis of Dorset, who had married Charles Brandon's daughter. Catherine died in 1580. Hertford and Dudley became the Dukes of Somerset and Northumberland respectively and, one after the other, ruled England during the reign of the young Edward VI. Each in turn ended his days on the scaffold. Gardiner like Norfolk survived the triumph of his enemies to take a leading part in the Catholic reaction under Queen Mary. Like Norfolk, also, he died peaceably in his bed before the end of the reign of that unhappy persecutress and thus did not have to witness the final overthrow of depapalized Catholicism by Elizabethan Anglicanism. Latimer and Cranmer were among those singled out for special attention during the rampant reaction under Mary. They were burned at Oxford in 1555 and 1556.

Wriothesley and Rich, by adroit manipulation of people and principles, survived to enjoy future honours. Wriothesley, by then Earl of Southampton, died in 1550. Baron Rich of Leighs died, a wealthy old man, in 1567. Posterity has served them ill, but no worse than they deserved. Wriothesley's biographer found nothing better to say of him than, 'It is difficult to trace in Southampton's career any motive beyond that of self-aggrandisement.'[21] Rich, who had a hand in the undoing of more great men of his age than any contemporary, has been described as 'a time-server of the least admirable type' and 'one of the most ominous names in the history of the age'.[22] Bishop Bonner was among the more active heresy hunters of Mary's reign and became one of the most hated men in London. Refusing the oath of supremacy to Queen Elizabeth, Bonner spent the last ten years of his life in prison. Even after that lapse of time, his burial in 1569 had to be carried out in secret for fear of disturbances. John Longland only outlived by a few months the King he had served so faithfully. He died in May 1547. Death saved him the agonizing decisions with which his conscience would have been confronted had he been called upon to serve the next two Tudors. Thus the troubled decade after Anne Ayscough's death removed from the stage most of the men and women who had dominated the final scenes of Henry VIII's reign.

In the shires those years passed less dramatically. George Lascelles continued to build the fortunes of his family, now centred at Elston. On his death he passed on extensive fair lands to his eldest son. Bryan Lascelles was knighted by Queen Elizabeth and this honour was bestowed on many of his descendants, all of whom for over a century were prominent landowners and administrators in Nottinghamshire. Whatever policy changes occurred in London, the Lascelles and many of their neighbours remained loyal to the cause for which John Lascelles had died. The family became markedly Puritan later in the century. When Sir George Lascelles's wife, Mary, died in 1615 it was recorded on her memorial brass,

> Her holy and religious care
> To have the Gospel taught,
> Did always argue public good
> Before her own she sought.[23]

Indeed the whole area of Nottinghamshire and Lincolnshire around Retford, Worksop, Gainsborough and Newark was a Puritan stronghold in the late sixteenth century and in the next century, it was this area that produced the Pilgrim Fathers. In 1705 the name of Lascelles vanished from Nottinghamshire after more than two hundred years, with the extinction of the male line, and the Lascelles lands, tenements, messuages and rents passed by marriage to the Thorolds of Lincolnshire.

Francis Ayscough also continued to prosper. He took every opportunity of adding to his estates. He built a fine new house at South Kelsey. When his wife, Elizabeth, died in 1559, he made a highly advantageous second marriage. He had for some years had his eyes on a large area of crown land and administration known as the Soke of Caistor. It comprised 'the Manor of Caistor, etc. and ten messuages, two hundred acres of land, one hundred acres of meadow, one hundred acres of pasture and forty shillings rent in Caistor, Gresby, Houghton, Fulnetby, North Kelsey, and Ancholme'.[24] Despite sustained efforts, Francis was unsuccessful in his suit for this land when the Queen disposed of it in 1557. Instead it went to the courtier Sir Thomas Hastings. Weeks of hard bargaining followed. Hastings was quite prepared to sell his new acquisition, but there were other suitors, namely Sir William Cardell and Lady Elizabeth Dalyson. On 14 October 1557 a deal was made; the Soke was granted jointly to the three suitors but was to revert eventually to the heirs of Elizabeth Dalyson. Francis Ayscough accepted this arrangement but his ambition refused to be contained by it. On 15 December he bought out Sir William Cardell. Thus matters remained for two years. Then fortune played into Sir Francis's hands as it had played into his father's hands in 1522. On the same day, 10 October 1559, Francis's wife and Lady Dalyson's husband died. After a decent delay the head of the Ayscough family married widow Dalyson and thus brought into the family, not only the property inherited by Elizabeth from her late husband, but also the Soke of Caistor. By such manoeuvres Sir Francis Ayscough prospered and was able to leave to his eldest son estates valued (in the opinion of the family chronicler) at over £20,000.

Francis died in 1564, a convinced Protestant. This is clearly shown by the wording of his will. Does it also suggest a still lingering remorse over the betrayal of his sister?

I bequeath my soul to Almighty God, by whose merits and passion I trust only to be saved and through no good deeds of my own but with the publican I do confess myself to be a sinner and do appeal to God's mercy and not to his justice, knowing him to be a merciful Lord in whom I only trust.[25]

Most of Francis's close friends were also Protestants. He enjoyed a lifelong relationship with Nicholas Bullingham, one-time chaplain to Archbishop Cranmer, and stood godfather to one of his sons (named Francis). Bullingham went into exile during Mary's reign and it was partly due to Francis's intercession that he was appointed to high office by Elizabeth and eventually became Bishop of Lincoln (1560). Another Marian exile, Laurence Meres, was also among Francis Ayscough's circle of intimates and became an executor of his will. His memorial bust in Stallingborough church shows a refined, melancholy face and reveals little of the energy and ambition which were characteristic of the man.

Perhaps Francis's greatest dynastic achievement was the marriage of his son, William, into the nobility. The girl in question was Anne, daughter of Edward Fiennes Clinton, Earl of Lincoln. Alas for Sir Francis Ayscough's ambition. The family chronicler records the subsequent history of this marriage and does not fail to draw a moral:

> ... For the sequel, this much I have since observed, that his [i.e. Francis's] son and heir in few years wasted the better part of his patrimony (not to be redeemed at this day with twenty thousand pounds) by yielding over much to the unbridled vanities of another Anne Ayscough, his wife. Thus it pleased the Lord in his wisdom to give honour to our family through such a person as the world then held reproachful [i.e. Anne Ayscough the martyr], and contrariwise to impair the state and reputation of the same, by such a match as, in the judgement of man (for she was honourably descended) should rather have given more estimation unto it.[26]

We might add that not only did Anne Clinton waste much of the carefully garnered Ayscough wealth but she also failed to provide her husband with an heir.

Though the senior male line died out, there were other sons to carry on the name. The Ayscoughs maintained a leading position in Lincolnshire and, from time to time, provided leading servants of the state. Admiral Sir George Ayscough, for example, served the Parliamentary cause well during the Civil War and suffered accordingly at the Restoration. Scarcely a decade went by in which there was not an Ayscough as sheriff in Lincolnshire. Until 1707. In that year the last male heir, Charles Ayscough, died.[27] Though the Boucherett family, who inherited the Ayscough lands, incorporated the name also with their own, the passing of Charles Ayscough brought to an end the story of a distinguished family.

Throughout England there were many families like the Ayscoughs, and the Lascelles, the Markhams, Babingtons and Tyrrwhits, whose fortunes were bound up with the social and religious changes of the Reformation. The scant details of births and deaths, land transactions and marriages, beliefs, hopes and fears lie recorded in wills, deeds and family documents in private and public archives all over the country. Their tales, incomplete though they may be, are worth piecing together and re-telling. The chronicle of those tumultuous years belongs as much to them as it does to the kings and queens, the nobles and councillors, the bishops and scholars of the realm. Without them the story of the English Reformation – its glory and heroism, its violence and destructiveness, its hypocrisy and greed, its faith, hope and charity – is incomplete.

## Abbreviations

*Cal. S.P. Span.*   *Calendar of State Papers, Spanish*
*DNB*   *Dictionary of National Biography*
Foxe   *Acts and Monuments* by J. Foxe
*L.P.*   *Letters and Papers of the Reign of Henry VIII*, ed. J. S. Brewer,
    J. Gairdner and R. H. Brodie
*Lollards and Protestants*   *Lollards and Protestants in the Diocese of York*,
    by A. G. Dickens
*S.P.*   *State Papers of Henry VIII*
*A.A.S.R.*   *Associated Architectural Societies Reports*
*Lincs N. and Q.*   *Lincolnshire Notes and Queries*
*Lincs A.A.S.R.*   *Lincolnshire Architectural and Archaeological Society
Reports*
L.R.S.   Lincolnshire Record Society
P.P.R.   Principal Probate Registry

# *Notes*

*Chapter 1*

1. There were many spellings of the name current in the sixteenth
   century – Ascue, Eskew, Askew, Ascough, etc. but Ayscough is the
   most common in family and local documents and is therefore used
   here. Sir William's daughter, who occupies the later pages of this
   book, is usually known as Anne Askew, but I have used the Ayscough spelling in her case, for consistency.
2. There has long been a confusion between this Sir William Ayscough
   and his father of the same name. This has led to a tradition that con-
   nects the family almost exclusively with Stallingborough. For the
   elucidation of this point see H. C. Brewster, *South Kelsey Notes*
   (1898), pp. 50–51 and *Lincs N. and Q.*, Vol. III, pp. 117–19.
3. Quoted in A. R. Maddison, *Lincolnshire Pedigrees*, i, 29.
4. Brewster, *op. cit.*, pp. 58–9.
5. Beside the present eighteenth-century church at Stallingborough,
   the outline of the ancient hall and the now lost village can still be
   made out.
6. Traditionally the King indicated his choice of Sheriff by pricking
   the man's name on a short list with a golden pin.
7. *Grey Friars Chronicle*, p. 27.
8. They were married by 1512 for Sir William Wrottesley's will dated
   26 December mentions bequests to 'my son-in-law Ayscough'.
   C. G. S. Fuljambe in *Lincs N. and Q.*, iii, pp. 177–9.
9. C. Ferguson, *Naked to Mine Enemies*, p. 108.
10. *Ibid.*, p. 109.
11. *Ibid.*, p. 109.
12. Brewster, *op. cit.*, p. 54.
13. W. C. Metcalf, *A Book of Knights*, p. 47. For a description of this
    campaign by an eye-witness, see the account by John Taylor, Clerk
    of the Parliaments in *L.P.*, i, pt ii, 1057 ff.

14. *Rutland Papers*, Camden Society, 1842, p. 42.
15. *L.P.*, iii, pt i, 906.
16. *L.P.*, iii, pt ii, 2531.
17. For a full description of the working of the Court of Wards see G. R. Elton, *The Tudor Revolution in Government*, pp. 219 ff.
18. *L.P.*, iii, pt ii, 2288.
19. Brewster, *op. cit.*, p. 52. *L.P.*, iii, pt ii, 2635. The parish register of St Mary's, South Kelsey for 1563–6 (now lost) contained a copy of a return made by the Archdeacon of Lincoln: 'Kelsey St Mary's. Rectory. 57 families. 1 Hamlet – Winghale with 1 family. Kelsey St Nicholas. Rectory. 31 families.' Thus the two Kelseys constituted a moderate-sized village community by sixteenth-century standards.
20. *Ibid.*
21. *Ibid.*, p. 53.
22. The grant of land at Spalding seems to have been made to Sir William by Henry VIII. For an interesting account of the history of Ayscoughfee Hall (which is still standing and is preserved by Spalding Urban District Council) see E. H. Gooch *A History of Spalding*, 1940. The house was originally built by a wool merchant, Richard Alwyn, in 1420.
23. Brewster, *op. cit.*, p. 253. Cf. also C. W. Foster, *Lincoln Wills*, ii, p. 165: 28 February 1529 Robert Wilkinson of North Coates, 'To Margaret my wife, the house that I was in for the term of my early years, doing her duty to the lord, Sir William Ayscough, Knight.' Wilkinson must have been just one of many Ayscough tenants.
24. A. R. Maddison, 'Lincolnshire Gentry During the Sixteenth Century', *Lincs A.A.S.R.*, xxii, (1893) p. 209.
25. J. W. F. Hill, *Tudor and Stuart Lincoln*, pp. 25–9.
26. Brewster, *op. cit.*, p. 255.
27. E. Peacock, *English Church Furniture*, pp. 125, 157. This book is an account of the destruction of 'objects of superstition' in a large number of Lincolnshire churches during the early years of Queen Elizabeth's reign.
28. H. C. Brewster drew a plan of South Kelsey Hall as it must have been in Elizabethan times. (*South Kelsey Notes*, ii.) Today only fragments of red-brick towers, walls and gateways survive, built into modern farm buildings.
29. John Williams to Thomas Cromwell, *L.P.*, xi, 888.
30. *Lollards and Protestants*, p. 140.
31. *DNB*.
32. *Lollards and Protestants*, p. 120.
33. Historical Manuscripts Commission. Appendix, pt 10, pp. 47–8.
34. W. Tyndale. Preface to the *Five Books of Moses*, 1530, ed.

F. F. Bruce in *Courtenay Library of Reformation Classics*, 1964, p. 34.

35. For an analysis of these writings see, M. Aston, 'Lollardy and the Reformation: Survival or Revival', in *History*, xlix, 1964.
36. E. Arber *English Reprints*, xxviii, p. 165.

## Chapter 2

1. It was cut by about one-third in 1540 when the dioceses of Peterborough and Oxford were created.
2. Foxe, iv, p. 227.
3. *A Dialogue Concerning Heresy*, T. More, *English Works*, p. 213.
4. *L.P.*, xi, 325.
5. Foxe, iv, pp. 241–2.
6. Sanders was assessed at the high figure of £200 in the subsidy roll of 1524.
7. Foxe, iv, pp. 231–2. J. A. F. Thomson, *The Later Lollards*, pp. 92–3.
8. For the proceedings against Joye and his flight, see C. C. Butterworth and A. C. Chester, *George Joye 1495?–1553: A Chapter in the History of the English Bible and the English Reformation*, pp. 37–45.
9. L.R.S., xii, 91 and 123.
10. *Lollards and Protestants*, pp. 25–7.
11. In recent years vigorous persecution at Worksop had resulted in the apprehension, trial and recantation of two notable heretics. Two friends and colleagues of Henry Burnett's had been forced to abjure Lutheran beliefs in Hull in 1528. In Rotherham, Jesus College was divided by a controversy caused by the opinions and activities of William Senes, chaplain in charge of the choir school – a controversy which was to drag bitterly on for several years (see below pp. 101–103).
12. Now in the British Museum. It bears the words 'Anna Regina Angliae' in red letters on the fore-edge.
13. '. . . we be credibly informed that the bearer hereof, Richard Herman, merchant and citizen of Antwerp . . . was in the time of the late Lord Cardinal put and expelled from his freedom and fellowship of and in our English house there, for nothing else . . . but only . . . that he, ~~like a good Christian man~~ [sic] did . . . help to the setting forth of the New Testament in English. We therefore desire and instantly pray you, with all speed and favour convenient, to cause this good and honest merchant . . . to be restored to his pristine freedom, liberty, and fellowship aforesaid . . .' H. Ellis, *Original Letters*, 1st Series, ii, p. 45.
14. Early writers were divided over the question of whether the divorce

was Henry's idea or whether it was suggested to him by Wolsey (and, some add, Longland). Polydore Vergil and Tyndale blamed Wolsey and so did the imperial and French ambassadors of the day. Nicholas Sander, a Catholic apologist writing in Mary's reign, depicted the King as the sole author of the idea. Popular opinion was almost unanimous in blaming Longland. When rebellion broke out in the north towards the end of 1536, one of the most common complaints was '. . . there are bishops of the King's late promotion who have subverted the faith of Christ . . . They think the beginning of this trouble was the Bishop of Lincoln.' *L.P.*, xi, 705. The matter had been on Henry's mind for a long time and he must have discussed it with his close advisers. Who more natural to be a party to the King's thoughts than his confessor? It is clear that Longland knew and supported Henry VIII's point of view in the 'great matter'. Cf. J. D. Mackie, *The Earlier Tudors*, pp. 322–5 for a summary of the various opinions.

15. The methods employed by the commissioners are clearly explained in their report to the King (*S.P.*, i, pt ii, pp. 377–9):

'. . . first we called before us the regents [i.e. the junior M.A.s], in whom we thought all the doubt lay, explaining unto them how much it would contribute to the ammendation of all such displeasures and inconveniences, as might ensue unto them as a result of your Grace's indignation, conceived most worthily against them for their bad behaviour used heretofore towards your Highness, if now at least they submitting themselves and their . . . opinions to such requirements as had been devised by the most sage and wise doctors of the University . . . Several answered us very frowardly. Albeit, finally causing them to divide . . . into two parts, we had of our opinion 27 and of the opposing party there were but 22.'

16. *Cal. S.P. Span.*, iv, 475.
17. H. Ellis, *Original Letters*, Second Series, v, cviii. John Coke to Thomas Cromwell, 22 May 1533.
18. *L.P.*, viii, 809.
19. *Cal. S.P. Span.*, v, 430. Garrett Mattingly, *Catherine of Aragon*, pp. 191 ff.
20. *L.P.*, viii, 583.
21. In a letter of 8 July following, Longland appealed to Cromwell desiring that the men of Newark might be so ordered that Foster might live in safety among them. He suggested that, if Cromwell were to look closely into the case, he would discover that 'Sir John Markham, Sir William Merying and Bevercottes, justices of the peace, are supporters of their tenants in this matter. Bevercottes' servants were in the riot, as Foster can prove'. *L.P.*, ix, 751.

22. *L.P.*, ix, 751.
23. In April 1539 the Newark city fathers appealed to Cromwell to put an end to episcopal rule in the town (*L.P.*, xiv, pt i, p. 392) but without success. Newark finally obtained its charter in 1549 – two years after Longland's death and during the liberal, Protestant regime of Protector Somerset.
24. *L.P.*, viii, pt i, p. 963.
25. *L.P.*, x, 172.
26. *L.P.*, viii, pt i, 955.
27. Longland's long and interesting letter is in *L.P.*, x, 804. On 16 May, the day after Anne's condemnation, he wrote again, thanking Cromwell for his prompt action and drawing the Vicar General's attention to Garrett, 'There is another like preacher, with the King's great seal, named Garrett, of little learning and less discretion, against whom Lincolnshire much grudgeth.' *L.P.*, x, 891.


*Chapter 3*

1. Taxation by papal officers had been erratic and usually incomplete.
2. The question of motivation in the Pilgrimage of Grace has recently been the subject of some interesting and informative articles: A. G. Dickens, 'Secular and Religious Motivation in the Pilgrimage of Grace' in *Studies in Church History*, ed. G. J. Cuming, vol. iv, 1967, pp. 39–64; C. S. L. Davies, 'The Pilgrimage of Grace Reconsidered' in *Past and Present*, No. 41, 1968, pp. 54–76; M. E. James, 'Obedience and Dissent in Henrician England: The Lincolnshire Rebellion 1536' in *Past and Present*, No. 48, 1970, pp. 3–78.
3. *L.P.*, ix, p. 380.
4. John Speed, *Theatre of the Empire of Great Britain*, Book 1 Fol. 63–4, p. 2.
5. e.g. Boston, Stickney and Tattershall.
6. J. Darby (ed.), *An Historical Geography of England Before 1800*, p. 334.
7. The standard work on the Pilgrimage of Grace including the Lincolnshire rising is M. H. and R. Dodds, *The Pilgrimage of Grace and the Exeter Conspiracy*. For the most recent study of the Lincolnshire Rebellion see M. E. James, 'Obedience and Dissent in Henrician England: The Lincolnshire Rebellion 1536'.
8. R. C. Dudding (ed.), *The First Churchwardens' Book of Louth*.
9. R. C. Dudding, *op. cit.* The spire was begun in 1501 and completed in 1515. It represented years of work, prayer and sacrifice on the part of the parishioners. The total cost was £305. 8s. 5d. Its completion was attended by scenes of rejoicing and thanksgiving.

'William Ayleby, parish priest, with many of his brethren priests, hallowing the . . . weathercock and the stone that it stands upon . . . and then the priests sang *Te Deum Laudamus*, with organs and the churchwardens rang all the bells, and caused all the people there present to have bread and ale.'

10. Quoted in H. Maynard-Smith, *Henry VIII and the Reformation* p. 38.

11. *L.P.*, xi, 324.

12. 'The contempt of human law, made by rightful authority, is to be punished more heavily and more seriously than any transgression of the divine law', Stephen Gardiner, *Answer to Bucer*, quoted by P. Janelle, *Obedience in Church and State*, p. 205.

13. Sir Edward Maddison, knighted at the coronation of Anne Boleyn (31 May 1533) was born in 1454. A. R. Maddison, *Lincolnshire Gentry During the Sixteenth Century*.

14. The figure of 10,000 was an exaggeration, but the reality of 3,000 men on the move would hardly have proved less disquieting to the gentlemen.

15. Thomas Moigne's deposition at his trial in *S.P.*, ii, 971.

16. *Ibid.*

17. *L.P.*, xi, 971. Dodds, *The Pilgrimage of Grace and the Exeter Conspiracy*, p. 97.

18. Here my interpretation is at variance with that of M. H. and R. Dodds, *The Pilgrimage of Grace and the Exeter Conspiracy*. The authors of that excellent book, in my opinion, oversimplified the attitude of the gentlemen by imputing the same motives to all of them. The Misses Dodds saw all the commissioners confronted by a dilemma:

'If they fought and were defeated those who did not fall in the field would end on the gallows, or at best in exile; their lands would pass to strangers, their children would be left destitute, and the old names would die out. Lincolnshire would be given over to fire and pillage. If they fought and won, it would mean the renewal of civil war in England, after fifty years of peace. The new war would be a religious war, with some prospect of foreign invasion . . .' (p. 123).

This underestimates the loyalty of most of the gentlemen, their involvement with the Tudor regime, their abhorrence of civil strife, and the rigid class divisions in sixteenth-century England. The Lindsey commissions never had any intention of leading the rebellion, nor were they tempted by anything less than self-preservation to take arms against the King. Throughout the entire sequence of sorry events, Sir William Ayscough and his fellow captives did all they could to delay and hinder the host. Their action is exactly what we would expect of loyal but powerless and outnumbered men. Their response makes more reprehensible the reaction of Sir Edward Dymock and the gentlemen captured by the Horncastle host (see below, pp. 71–2). Their motives were equally clear, and their actions unambiguous: they actively supported the aims and methods of the rebels and did not hesitate to lead the insurgents.

19. *L.P.*, xi, 534.
20. Moigne's deposition, *op. cit.*
21. The Dymocks were a family of long standing in the royal service. At the coronation of the sovereign a member of the family performed the function of royal champion, an honour claimed by a Dymock at almost every coronation from Richard II's to George IV's (after which the custom fell into abeyance). They were supporters of the old religion. Later, in the reign of Queen Elizabeth, Sir Edward's son, Robert, was involved in recusancy proceedings.
22. *L.P.*, xii, pt i, 70 (iii, vii, x, xi); and 380.
23. Lord Hussey of Sleaford was concerned at the spread of unorthodox views which threatened to engulf the traditional faith. His anxiety was revealed in a conversation with Thomas Rycord of 'Haitefield', Yorkshire some time in 1535 or 1536, which was reported at his trial in 1537. Hussey asked about the spread of heresy in the north. Rycord replied 'it was little there except in a few particular persons who carried in their bosoms certain books, praying to God that some noble men might put the King's grace in remembrance for reformation thereof'. Hussey replied: 'That we can never do without help . . . and it will never mend without we fight for it.' *L.P.*, xii, pt i, 576.

24. *Select Pedigree of the Heneages of Hainton, Lincs*

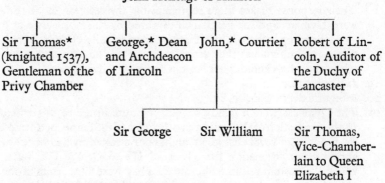

John Heneage of Hainton

Sir Thomas* (knighted 1537), Gentleman of the Privy Chamber

George,* Dean and Archdeacon of Lincoln

John,* Courtier

Robert of Lincoln, Auditor of the Duchy of Lancaster

Sir George     Sir William     Sir Thomas, Vice-Chamberlain to Queen Elizabeth I

\* Involved in the Lincolnshire Rising.

25. *L.P.*, xii, pt i, p. 35, No. 70.
26. The gentleman referred to here is Sir John Harrington of Exton, Rutland. The Harringtons were big landowners in the border area. A junior branch of the family was headed by Sir Robert Harrington and seated at Witham, just inside the Lincolnshire boundary.
27. *L.P.*, xi, 567.
28. For the later unfortunate history of Sir Christopher Ayscough see below pp. 152–4. See also the Ayscough pedigree on p. 10.
29. Morland's deposition in *L.P.*, xii, pt i, 380.
30. *S.P.*, i, 463–70.
31. *L.P.*, xii, pt i, 590.
32. The record of his conviction gives Tyburn as the place of execution but some traditions connect his death with Sleaford or Lincoln. It is quite possible that he was transported back to his county for execution – *pour encourager les autres*.
33. See below, Chapter 6.
34. By far the greatest beneficiary of the Dissolution in Lincolnshire was Charles Brandon, Duke of Suffolk. Edward Fiennes Clinton, Lord Clinton and Saye, received substantial grants also. The only gentry families to benefit substantially were the Tyrrwhits and Heneages, who, as well as having influence at court, could claim not to have been deeply involved in the rising. The following list shows the monastic lands obtained by these magnates.

Duke of Suffolk: Barlings, Boston Black Friars, Bruern, Bullington, Burwell, Ellesham, Greenfield, Kirkstead, Lincoln Friars, Louth, Maltby, Markeby, Newhouse, Nocton, Revesby, Skirbeck, Stamford, Tattershall, Thornholm, Vaudey, Willesford.

Lord Clinton: Alvingham, Aslakby, Crowland, Fosse, Haverholm, Holland Brigge, Sempringham, Stamford, Swineshead.

The Tyrrwhits: Bardney, Belvoir,\* Cameringham, Eagle Comandry,\* Gokwell, Kyme,\* Stanfield, Urford.

(\* Held in partnership with Thomas Manners, Earl of Rutland.)

The Heneages: Heynings, Legbourne, Newstead, North Ormesby, Sixhills, Tupholm, Wellow.

The Skipworths: Nun Cotham, Caversham.

Many of these estates did not stay very long with their original grantees. The local landowners, like many courtiers and London merchants, became speculators in monastic lands. Notable among the Lincolnshire speculators were John Bellow of Grimsby, one of Cromwell's agents, and John Broxholme. Cf. T. Tanner, *Notitia Monastica*, and S. B. Liljegren, *The Fall of the Monasteries and the Social Changes in England.*

35. *L.P.*, xv, pt i, 295.

*Chapter 4*

1. H. Ellis (ed.), *Original Letters Illustrative of English History*, Series ii, ii, 142.
2. G. R. Elton, *The Tudor Revolution in Government*, pp. 6–8. A. G. Dickens, *Thomas Cromwell and the English Reformation*, pp. 174–85.
3. Stephen Gardiner in his *Answer to Bucer*, quoted in P. Janelle, *Obedience in Church and State*, p. 205.
4. Quoted by A. G. Dickens in *Thomas Cromwell and the English Reformation*, p. 185.
5. *L.P.*, xv, pt i, 295.
6. The Skipworths had a long and honourable connection with Lincolnshire extending back to the thirteenth century. Their principal seat was at South Ormsby, between Horncastle and Louth. Skipworths frequently served as sheriff in the county and were supporters of Henry VIII's policies. However, later in the century they, like the Dymocks and Tyrrwhits, became involved in recusancy proceedings. See A. R. Maddison, *Lincolnshire Pedigrees.*
7. P.P.R. F.39 Hogen. A study of the wills made by educated men and women during the years 1530–60 is one way of assessing the reaction of the upper classes to the forces of the Reformation and the Counter Reformation. The standard form used by testators before 1530 was 'I bequeath my soul to God Almighty, Our Lady St Mary and to all the whole company of heaven'. Frequently the prayers of the Virgin and saints were invoked. During the period

mentioned more and more people forsook this form. Many omitted reference to 'Our Lady' and the saints. An increasing number gave expression to such distinctly Protestant doctrines as justification by faith only and assurance of salvation. This evidence suggests that the new beliefs took root very rapidly among the educated classes.

8. *L.P.*, iii, pt i, 703.

9. His name appears on the list of subsidy commissioners for that year. *L.P.*, iii, pt ii, 3289.

10. The official sheriff lists supply the name of Nicholas Strelley as sheriff for this year but a grant recorded in *L.P.*, xii, pt ii, 1150g mentions Hercy as being appointed to that position.

11. The Topcliffes of Somerby were one of the leading families of the Lincolnshire/Nottinghamshire border and closely related by ties of friendship and kinship with the Burghs of Gainsborough. The most famous (or notorious) member of the family was Richard (born 1532), son of Robert Topcliffe by his wife Margaret, daughter of Lord Burgh. Richard was an active seeker out and persecutor of Roman Catholic recusants in Elizabeth's reign.

12. He is called George in the heralds' visitations 1569–1614 (cf. *Select Pedigrees*, pp. 57 ff.), but Harleian MS 1400 and the Elston Parish Register MS in Notts. Record Office confirm the name as Richard and he can confidently be identified with the Richard Lascelles whose will, dated September 1520, is preserved in the Borthwick Institute, York.

13. *Select Pedigrees from Visitations of the County of Nottingham 1569–1614*, Harleian Society, 1871.

14. Humphrey Hercy was an executor of Richard's estate as was 'the right worshipful and honourable Lord, and my good Lord, the Earl of Shrewsbury', cf. Richard Lascelles' Will.

15. Thomas Starkey in a report presented to Cromwell and the King in 1535 and later published under the title *A Dialogue between Reginald Pole and Thomas Lupset*, ed. K. M. Burton. For a full discussion see Joan Simon, *Education and Society in Tudor England*, pp. 148–62.

16. This is deduced from his later theological ideas which certainly show a close understanding of the views of some of the German reformers, particularly Carlstadt. He may of course have read all the continental writers in Latin or in English translation.

17. Certainly there was a John Lascelles at Oxford then, who is recorded by Wood in *Athenae Oxonienses*, but there is no way of proving that this is the same person.

18. Furnivall's Inn was founded in 1406 as an adjunct of Lincoln's Inn.

19. Cf. Joan Simon, *op. cit.*, pp. 13, 53–5.

20. More was put to the Inn in 1501 after two years at Oxford where, in the opinion of his father, he was wasting his time on such sub-

jects as Greek and Philosophy. He proceeded to Lincoln's Inn in 1504.

21. Plumpton Correspondence in *Dugdale's Visitation of Yorkshire*, ed. J. W. Clay, pt 8, pp. 231–93.

22. Elizabeth Plumpton came to share her son's faith as the tenor of her will, sealed 6 January 1552, indicates: '. . . I commend my soul into the most merciful hands of my Saviour and Redeemer, Jesus Christ, through whose painful passion I undoubtedly believe to be eternally saved.' Test. Ebor. vi, 260 ff. For a full study of the Plumptons see *Lollards and Protestants*, pp. 131–7.

23. Quoted by J. R. Tanner, *Tudor Constitutional Documents*, p. 192 n.

24. A quick study of the selected pedigrees on pp. 12–14 will show how closely interrelated these four families were. Note particularly the touching evidence of a long-standing friendship in the naming of George Lascelles' youngest child – 'Hercye'.

25. *L.P.*, v, 628.

26. For a full discussion of the suppression of the Observants see D. Knowles, *The Religious Orders in England*, iii, pp. 206–11.

27. *L.P.*, vi, 1664.

28. *L.P.*, vii, 939, 1020, 1652.

29. *L.P.*, vii, 1510.

30. *L.P.*, viii, 560.

31. A. R. Maddison, *Lincolnshire Pedigrees*. For a fuller treatment of the Disney family see *Parish Memorials relating to Norton Disney* by 'A Country Vicar'.

32. The editor of *L.P.* assigns this note to 1538 but it is undated and there are reasons for suspecting that it may have been written somewhat earlier. The list contains the name of Miles Coverdale, who was in France from the spring of 1538. (Cf. J. F. Mozley, *Coverdale and His Bibles*, p. 7.)

33. *L.P.*, xiii, pt ii, 1184, iii.

34. For an accurate but imaginative account of life in such a household see Lacey Baldwin Smith, *A Tudor Tragedy*, pp. 52–4.

35. York Diocesan Registry, folios 129, 148v, 149, 154, 154v, 156v. Also *L.P.*, xii, pt ii, 436; xiii, pt ii, 149. Also *Lollards and Protestants*, pp. 37 ff.

36. One member of this group, Sir Nicholas Carew, Master of the King's Horse, made a gallows speech which impressed many of the Londoners who had come to witness his end. In it he urged the people to read evangelical books, explaining that his downfall was the result of his hatred of the Gospel. This provides an interesting illustration of the fact that politics and religion were inseparably linked in Tudor minds. *L.P.*, xiv, pt i, 466.

37. The following is an example of the extreme rumours that were

circulating and the alacrity with which they were believed in some quarters. In 1539 a very distressed John Foster wrote to Cromwell:

'. . . my misfortune hath been to have conceived untruly God's word and not only with the intellect to have thought it, but externally and really I have fulfilled the same. For I, as then being a priest, have accomplished marriage – nothing pretending but as an obedient subject. For if the King's Grace could have found it lawful that priests might have been married, they would have been to the Crown [doubly] faithful. First, in love; secondly for fear that the Bishop of Rome should re-establish his power unto their desolation. But now by rumour among the people, I perceive I have done amiss . . . as soon as I heard it to be true, I sent the woman to her friends threescore miles from me . . .'. H. Ellis (ed.), *Original Letters*, First Series ii, cxli.

Foster was only one among many simple people to be thoroughly confused by the religious changes of the 1530s.

38. For the examination of treasons and felonies.
39. *L.P.*, xii, pt i, 537; xiii, pt i, 604.
40. *L.P.*, xii, pt i, 892; xiii, pt i, 287, 877; F. A. Gasquet, *Henry VIII and the English Monasteries*, pp. 282–3; J. C. Cox in *Victoria County History – Nottinghamshire*, li, pp. 99–100; Knowles, *op. cit.*, pp. 372–3.
41. *L.P.*, xiii, pt i, 787, 788.
42. *L.P.*, xiii, pt i, 861, 871.
43. The Anthony Neville referred to here is Sir Anthony Neville of South Leverton, Notts. Nothing is now known of his conflict with the people of Cottam nor of the 'lunatic priest' he was forcing on them. If he was an opponent of the new religious beliefs, his views obviously changed later, for his will, dated November 1557, has a decidedly 'Protestant' flavour: 'I bequeath my soul to God Almighty and to Jesus Christ his only Son our Lord, who hath redeemed my soul upon(?) the holy cross by his merits and bitter passion. Therefore into his hands I commit my soul.' York Diocesan Records at the Borthwick Institute, Vol. 15.2., fol. 107.
44. *L.P.*, xiii, pt i, pp. 387–8. The 'Lady' in question was a locally popular statue of the Virgin Mary, reputed to have miraculous powers.
45. *L.P.*, xv, 229.
46. *L.P.*, xiii, pt ii, 726.
47. There were other reasons for the monasteries to alienate land and realize wealth. Abbots and priors granted land to relatives to enable them to establish or increase their estates. Other grants were made to powerful local landlords in order to win their support.

48. *L.P.*, xiv, pt ii, App. 2.
49. *L.P.*, xiii, pt ii, 726.
50. *L.P.*, xiv, pt ii, App. 2.
51. *L.P.*, xvi, 381–5.
52. R. Thoroton, *Antiquities of Nottinghamshire*, p. 460. T. Bailey, *Annals of Nottinghamshire*, ii, p. 424.
53. For Augmentations see G. R. Elton, *The Tudor Revolution in Government*, pp. 203–19.
54. H. Gee and W. J. Hardy, *Documents Illustrative of English Church History*, p. 276.
55. e.g. *S.P.*, i, pt ii, pp. 518–19.
56. *S.P.*, i, pt ii, p. 568.
57. *Cranmer's Works*, Parker Society ii, p. 168. It was suggested by H. Maynard-Smith that 'the ordinary man welcomed the settlement' (*Henry VIII and the Reformation*, p. 166). Such an interpretation of the religious situation is hardly supported by the facts. In both houses and in convocation the measure was resisted by more than a minority 'both of divines and lawyers', Cranmer, *op. cit.* A considerable number of Englishmen fearing persecution, fled abroad. Furthermore, the Act of Six Articles far from bringing religious unity to the realm only added fuel to the flames of controversy. Christian men and women were, on the one hand being encouraged to read the Bible, while on the other hand required to assent to doctrines founded on the authority not of Scripture but tradition.
58. A. G. Dickens, *Thomas Cromwell and the English Reformation*, p. 109.
59. Equivalent to perhaps £10,000 in modern currency.
60. Cf. A. G. Dickens, *op. cit.* and J. F. Mozley, *Coverdale and His Bibles*, pp. 201–220.
61. By September Cromwell had completely regained his ascendancy over his rivals. He was even able to secure the dismissal of his arch enemies, the Bishops of Winchester and Chichester, from the Council.
62. *L.P.*, xiv, pt ii, 751.
63. *L.P.*, xvi, 61.
64. G. R. Elton, *The Tudor Revolution in Government*, pp. 385–97.
65. *L.P.*, xiii, pt ii, 400.
66. R. B. Walker, *A History of the Reformation in the Archdeaconries of Lincoln and Stow, 1534–94* (Liverpool Ph.D. Thesis 1959), pp. 90–92. This despoliation of the shrine of St Hugh proved inadequate to Henry. Having seen the remains of it on his northern progress in August 1541, he wrote to Longland from Hull on 4 October ordering the Bishop to enforce the royal injunction concerning the removal of objects of superstition. The tomb of St Hugh was to be 'taken away until there remain no memory of it'. *Ibid.*

67. For a full and fascinating account of Cromwell's fall and the events leading up to it see G. R. Elton, 'Thomas Cromwell's Decline and Fall' in *Cambridge Historical Journal* (1951), pp. 15 ff.

## Chapter 5

1. Just how generous Henry was can be seen from his New Year gifts to the Queen in 1541. These included a square containing 27 table diamonds and 26 clusters of pearls, a brooch made up of 60 rubies and 33 diamonds and edged with pearls and a muffler of velvet and fur sewn with 38 rubies and 572 pearls. C. Camden, *The Elizabethan Woman*, p. 100.
2. As Lord Treasurer, Norfolk had oversight of the Exchequer, though he rarely put in an appearance there, leaving most of the work to the Chancellor of the Exchequer. Cf. G. R. Elton, *The Tudor Revolution in Government*, pp. 107–9.
3. *L.P.*, xvi, 101.
4. *DNB.*
5. *L.P.*, xvi, 101.
6. He and Garrett were both, for a time, chaplains to Sir Francis Bigod, the strange Yorkshire gentleman. They had been friends in their Cambridge days and, despite their divergent views, their relationship since then had often been close. Eventually, however, friendship soured to hatred. Cf. *DNB.*

   Bigod's strange career serves as a warning against trying to fit people into neat categories – 'Protestant', 'Catholic', 'Reformer', 'Conservative', etc. Born in 1508 of Yorkshire gentry stock, he went to Oxford and imbibed a scholarly Protestantism. Yet he opposed the royal supremacy. This and other grievances moved him to take a leading part in the Pilgrimage of Grace. He was executed as a traitor in 1537. *DNB* and *Lollards and Protestants*, pp. 53 ff.
7. *DNB.*
8. For the careers of Alexander Seton and John Parkhurst see below pp. 131–2 and p. 175 respectively. John Parkhurst ended his days as Bishop of Norwich under Queen Elizabeth.
9. *L.P.*, xiv, pt i, 1275. H. Ellis, *Original Letters*, First Series, ii, cxliii.
10. *DNB.*
11. The first pair of secretaries were Sir Thomas Wriothesley and Sir Ralph Sadler.
12. By 1540 a Privy Council of nineteen regular members had emerged. The numbers were always kept up and vacancies immediately filled. Beyond the Privy Council there was a larger and vaguer group of 'councillors', whose advice and services might be called upon from time to time. The creation of this new kind of Privy Council may

confidently be credited to the administrative genius of Thomas Cromwell. Cf. Elton, *op. cit.*, pp. 316 ff.

13. It is perhaps valid to mention here as further evidence of changing religious trends the case of Humphrey Monmouth, a wealthy London cloth merchant who left money in his will, not for the saying of masses for his soul, but for the preaching of sermons to edify others. For the activities of Monmouth and his colleagues, see E. G. Rupp, *Studies in the Making of the English Protestant Tradition*, p. 11.

14. The story which John told the Council later was that he knew nothing of Catherine Howard's conduct until the summer of 1541. It seems, however, inconceivable that Mary Lascelles should have said nothing about the goings-on at Lambeth to members of her own family. John, of course, dared not reveal prior knowledge of these matters for fear of being accused of having concealed them from the King.

15. For the fullest modern treatment of Catherine Howard's affairs see L. B. Smith, *A Tudor Tragedy*, pp. 54–65.

16. *Acts of the Privy Council*, vii, pp. 354–5.

17. *L.P.*, xvi, 1430, 1433.

18. J. Ridley, *Thomas Cranmer*, p. 223.

19. Burnet, *The History of the Reformation* (1839), iv, No. xxv, p. 139.

20. Foxe, v, pp. 465 ff.

21. *L.P.*, xviii, pt i, 310.

22. There are numerous accounts of this popular story. Foxe had it from Ralph Morice, Cranmer's secretary, and it appeared in *Acts and Monuments*, viii, pp. 24–6. It can also be found in J. G. Nichols, *Narratives of the Reformation* (Camden Society, 1859), pp. 254–8 and in Strype, *Memorials of Archbishop Cranmer* (1694), Book I, xxviii, pp. 124–6.

23. Denny was himself a convinced Protestant and one of the courtiers whose influence with the King was increasingly resented by the conservatives. See below, p. 173.

24. John Lord Russell, Lord Privy Seal, was an able soldier. He lost an eye at the siege of Morlaix in 1522. He was a moderate on the Council and was clearly not a willing supporter of the plot against Cranmer. *DNB*.

25. William Turner (*alias* William Wroghton), *The Man of Sin – With His Disclosing* (Basle 1543), Postscript.

26. Perhaps it never dawned on Henry, who seemed convinced until the end of his days, that he could manipulate the thoughts and beliefs of his people just as he could manipulate their goods and their bodies.

27. *L.P.*, xviii, pt i, 500.

28. C. Wriothesley, *A Chronicle of England*, i, 142. Strype, *Ecclesiastical Memorials*, i, 367.
29. Foxe, v, p. 495.
30. Sir Philip Hoby (1505–58) was a Gentleman Usher of the Privy Chamber. He came to prominence in the royal service, like so many others in the early 1530s, because of his zealous support of the political Reformation. He was an experienced diplomat and a soldier, an amiable courtier and a convinced Protestant. *DNB*.
31. Foxe, v, pp. 495–6.
32. Strype, *Memorials of Archbishop Cranmer*, Book I, xxviii, p. 123.
33. *Ibid.*
34. *Ibid.*
35. Strype, *op. cit.*, Book XXVII, p. 123.
36. *Ibid.*

*Chapter 6*

1. For Sir Francis Bigod's rising see *Lollards and Protestants*, pp. 53 ff.
2. *L.P.*, xii, pt i, 140.
3. *L.P.*, xii, pt i, 179.
4. *L.P.*, xii, pt i, 951.
5. *L.P.*, xii, pt ii, 1322.
6. He died in 1571. Will in Lincs Archives, 1534. x. 57.
7. *L.P.*, xiii, pt ii, 245 (i).
8. *L.P.*, xiii, pt ii, 245 (ii).
9. *L.P.*, xv, 601.
10. The Kyme pedigree is very incomplete but research has indicated that the Thomas Kyme born at Friskney *c.* 1515 is almost certainly the man with whom we are concerned here. The de Kymes were a very ancient family and a thirteenth-century ancestor had built a castle at South Kyme on the edge of the fen (one tower of which still survives). Since those days all branches of the family had sunk to yeoman or peasant status. Through farming and trade the Friskney Kymes had prospered and by the mid-sixteenth century could contemplate marriage into the leading families of the shire. Thomas's father took as his third wife, about 1532, Margaret, daughter of John Heneage, cf. A. R. Maddison, *Lincolnshire Pedigrees*, i (1902), pp. 58–68; E. Trollope, *Anne Askewe, the Lincolnshire Martyr*, in *A.A.S.R.*, vi, pt ii, pp. 117 ff.; A. Gibson, *Notes on the Heralds' Visitation of Lincolnshire 1634* (1898), pp. 75–97; and the same author's remarks in *Lincolnshire Notes and Queries*, iii, pp. 117–19, 177–9.
11. This created for the head of the family a knotty legal problem over the claim to the land Elizabeth had brought to the marriage – the

manor of Oxton, Nottinghamshire. For two years after his father's death Francis Ayscough was fighting for possession of this land, only to lose the case which was decided in favour of Sir Nicholas Strelley (who claimed the manor as the nearest male descendant of his uncle) by Act of Parliament in 1543. *L.P.*, Addenda i, pt ii, 1515, 1895 and *L.P.*, xviii, pt i, 66, Cap. xxxix.

12. The Ancaster deposits in the Lincolnshire archives contain many documents relating to the Suffolk estates which mention George St Paul. He is frequently referred to in such terms as 'our counsellor and servant'. See especially 3 Ancaster, 8. i. p. 15, a document dated 30 September 1541, appointing St Paul steward of 'the manors of Donnington, Frampton, Waslingborough, Leadenham, Fulbeck, the sokes of Kinton Holland, Shirbeck, Gayton and Munby and the manors of Kirkstead, Woodhall, Buckland, Roughton, Barlings, Scothorne, Carlton, Stainton, Scampton, Caenby and Glentham, parcels of Kirkstead and Barlings and Allington. Charles Duke of Suffolk to George St Paul for his good counsel'. The Protestant convictions of the family are shown in the wording of their wills. Sir John St Paul, George's father, died in 1545 at the ripe old age of 84 or 85 and stated, 'I give and freely bequeath my soul to God Almighty which hath redeemed the same by the merits of his blessed passion' – C.P.R. 27 Allen. George's own will was even more explicit: 'I bequeath my soul unto God, trusting by the merits of his only Son, our alone Lord and Saviour, to have forgiveness of all my sins and to be in the number of those whom he, by his Holy Spirit hath sanctified to everlasting life.' P.P.R. 43 Welles.

13. Richard Disney's Will in Lincolnshire Archives Office: 'I bequeath my soul into the hands of Almighty God, in whom I only trust, praying him to receive me to his mercy, and my body to be buried in my chapel in the church without superfluous pomp and decently.' L.R.S. 1578.88. dated 22 January 1577. Jane lived at South Kelsey after Richard's death and was buried there 27 December 1590.

14. *L.P.*, xv, 601.

15. P.P.R. 29 Alenger.

16. *L.P.*, xiii, pt i, p. 581, No. 60.

17. Pat. 32. Hen. VIII, p. 7. m. 28. *L.P.*, xv, 831, (46).

18. Matthew V, vs. 11–12.

19. I Corinthians VII, vs. 13, 15.

20. Bale, *op. cit.*, pp. 173–4.

21. *Ibid.*

22. So strong were Parkhurst's Protestant convictions and so undaunted was he in his advocacy of them that he considered it prudent to flee to Zürich on the accession of Queen Mary. When the persecutions of that reign were over and Elizabeth was secure on the throne of

England, Parkhurst returned, to be appointed to the bishopric of
Norwich (1560), where he enthusiastically sought out secret papists
but allowed Puritan excesses to continue unchecked. He died in
1575. *DNB*.

23. The extent of real Protestant conviction among the wealthier classes
is something which has always been very difficult to define. Few
documents exist in which gentlemen and noblemen have expressed
their faith. It was then, as ever, hard for men with great treasures on
earth to value more highly treasures in heaven. So we find few
instances of men of substance taking a stand for their faith and
thereby risking disgrace, prosecution, loss of royal favour and confiscation of property (which makes the cases of Anne Ayscough and
John Lascelles particularly interesting). A large Protestant middle
class existed by the beginning of Elizabeth's reign, therefore the
middle years of the century must have been a period of transition.
When we seek fuller information about this period of transition we
rely primarily on the wording of wills. Professor Dickens' (*The
English Reformation*, p. 192) researches among Yorkshire and
Nottinghamshire wills indicated that testaments with a Protestant
flavour increased from 25 per cent to 40 per cent of the yearly toal
between 1545 and 1547. My own studies of over 200 wills signed by
East Midlands testators indicate a slight increase between 1530 and
1544, a more rapid increase between 1545 and 1552 and only a slight
levelling out during the reign of Mary Tudor. This evidence is a
fairly clear indication of the numbers of educated, well-to-do men
and women who were committed to the new beliefs. Other scraps of
evidence from official and private documents (such as I have cited in
relevant places throughout this book) seem to me to support the view
that the years 1535–50 were decisive for the spread of Protestantism
among the English middle classes – and, therefore, decisive in deter-
mining whether England was to be a Protestant or Catholic country.

*Chapter 7*

1. *L.P.*, xxi, pt i, 836.
2. *Grey Friars Chronicle*, p. 48.
3. 1543 edition, p. 98.
4. *L.P.*, xix, pt ii, 797.
5. *Grey Friars Chronicle*, p. 48.
6. See J. J. Scarisbrick, *Henry VIII*, pp. 443–4. Hertford's criticisms
   of the royal plan of campaign were soon justified. The 1544 raid
   stirred bitter resentment and lost England the support of many
   friendly Scottish nobles.
7. Cranmer's attitude to the work of translation is made clear in a letter

sent to the King with the first draft of his revised litany – a draft which was either shelved for seven months or sent back by Henry for further revision. Part of the letter, dated 7 October 1543, reads as follows:

'. . . for as much as many of the processions in the Latin were but barren (as me seemed) and little fruitful, I was constrained to use more than the liberty of a translator. For in some processions I have altered divers words. In some I have added parts; in some taken parts away. Some I have left out completely, either because the matter appeared to me to be to little purpose, or because the days are not, with us, festival days. Some processions I have replaced completely, because I thought I had better matter for the purpose, than the Latin procession . . .' *S.P.*, i, pt ii, cxcvi.

8. John Thirlby, the diocesan of this short-lived see, was at this time a close friend of Cranmer, who had frequently been 'good lord' to him and had advanced him to the royal service. He was influenced by the new religious opinions, though he afterwards became an enemy of the Reformation. *DNB.*

9. *S.P.*, i, pt ii, cxcix.

10. The comparison of this regency council with the one appointed by Henry shortly before his death has, perhaps, not been sufficiently drawn by earlier historians. On both occasions Henry was concerned to appoint men whom he trusted and who would be capable of working together. He tolerated, and even encouraged, factions among his own privy councillors but his prime concern when appointing advisers for his wife and son was for stability. Men whom Henry knew to be intriguers (such as Gardiner) were omitted from the Council on both occasions.

11. Chapuys writing to the Queen of Hungary on 9 April 1543 reported how the Earl of Surrey had been imprisoned for rioting in London and remarked, 'I suspect he will remain long in prison because he is suspected of Lutheranism.' The 'foolish proud boy' may well have dabbled in Protestantism because it was forbidden. He was certainly not a serious convert. (*L.P.*, xviii, pt i, 390.)

12. Perhaps Underhill was the first Englishman to whom that epithet was applied.

13. John Dudley made his career as a soldier, was created Viscount Lisle in 1543 and appointed Lord Admiral in the same year. He was later to become Duke of Northumberland. During the reign of Edward VI, Dudley was largely responsible for the downfall of the Duke of Somerset, whose position as Protector he assumed.

14. Her mother was Mary de Salines, a lady-in-waiting to Catherine of Aragon. *DNB.*

15. *Cal. S.P. Span.*, 1547–53, p. 101.

16. 'Of a Lady that Refused to Dance with Him.'
17. Clearly not all the Tyrrwhits were conservatives. This Robert, a cousin of Sir Robert of Kettleby, and his wife, being continuously open to the influence of the new learning, had a more liberal outlook than their Lincolnshire relatives.
18. *Cal. S.P. Span.*, xxi, p. 1. No. 289.
19. For a fuller discussion see W. K. Jordan, *Edward VI: The Young King*, pp. 40 ff.
20. J. J. Scarisbrick, *Henry VIII*, p. 454.
21. *L.P.*, xx, pt ii, 455, and J. J. Scarisbrick, *Henry VIII*, pp. 458–9.
22. J. A. Muller, *The Letters of Stephen Gardiner*, pp. 152–4.
23. Wriothesley to Paget 11 November 1545, *S.P.*, i, pt ii, p. 840.
24. Gardiner to Paget cf. J. A. Muller, *The Letters of Stephen Gardiner*, pp. 185 ff. and 198 ff. Also J. J. Scarisbrick, p. 455 and p. 456 n.
25. When Thomas Howard complained of the laxity of the Essex subsidy commissioners they replied 'a great number of people have lamentably complained . . . that for lack of payment for such grain as is taken for the King's Highness' use, they have no money to pay the subsidy'. *S.P.*, i, pt ii, pp. 789–90.
26. Russell to Paget from Exeter 18 August, *S.P.*, i, pt ii, p. 818.
27. *S.P.*, i, pt ii, pp. 817–18.
28. Wriothesley to Paget from Ely Place, 11 November, *S.P.*, i, pt ii, p. 840.
29. Probably in the middle of 1544 when the Act of Six Articles had been considerably modified. By the new legislation suspected heretics could not be punished for offences over a year old, nor could witnesses be called to testify about a sermon more than forty days after it had been preached.
30. See above p. 175.
31. Legend, supported by some writers, confidently asserts that Anne *was* a member of the study group meeting in the Queen's rooms and that she presented Catherine and her ladies with copies of Tyndale's New Testament. Certainly she was known by some of the Queen's ladies, who later comforted her in prison. She may have met Catherine, for the Catholic faction later believed that Anne's condemnation for heresy could be used as a means of implicating the Queen. That Anne 'introduced' Tyndale's works to the Queen's circle is highly unlikely for no better reason than that Catherine Parr, the Duchess of Suffolk, Lady Denny and the others would have been already familiar with current New Testament translations. See H. Chapman, *Lady Jane Grey*, p. 30.
32. C. Wriothesley, *Chronicle*, i., pp. 155–6.
33. *S.P.*, i, pt ii, 806–7, x, 583–5.
34. *DNB*.

35. E. Hall, *Chronicle*, p. 865. J. Stow, *Annals*, p. 590.
36. F. G. Emmison, *Tudor Secretary*, p. 59.
37. *Cal. S.P. Span.*, 1547–53, No. 491. See also *DNB*.
38. He had studied at Winchester College. J. Strype, *Ecclesiastical Memorials*, I. i, 595.
39. *Ibid.*
40. During Anne's second imprisonment in 1546 she wrote an account of her various examinations. This account fell into the hands of John Bale in Germany and he published it in English, with his own, typically scurrilous, running commentary. This work was published in 1547 and was reprinted in full in *Select Works of Bishop Bale* (Parker Society 1849). It is on this edition that the account here is based. Later John Foxe used Bale's version as the basis of his own account of Anne's trials in *Acts and Monuments*. He had access to more material and he was able to correct Bale in some places. It is unfortunate that the only accounts of the 'Troubling of Anne Ayscough' should be so one-sided but Foxe, at least, was an accurate historian who did not sink to distortion of facts. Judicious reading between the lines enables us to form a reasonably clear impression of the sequence of events between March and July 1546.
41. Some earlier writers ascribed this arrest to March 1545, thus making it the first occasion on which Anne ran foul of the authorities. In this they were following the accounts of Bale and Foxe who gave the date as 10 March 1545. But the sixteenth-century accounts used the old calendar employed in legal and official circles whereby the new year was not begun until 26 March. There can be no doubt that the correct date is 10 March 1546, as was pointed out by Pratt in his edition of *Acts and Monuments*, v, p. 836. Only this dating makes sense of the sequence of Anne's three trials. Furthermore the accounts specifically name the Lord Mayor who examined her as Sir Martin Bowes and he was not installed until November 1545.
42. There is some contradiction among the authorities as to what happened next. Anne's own account published by Bale states clearly 'then they had me from thence to my Lord Mayor'. Archdeacon Loud, a scholar and tutor in the pay of Rich and Sir Richard Southwell (a member of the Privy Council), expanded on this in a letter to Foxe with the express intention of providing the Martyrologist with more information. Yet his narrative was written some fifteen troubled years after the events described and Foxe did not apparently think sufficiently highly of it to incorporate it in later editions of the 'Book of Martyrs'. According to Loud, Anne was immediately lodged in the Tower, whither the Lord Mayor, Sir Martin Bowes, repaired to interview her. The improbability of her being lodged in the Tower

by the quest hardly needs stressing and Loud is almost certainly confusing this period of Anne's persecution with a later one when she was imprisoned in the Tower (this was only after her conviction as an unrepentant heretic). Furthermore, Loud has some fun at Bowes's expense and seems intent upon ridiculing him. He makes the puzzling assertion that the Lord Mayor was 'sitting with the council, as most meet for his wisdom' – clearly a confusion with Anne's second examination – and puts into his mouth some absurd questions which enabled Anne to ridicule him most effectively. Eventually, according to Loud, the assembly broke up with much laughter and the complete confusion of the Lord Mayor. We are probably wiser to trust in Anne's, simpler, account of this particular section of her examination.

43. Standish was a man of pronounced conservatism and the author of *A Little Treatise against the Protestation of Robert Barnes at the time of his Death* (1540) and *A Discourse wherein is debated whether it be expedient that the Scripture should be in English for all men to read* (1544). However, his opinions were not so strongly held as to prevent him holding various preferments under Henry VIII, Edward VI, Mary and Elizabeth I. *DNB*.

44. J. Bale, *op. cit.*, p. 154.

45. J. Bale, *op. cit.*, p. 155.

46. Bale's first edition (1546) gave it as 'XII' days. This was changed to 'VII' in the second edition. Foxe gives 'eleven'. Since her confession was dated 20 March in the Bishop's register, the interval must have been seven days. Cf. Bale, *op. cit.*, p. 156.

47. *Ibid.*, p. 159.

48. The identity of this man has defied all attempts at discovery. The name is variously spelled – e.g. Brittanye, Brittayne, Britaine, etc. – and he is always referred to as 'my cousin'. Presumably he was therefore a relative of Anne's and the term 'cousin' is not used loosely. He was a student of law and probably at Gray's Inn.

49. This was none other than the author of the famous *Chronicle*. Hall was a member of Gray's Inn and a convinced if circumspect reformer. His parents were not so cautious; John Hall and his wife were known as ardent supporters of the Protestant cause and were imprisoned for their faith during Mary's reign. They both outlived their son, who died in 1547. *DNB*.

50. Foxe, v, p. 543.

51. Among those present, according to Foxe, was one Richard, a servant to Sir Anthony Denny. This affords further proof of Anne's close connection with the court. Foxe, *ibid*.

52. There is some doubt about Anne's confession. The document which Foxe quoted from the episcopal register did not contain the

qualifying subscription mentioned. Foxe's answer was that the confession was copied out again at a later date and the subscription omitted so that the authorities could claim that Anne had gone back on her oath. Against this it can be argued that Bonner is unlikely to have tolerated the addition which Anne (by her own report) made to the document, since it went a long way towards nullifying all that he was trying to achieve by making her sign a confession. Can it be that Anne was forced to withdraw her qualification but afterwards insisted that she had not done so, or was there genuine confusion over the issue? Whatever the truth of the matter, the authorities were now possessed of a document which, whether tampered with or not, served to discredit Anne Ayscough in the eyes of her admirers and co-religionists. This was primarily why it was necessary for Anne to publish her own account of her examinations, which in versions edited by Foxe and Bale are now the only evidence we have to go on.

53. Bale has a somewhat fantastic explanation of this curious event: 'The other woman, whom they would here have most craftily delivered . . . (as I am credibly informed) was a popish slut, which they had before provided both to betray her and accuse her . . . she was now detained for perjury. Fain would the prelates . . . have had her at liberty, but they feared much to be noted partial.'
*Op. cit.*, p. 180.

### Chapter 8

1. Henry suffered increasingly frequent attacks of fever brought on by his ulcerated legs. In February 1546 he was seriously ill for three weeks. The ravages of pain were, by now, almost permanently visible on his face. J. J. Scarisbrick, *Henry VIII*, pp. 486–7.
2. *L.P.*, xxi, 744.
3. J. Strype, *Memorials*, iii, i, 160.
4. *L.P.*, xxi, 790.
5. C. Wriothesley, *Chronicle*, p. 167.
6. *DNB*.
7. *L.P.*, xxi, pt i, 810.
8. *Ibid.*
9. *L.P.*, xxi, pt i, 823.
10. *Ibid.*
11. *Ibid.*
12. *L.P.*, xxi, pt i, 848.
13. *L.P.*, xxi, pt i, 836, 845.
14. *L.P.*, xxi, pt i, 835.
15. *L.P.*, xxi, pt i, 790.

16. Shaxton had clearly beaten a diplomatic retreat when things began to 'hot up' in London, but his exit had not been swift enough. Despite his gesture in 1539, he was not of the stuff that martyrs are made of. His examinations and recantation in 1546 broke him utterly and he never returned to the Protestant fold. He ended his days as a minor persecutor under Queen Mary.

17. For a clear examination of the troubled career of Robert Wisdom, see Sherwin Bailey, 'Robert Wisdom under Persecution, 1541–1543', in *Journal of Ecclesiastical History*, ii, 180 ff. See also *Lollards and Protestants*, pp. 194–6.

18. *L.P.*, xxi, pt i, 898.

19. Edward Ayscough, *A History Containing the Wars, Treaties, Marriages, and Other Occurrents between England and Scotland* . . . pp. 106 ff.

20. *Ibid.*

21. *L.P.*, xxi, pt i, 946.

22. *L.P.*, xxi, pt i, 1013.

23. *Grey Friars Chronicle*, p. 55.

24. *Acts of the Privy Council*, I, 462.

25. J. Bale, *Selected Works*, pp. 196 ff., and Foxe, v, 544 ff.

26. H. Ellis, *Original Letters*, second series, Vol. ii, p. 176. C. Wriothesley, *Chronicle*, I, pp. 166–7.

27. *Acts of the Privy Council*, I, p. 464.

28. *Ibid.*

29. Foxe, v, p. 553.

30. *Acts of the Privy Council*, I, 462. This Christopher White was a friend of the merchant Johnson Brothers. He was a stepson of a formidable London businesswoman, 'Mistress Fayrey'. For details of this group see B. Winchester, *Tudor Family Portrait, passim*.

31. J. D. Mackie, *The Earlier Tudors*, p. 442.

32. Foxe, v, pp. 553 ff.

33. *L.P.*, xxi, pt i, 1491.

34. Foxe, v, p. 557.

35. *Ibid.*

36. J. Bale, *op. cit.*, pp. 220 ff.

37. *Ibid.*

38. H. Ellis, *Original Letters*, second series, Vol. ii, p. 176.

*Chapter 9*

1. Foxe, v, p. 565.

2. The exact dating of these events is difficult. According to Foxe they occurred while the court was at Westminster (i.e. between mid-June and mid-August). They also coincided with a bad attack of Henry's

illness, which took place in July. By mid-July the King seems to have turned his back on persecution. On the thirteenth he pardoned his favourite, George Blagge. No more executions of high-born heretics occurred after 16 July. On 25 July Hertford returned from France to be followed a few days later by Dudley. The ascendancy of the Catholic party was then at an end. It seems most probable that the train of events began (as suggested in Chapter 8) shortly after Gardiner's return from the Continent on 12 June. If we are correct in seeing the proclamation of 8 July as part of the Catholic plot, the final attack on Catherine Parr must have been made between then and the twentieth.

3. Foxe, v, p. 558.
4. Foxe, v, p. 560.
5. Hemsley was a priest and a former Observant friar of Richmond. Foxe states that this man was Nicholas Bellenian, a Shropshire priest, but is almost certainly mistaken. The contemporary *Grey Friars Chronicle* and Wriothesley's *Chronicle* agree in naming the third examinee as John Hemsley.
6. Lascelles's doctrine, Foxe, v, pp. 551 f. The salient passages from this interesting document are as follows:

'. . . as at God's hand the breaking of the most innocent and immaculate body and blood of Christ is the quietness of all men's consciences, the only remedy of our sins, and the redemption of mankind . . . so the mass, which is the invention of man (whose author is the Pope of Rome, as it doth appear in Polydore Virgil and many others) is the unquietness of all Christendom, a blasphemy unto Christ's blood, and (as Daniel calleth it) the abominable desolation, as the Scripture shall hereafter more manifest it.'

St Paul, says Lascelles, would not presume to breathe on the host, to use other ceremonies and to say on behalf of Christ, '*Hoc est corpus meum*'.

'. . . it was the Lord Jesus that made the supper; who also did finish it, and made an end of the only act of our salvation, not only here in this world, but with his Father in heaven; as he declareth himself, that he will drink no more of this bitter cup, till he drink it new in his Father's kingdom, where all bitterness shall be taken away.'

He suggests that no man is able 'to finish the act of our Saviour, in breaking of his body and shedding of his blood here'. The Lord Jesus said it, once for all and he was the only fulfiller of it.

'For these words "*Hoc est corpus meum*" were spoken of his natural presence (which no man is able to deny), because the act was finished on the cross, as the story doth plainly manifest it to them that have eyes. Now this bloody sacrifice is made an end of; the supper is finished.' 1 Peter iii, v. 18, Hebrews ix, v. 12.

After his resurrection Christ was known to his followers in the breaking of bread. So John Lascelles will receive it at His hands after the resurrection.

The apostles continued the practice (Acts ii, v. 47). Paul taught how it was to be administered and received (1 Cor. xi, v. 26). 'Here I do gather, that the minister hath no further power and authority, than to preach and pronounce the Lord's death, or else to say, the Lord Jesus said it, who did fulfil it on the Cross.'

'Furthermore, I do steadfastly believe, that where the bread is broken according to the ordinance of Christ, the blessed and immaculate Lamb is present to the eyes of our faith, and so we eat his flesh, and drink his blood, which is to dwell with God, and God with us. And in this we are sure we dwell with God, in that he giveth us his Holy Spirit, even as the forefathers, that were before Christ's coming, did presently see the Lord's death, and did eat his body, and drink his blood.'

'In this I do differ from the Pope's church, that the priests have authority to make Christ's natural presence in the bread, for so doth he more than our Lord and Saviour did; as the example is manifest in Judas, who at Christ's hands, received the same wine and bread as the other apostles did.'

The Pope and his adherents were foretold by Daniel (ix, v. 36).

'. . . I leave the commemoration of the blessed supper of the Lord, and the abominable idol, the mass, which is it that Daniel meaneth by the god Maozim.' He refers to the second and last chapters of the book of Daniel, to 2 Thessalonians ii, Matthew xxiv, v. 15 and Mark xiii, v. 14, 'Further Luke saith "the time is at hand" (xxi, v. 32).' 'Paul saith, "the mystery of iniquity worketh already, yea, and shall continue till, the appearance of Christ," which in my judgement is at hand.'

'Now for the supper of the Lord, I do protest to take it as reverently as Christ left it, and as his apostles did use it, according to the testimonies of the prophets, the apostles, and our blessed Saviour Christ.'

In this confession Lascelles shows himself nearer to such extreme continental reformers as Carlstadt than to any mainstream of Protestant doctrine. His opinions are clearly the result of wide reading in the Fathers and the works of contemporary reformers but spring above all from a literal interpretation of the vernacular Bible.

He never for one moment contemplated forsaking his beliefs and cheerfully embraced his martyrdom. He signed his declaration of faith with a brave and touching flourish:

'John Lascelles, late servant to the King, and now, I trust, to serve the ever lasting King, with the testimony of my blood in Smithfield.'

7. J. Strype, *Narratives of the Reformation*, p. 148.
8. Foxe, v, p. 549.
9. Foxe, v, p. 546.
10. While in prison Anne wrote a clear account of her belief concerning the Holy Communion. It is not possible to quote it here in full but the significant passages are as follows:

'The bread and wine were left us for a sacramental Communion, or a mutual participation in the inestimable benefits of his most precious death and blood-shedding, and that we should in the end thereof be thankful . . .' '. . . The bread is but a remembrance of his death, or a Sacrament of thanksgiving for it, whereby we are knit unto him by a communion of Christian love', 'the . . . Son of God . . . is now glorious in heaven . . . that he call God . . . is a piece of bread.' 'I believe . . . the eternal Son of God not to dwell there', 'the sacramental bread was left us . . . in remembrance of Christ's death . . . and . . . thereby we also receive the whole benefits and fruits of his most glorious passion'. 'They [her enemies] both say, and also teach it for a necessary article of faith, that after the words of consecration be once spoken, there remaineth no bread, but even the selfsame body that hung upon the Cross on Good Friday, both flesh, blood and bone. To this belief of theirs say I nay', 'the bread [is] an only sign or sacrament'. This, her final position, amounts to sacramentarianism and memorialism. Christ is completely absent from the elements. A sacrament is only a sign and, in no way the object signified. This standpoint is akin to Zwingli's, yet some of her other remarks are reminiscent of Lollardy; such are her use of the old argument that Christ cannot be in the elements because he is in heaven, and her rejection of transubstantiation on the grounds that the consecrated bread if kept for a long time would go mouldy. Here is no attempt to understand transubstantiation or to grapple with the implications of the words of institution, '*Hoc est corpus meum*'. Foxe, v, pp. 543 and 549.

Her doctrine is similar to, but not as sophisticated as John Lascelles's. Like John her sheet-anchor is the English Bible and her pilots Tyndale, Frith and other English reformers. Confronted with the problem of interpreting the exact nature of Christ's presence in the communion service, she is motivated by a complete rejection of sacerdotalism and the priestly miracle and can only reject along with it any kind of divine presence in the elements.

This last statement of her belief is simpler and clearer than comments made earlier during her first trial. The probable reason for this difference is that Anne came to London a simple sacramentarian, having evolved her theology from her understanding of the Bible and whatever instruction she had received in Lincolnshire. Then, through John Lascelles and other members of their group, she came into contact with a greater variety of heretical opinion. Bale asserted confidently that Lascelles had been her tutor and Anne's beliefs as stated in March 1546 bear much closer relationship to Lascelles's than her later sacramentarianism. Under his tutelage she accepted the more sophisticated doctrine of the spiritual presence. When she was removed from court circles after her release, her more extreme beliefs reasserted themselves and were reinforced by other arguments of a Zwinglian nature which she had encountered in London. This, at least, is one explanation which fits all the facts. It is undoubtedly wrong to assess the opinions of a heretic like Anne in terms of what elements stemmed from Zwinglianism, what from Lollardy, what from Frith, Tyndale, Luther, etc.; her ideas sprang from a much more complicated general background in which it is impossible to distinguish clearly individual elements. Her only textbook was the Bible and there appear in her writings no clear quotations from or references to contemporary theological works. However, her basic faith, and that for which she died, seems to have been compounded of elements shared by Lollardy and Zwinglian sacramentarianism.

11. Foxe, v, 550.
12. J. Strype, *Memorials of Archbishop Cranmer*, i, p. 596.
13. A. L. Rowse, *Raleigh and the Throckmortons*, p. 11.
14. J. Strype, *Ecclesiastical Memorials*, I, i, p. 595.
15. Foxe, v, p. 551.
16. The Council of the North to the King, 22 December 1546. *S.P.*, v, p. 577.
17. It will not have escaped the attention of the reader that though Anne's joints were so dislocated by her racking that she had to be taken to Smithfield in a chair, yet she had sufficient command of her

hands to be able to write lengthy letters to her friends. We must conclude that Anne did not endure a severe racking and that Wriothesley and Rich, though they obviously went too far with their torture, had only intended to frighten her. All her limbs were not equally affected by the racking and there seems little need to concur with Foxe that she was near to death. However, she was evidently in considerable pain and her legs were unable to support her.

18. Foxe, v, 691.
19. J. Strype, *Memorials of Archbishop Cranmer*, ii, 335.
20. Thomas Seymour became Lord Admiral in 1548.
21. *DNB.*
22. *DNB.*
23. Worksop Parish Church.
24. H. C. Brewster, *South Kelsey Notes*, p. 67.
25. P.P.R. Morison 1.
26. Edward Ayscough, *op. cit.*, pp. 306 ff.
27. A. R. Maddison, *Lincolnshire Pedigrees.*

# Bibliography

(Unless otherwise noted, the place of publication is London.)

## Manuscript Sources

Wills in the Principal Probate Registry, Somerset House, London W.C.2 (individual references given in notes).

Wills in the Lincolnshire Archives Office, the Castle, Lincoln (individual references given in notes).

Wills in the Nottinghamshire County Archives, Shire Hall, Nottingham (individual references given in notes).

Wills in the York Diocesan Records at the Borthwick Institute, York (individual references given in notes).

The Ancaster deposit in the Lincolnshire Archives Office.

Brewster, H. C., *South Kelsey Notes* (1898), two manuscript volumes in Lincoln Cathedral Library, Nos. 262–3.

## Printed Sources

*Acts of the Privy Council of England*, ed. J. R. Dasent, 32 Vols, 1890–1907.

Arber, E., *English Reprints*, xxviii, 1871.

Bale, J., *Select Works*, ed. H. Christmas, Parker Society, 1849.

Bateson M., ed. *A Collection of Original Letters from the Bishops to the Privy Council*. Camden Society, 2nd Series, liii (1895).

*Calendar of State Papers, Spanish*, ed. Bergenroth, Gayangos and Hume (1862).

*Chapter Acts of the Cathedral Church of St Mary of Lincoln, 1520–36*, Lincolnshire Record Society, ed. R. F. G. Cole, xii (1915).

Cranmer, T., *Miscellaneous Writings and Letters*, ed. J. E. Cox, Parker Society (1846).

*Chronicle of the Grey Friars of London*, ed. J. G. Nichols, Camden Soc., 1st Series, liii (1852).

Dudding, R. C., *The First Churchwardens' Book of Louth*, Oxford (1941).

Duffield, G. E., *The Work of William Tyndale. The Courtnay Library of Reformation Classics* (1964).

*Dugdale's Visitation of Yorkshire*, ed. J. W. Clay (1890).

Ellis, H. ed., *Original Letters Illustrative of English History*, 1st and 2nd Series (1824–7).

Foster, C. W., ed., *Lincoln Wills 1271–1530*, Lincolnshire Record Society (1914, 1918).

Foxe, J., *Acts and Monuments*, ed. J. Pratt (1877).

Fuller, T., *The Worthies of England* (1662).

Gee, H. and Hardy, W. J., *Documents Illustrative of English Church History* (1896).

*Letters and Papers Foreign and Domestic of the Reign of Henry VIII preserved in the Public Record Office, the British Museum and elsewhere*, ed. J. S. Brewer, J. Gairdner and R. H. Brodie (1862–1910).

*Lincolnshire Notes and Queries.*

Maddison, A. R. ed., *Lincolnshire Pedigrees*, Harleian Society, l–lv (1902–6).

Metcalf, W. C., *A Book of Knights* (1885).

More, Sir T., *The English Works*, ed. W. Rastell (1557).

*Narratives of the Reformation*, ed. J. G. Nichols, Camden Society, 1st Series, lxxvii (1859).

Peacock, E., *English Church Furniture, Ornaments and Decorations at the Period of the Reformation* (1866).

*Rutland Papers*, ed. W. Jerdan, Camden Society, 1st Series, xxi (1842).

*Select Pedigrees from Visitations of the County of Nottingham 1569–1614*, Harleian Society, iv, (1871).

Speed, J., *Theatre of the Empire of Great Britain* (1611).

*State Papers of Henry VIII* (1830–1852).

*Statutes of the Realm* (1810–28).

Tanner, J. R., *Tudor Constitutional Documents 1485–1603*, Cambridge (1930).

Turner, W., *The Hunting and Finding Out of the Romish Fox*, Basle (1543).

Turner, W., *The Man of Sin – With His Disclosing*, Basle (1543).

Wriothesley, C. A., *Chronicle of England*, Camden Society, 2nd Series, xi, (1875).

*Visitations of the County of Nottingham 1569–1614*, ed. G. W. Marshall, Harleian Society, iv (1871).

*Yorkshire Archaeological Society Indexes*, Vols. vi, xi, xiv, xix.

## Secondary Works

Allen, T., *A History of the County of Lincoln* (1834).

Aston, M., 'Lollardy and the Reformation: Survival or Revival', in *History* Vol. xlix (1964).

Ayscough, E., *A History Containing the Wars, Treaties, Marriages and Other Occurents between England and Scotland* . . . (1607).

Bailey, S., 'Robert Wisdom under Persecution, 1541–1543', in *Journal of Ecclesiastical History*, ii (1953).

Bailey, T., *Annals of Nottinghamshire* (1835).

Bainton, R. H., *Erasmus of Christendom* (1970).

Besant, W., *London in the Time of the Tudors* (1904).

Bowker, M., *The Secular Clergy in the Diocese of Lincoln, 1495–1520*, Cambridge (1968).

Brooks, F. W., *The Social Position of the Parson in the Sixteenth Century*, British Architectural Assn Journal 3rd Series (1948).

Burgess, W. H., *John Robinson, Pastor of the Pilgrim Fathers* (1920).

Burnet, G., *The History of the Reformation of the Church of England*, Oxford (1865).

Butterworth, C. C. and Chester A. G., *George Joye 1495?–1553. A chapter in the History of the English Bible and the English Reformation*, Philadelphia (1962).

Camden, C., *The Elizabethan Woman: A Panorama of English Womanhood, 1540 to 1640* (1952).

Chapman, H., *Lady Jane Grey* (1962).

Chapman, H., *Two Tudor Portraits* (1960).

Clebsch, W. A., *England's Earliest Protestants* (1965).

Constant, G., *The Reformation in England*, trans. R. E. Scantlebury (1934).

Darby, H. C., 'The Human Geography of the Fenland Before the Drainage' in *Geographical Journal*, lxxx (1932).

Darby, H. C., ed., *An Historical Geography of England before 1800*, Cambridge (1936).

Darby, H. C., *The Medieval Fenland*, Cambridge (1940).

Davies, C. S. L., 'The Pilgrimage of Grace Reconsidered' in *Past and Present*, No. 41 (1968).

Deanesly, M., *The Lollard Bible and Other Medieval Biblical Versions*, Cambridge (1940).

*Dictionary of National Biography*, 22 vols. 1963–4 edition.

Dickens, A. G., *Lollards and Protestants in the Diocese of York, 1509–1558*, Oxford (1959).

Dickens, A. G., 'Heresy and the Origins of English Protestantism' in *Britain and the Netherlands*, ii, ed. J. S. Bromley and E. H. Kossmann (1964).

Dickens, A. G., 'Secular and Religious Motivation in the Pilgrimage of Grace' in *Studies in Church History*, ed. G. J. Cuming, vol. iv (1967).

Dickens, A. G., *Thomas Cromwell and the English Reformation* (1959).

Dickens, A. G., *The Marian Reaction in the Diocese of York*, 2 parts (1957).

Dickens, A. G., *The English Reformation* (1964).

Dodds, M. H. and R., *The Pilgrimage of Grace and the Exeter Conspiracy*, Cambridge (1915).

Elton, G. R., *The Tudor Revolution in Government. Administrative Changes in the Reign of Henry VIII*, Cambridge (1953).

Elton, G. R., 'Thomas Cromwell's Decline and Fall' in *Cambridge Historical Journal*, x (1951).

Emmison, F. G., *Tudor Secretary* (1961).

Faludy, D., *Erasmus of Rotterdam* (1970).

Ferguson, C., *Naked to Mine Enemies. The Life of Cardinal Wolsey* (1958).

Fines, J., 'Heresy Trials in the Diocese of Coventry and Lichfield, 1511–12' in *Journal of Ecclesiastical History*, Vol. xvi, No. 2 (1965).

Foster, C. W., Calendar of Lincoln Wills 1320–1600 Index Library. British Record Society, xxviii (1902).

Garrett, C. H., *The Marian Exiles*, Cambridge (1938, reprinted 1966).

Gasquet, F. A., *Henry VIII and the English Monasteries* (1888).

Gee, H., *The Elizabethan Clergy and the Settlement of Religion, 1558–1564*, Oxford (1898).

Gibbons, G. S., *Notes on the Ayscoughs and S. Kelsey Hall. Lincs N. and Q*, Vol. xx, (1928–9).

Gibson, A., *Notes on the Heralds' Visitation of Lincolnshire 1634* (1898).

Gooch, E. H., *A History of Spalding* (1940).

Hall, E., *The Union of the Noble and Illustre Famelies of Lancastre and York* ('Hall's Chronicle') ed. H. Ellis (1809).

Harris, J. W., *John Bale, a Study in the Minor Literature of the Reformation*, Urbana (1940).

Heath, P., *English Parish Clergy on the Eve of the Reformation* (1969).

Herbert, W., *Antiquities of the Inns of Court and Chancery* (1804).

Hillerbrand, H. J., *The Reformation in its own words* (1964).

Hill, J. W. F., *Tudor and Stuart Lincoln*, Cambridge (1956).

Hodgett, G. A. J., *The Dissolution of Religious Houses in Lincolnshire and the Changing Structure of Society, Lincs. A.A.S.R.*, Vol. iv, pt i (1951).

Holland, J., *A History of Worksop* (1826).

Hughes, P., *The Reformation in England* (1950–6).

Huizinga, J., *Erasmus of Rotterdam* (1952).

James, M. E., 'Obedience and Dissent in Henrician England: The Lincolnshire Rebellion 1536' in *Past and Present*, No. 48 (1970).

Janelle, P., *Obedience in Church and State – Three Political Tracts by Stephen Gardiner*, Cambridge (1930).

Jordan, W. K., *Edward VI : The Young King* (1968).

Knowles, D., *The Religious Orders in England* (3 vols), Vol. iii, *The Tudor Age*, Cambridge (1959).

Knox, D. B., *The Doctrine of Faith in the Reign of Henry VII* (1961).

Leland, J., *Itinerary in England and Wales*, ed. L. Toulmin Smith (1906–10).

Liliegren, S. B., *The Fall of the Monasteries and the Social Changes in England*, London and Leipzig (1924).

Mackie, J. D., *The Earlier Tudors, 1485–1558*, Oxford (1952).

Maddison, A. R., *Lincolnshire Gentry During the Sixteenth Century*, Lincs. *A.A.S.R.* Vol. xxii (1893).

Major, K., *A Handlist of the Records of the Bishop of Lincoln and of the Archdeacons of Lincoln and Stow*, Oxford (1953).

Marchant, R., *The Puritans and the Church Courts in the Diocese of York 1560–1642* (1960).

Maynard-Smith, H., *Henry VIII and the Reformation* (1948, reprinted 1962).

Maynard-Smith, H., *Pre-Reformation England* (1938).

Mattingly, G., *Catherine of Aragon* (1942).

McFarlane, K. B., *John Wycliffe and the Beginnings of English Nonconformity* (1952).

Mozley, J. F., *Coverdale and His Bibles* (1953).

Muller, J. A., *The Letters of Stephen Gardiner*, Cambridge (1933).

Muller, J. A., *Stephen Gardiner and the Tudor Reaction* (1926).

Newton, A. P., 'Tudor Reforms in the Royal Household' in *Tudor Studies*, ed. R. W. Seton-Watson (1924).

Nugent, E. M., *The Thought and Culture of the English Renaissance* (1956).

Oxley, J. E., *The Reformation in Essex to the Death of Mary*, Manchester (1965).

*Parish Memorials relating to Norton Disney in the Diocese and County of Lincoln* by 'A Country Vicar', Newark (1893).

Pearce, R. R., *A History of the Inns of Court* (1848).

Pollard, A. F., *Henry VIII* (reprinted 1951).

Pollard, A. F., *Wolsey* (1929).

Porter, H. C., *Reformation and Reaction in Tudor Cambridge*, Cambridge (1958).

Purvis, J. S., *The Archives of the York Diocesan Registry* (1952).

Purvis, J. S., *Tudor Parish Documents in the Diocese of York*, Cambridge (1948).

Ridley, J., *Thomas Cranmer*, Oxford (1962).

Rowse, A. L., *Raleigh and the Throckmortons* (1962).

Rupp, E. G., *Studies in the Making of the English Protestant Tradition*, Cambridge (1949).

Rupp, E. G., *The Righteousness of God, Luther Studies* (1953).

Scarisbrick, J. J., *Henry VIII* (1968).

Simon, J., *Education and Society in Tudor England*, Cambridge (1966).

Smith, J. C. C., *Prerogative Court of Canterbury Wills 1383–1558*, Index Library British Record Society, Vols. x, xi and xviii (1893–7).

Smith, L. B., *Tudor Prelates and Politics 1536–58*, Princeton (1953).

Smith, L. B., *A Tudor Tragedy, The Life and Times of Catherine Howard* (1961).

Strype, J., *Annals of the Reformation and Establishment of Religion and other Various Occurrences in the Church of England during Queen Elizabeth's Happy Reign*, Oxford (1824).

Strype, J., *Ecclesiastical Memorials relating chiefly to Religion and the Reformation of it and the emergencies of the Church of England under King Henry VIII, King Edward VI, and Queen Mary I*, 3 Vols, Oxford (1820–40).

Strype, J., *Memorials of the Most Reverend Father in God Thomas Cranmer, Sometime Lord Archbishop of Canterbury*, Oxford (1840).

Stow, J., *A Survey of London*, ed. C. L. Kingsford, Oxford (1908).

Stow, J., *Annals* (edn 1601).

Tanner, T., *Notitia Monastica or an account of all the abbeys, priories and houses of friars heretofore in England and Wales* (1749).

Thirsk, J., *English Peasant Farming* (1957).

Thirsk, J., *Fenland Farming in the Sixteenth Century*, Leicester (1953).

Thomson, J. A. F., *The Later Lollards, 1414–1520*, Oxford (1965).

Thoroton, R., *Antiquities of Nottinghamshire*, ed. J. Throsby (1797).

Train, K. S. S., ed., *Lists of the Clergy of Central Nottinghamshire*, Thoroton Society Record Series, Vol. xv, pts i, ii (1953–4).

Trollope, E., *Anne Askew, the Lincolnshire Martyr*, Lincs. *A.A.S.R.*, Vol. vi (1862).

Venn, J. and J. A., *Alumni Cantabrigienses*, Cambridge (1922–7).

*Victoria County History – Nottinghamshire*, ed. J. C. Cox (1906).

Wharhirst, G. A., *The Reformation in the Diocese of Lincoln as Illustrated by the Life and Work of Bishop Longland*, Lincs. *A.A.S.R.*, Vol. i, pt ii (1937).

White, H. C., *Social Criticism in Popular Religious Literature of the Sixteenth Century*, New York (1944).

White, R., *Worksop, The Dukery and Sherwood Forest* (1875).

Williams, G. H., *The Radical Reformation* (1962).

Winchester, B., *Tudor Family Portrait* (1955).

Wood, A., *Athenae Oxonienses*, ed. P. Bliss, 4 vols (1813–1820).

*Unpublished Theses*

Ashby, E. G., *Some Aspects of Parish Life in the City of London, 1429–1529*, London M.A. Thesis (1951).

Hodgett, G. A. J., *The Dissolution of the Monasteries in Lincolnshire*, London M.A. Thesis (1947).

Scarisbrick, J. J., *The Conservative Episcopate in England 1529–1535*, Cambridge Ph.D. Thesis (1956).

Walker, R. B., *A History of the Reformation in the Archdeaconries of Lincoln and Stow 1534–94*, Liverpool Ph.D. Thesis (1959).

# Index

Act for the Advancement of True Religion (1543), 144, 164, 181

Act for the Dissolution of the Greater Monasteries (1539), 114

Act for the Dissolution of the Smaller Monasteries (1536), 58, 110, 114

Act of Six Articles (1539), 109, 113–14, 119, 124, 127, 130, 131, 133, 139, 146, 147, 168, 172, 183, 203, 209, 213, 216, 228, 234, 255 *n* 57

Act of Supremacy (1543), *see* Royal Supremacy

Act of Ten Articles ('Articles of Faith To Establish Christian Quietness' 1536), 59

Aglyonby, Henry (heretic), 42

Aleyn, Sir John, 153

Algar (*alias* Jones, heretic), 42

Annebault, Claude d', Admiral and Marshal of France (French ambassador), 235

Aragon, Catherine of, *see* Catherine of Aragon

Arthur, Prince of Wales, 9, 15*n*

Arundel, Henry Fitzalan, 18th Earl of, 178

Ascham, Roger (writer, scholar and tutor of Elizabeth I), 176

Ashwell, Prior of Newnham, 41

Aske, Robert (leader of Pilgrimage of Grace), 101

Askew family name, *see* Ayscough

Atwater, William, Bishop of Lincoln 1514–21, 38

Audley, Sir Thomas (later Lord Audley of Walden), Lord Chancellor 1532–44, 110, 134

Ayleby, William, Vicar of Louth, 247 *n* 9

Ayscough family, 7 *et seq*, 10–11, 83, 90, 167, 243 *n* 1

Ayscough, Anne (Mrs Thomas Kyme, Protestant martyr): early years of, 18, 35, 36, 155; marriage of, 160; her Protestant beliefs and matrimonial difficulties, 162–7; her life in London and first arrest, 180–3; her second arrest, examination and release, 186–97, 198; her recall to London, 203–5; her last examination and trial, 216–17, 218–24, 225; her martyrdom, 229–35, 236–7, 238, 240; *see also* 243 *n* 1, 260 *n* 23, 262 *n* 31, 263 *ns* 40, 41 and 42, 264 *ns* 48, 51 and 52, 265 *n* 53, 269 *ns* 10 and 17

——, Anne ( *née* Clinton, wife of William), 240

——, Charles (died 1707), 241

——, Christopher (Gentleman of Privy Chamber, died 1543), 18, 35, 36, 64, 74–5, 116, 162, 166, 174

——, Sir Christopher (of Ashby), 152–4, 250 *n* 28

——, Edward (Gentleman Pensioner and Cup-Bearer to Henry VIII, died 1558), 16, 18, 34, 115–16, 159, 162, 166, 174

——, Eleanor (*née* Tunstall, second wife of John), 9

——, Elizabeth (*née* Hansard, second wife of Sir William), 21, 22, 23, 24, 155

——, Elizabeth (*née* Hansard, first

wife of Sir Francis), 22, 23, 24, 35, 159, 162

——, Elizabeth (*née* Strelley, wife of Thomas), 160, 258 *n* 11

——, Elizabeth (*née* Wrottesley, first wife of Sir William), 15, 16, 18, 21

——, Sir Francis (died 1564), 16, 18, 24, 25, 26, 33–4, 36, 164, 165, 171, 204–5, 231, 239–40, 258 *n* 11

——, Admiral Sir George (died 1671), 240

——, Jane (Mrs St Paul, then Mrs Disney), 21, 35, 160, 259 *n* 13.

——, John (died 1491), 8–9

——, Margaret (formerly Mrs Skipworth, *née* Gibson, wife of Edward), 159

——, Margaret (*née* Tailboys, first wife of John), 8, 15

——, Martha, 16, 18, 35, 159

——, Thomas (died 1540), 34, 160

——, William, Bishop of Salisbury (died 1450), 7, 8

——, Sir William (died 1456), 8

——, Sir William (died 1509), 9, 15

——, Sir William (died 1541), 7, 15–16, 17, 18–19, 20, 21, 23–5, 26, 27, 31, 34–6, 63–4, 66–70, 73, 74, 75, 76, 115, 155, 156–62, 248 *n* 18

——, Sir William (of Louth), 152, 153

——, William (son of Sir Francis), 240

Babington family, 12, 96, 99, 107, 167, 241

Babington, Sir Anthony, 89, 90, 96–7

Babington, John, 90–1, 98, 100, 102–3, 104, 107, 108

Baker, Sir John (member of Privy Council), 220, 222

Bale, John (Protestant writer and later Bishop of Ossory), 43–4, 51, 132, 225, 234, 263 *ns* 40, 41 and 42, 264 *ns* 46 and 52, 265 *n* 53, 269 *n* 10

Bard, William (servant), 70

Barnes, Robert (chaplain to Henry VIII and Protestant martyr), 33, 51, 117, 126, 127, 225, 264 *n* 43

Bawmborough, Laurence, 157

Bawmborough, Thomas, 157

Becket, St Thomas à, shrine of, 109–10

Becon, John (priest), 145

Bellenian, Nicholas (priest), 267 *n* 5

Bellow, John (agent of Cromwell), 153, 250 *n* 34

Belmain, John (French Calvinist and tutor to Edward VI), 176

Bennet, Robert (serving-man), 147

Bertie, Richard (courtier), 237

Bigod, Sir Francis (landowner), 126, 256 *n* 6

Bilney, Thomas (Protestant martyr), 33

Blagge, Sir George (courtier), 132, 173, 174, 201, 228, 229, 235, 266 *n* 2

Bocher, Joan (Protestant martyr), 236

Boleyn, Anne, Queen, 36, 44, 46, 47, 53, 97, 114, 129, 131, 248 *n* 13

Bonner, Edmund, Bishop of London 1540–9, 1553–9, 126, 131, 138, 168–9, 175, 181, 186, 190, 191–7, 199, 203, 212, 213, 216, 228, 238, 264 *n* 52

Booth, William (landowner), 64, 67

Bosset, Anne (daughter of Lady Lisle), 106

Bowes, Sir Martin, Lord Mayor of London, 190–1, 195, 232, 233, 263 *n* 41 and 42

Brandon, Charles, *see* Suffolk, Duke of

Brian, Sir Francis (courtier), 75

Britain (relative of Anne Ayscough), 191–2, 193, 196, 197, 264 *n* 48

Brown, Sir Humphrey (Justice of King's Bench), 183

Browne, George, Archbishop of Dublin, 67

Broxholme, Robert (landowner), 24, 250 *n* 34

Brynton, Sir Edward (Vice-Chamberlain of the Queen), 116

Bullingham, Nicholas (Protestant reformer and later Bishop of Lincoln and then of Worcester), 240

Burdone, Richard (Protestant sacramentary), 234

Burgh, Sir Thomas, 1st Baron, 19, 64, 66, 67, 69, 71, 72, 252 *n* 11

Burnett, Henry (merchant), 42–3, 245 *n* 11

Butts, Edmund (son of Sir William), 193

Butts, Sir William (Henry VIII's physician), 131, 172–3, 174, 186, 193

Cade, Jack (rebel), 7

Calverley, Sir Hugh (courtier), 228

Calvin, John (Protestant reformer), 174

Caradine, Sir Thomas (courtier), 139, 146, 147, 148, 174

Cardell, Sir William (landowner), 239

Cardmaker (*alias* Taylor), John (Vicar of St Bride's, Fleet Street), 181

Carew, Sir Nicholas (Master of King's Horse), 253 *n* 36

Carnbull, Henry, chantry of, 101

Catherine of Aragon, Queen, 9, 15 *n*, 18, 19, 20, 36, 45, 47, 48, 55, 261 *n* 14

Cecil, Sir William (later Lord Burghley), 25

Chapuys, Eustace (Imperial ambassador, 111, 261 *n* 11

Charlemagne, Emperor, 18

Charles V, Emperor, 18, 19–20, 23, 119, 120, 121, 170, 171, 176, 180, 215

Cheke, Sir John (Regius Professor of Greek and tutor to Edward VI), 176

Chichester, Bishop of (Richard Sampson 1536–43), 255 *n* 61

Clarke, James, Constable of Barrow, 156–7, 158

Cleves, Anne of, Queen, 109, 119–20, 129

Cleves, Wiliiam, Duke of, 119, 120

Clinton, Anne *see* Ayscough, Anne

Clinton, Edward Fiennes Clinton, 9th Baron (later 1st Earl of Lincoln), 83, 240, 250 *n* 34

Cobbler, Captain (rebel), 62, 68, 81, 82

Colet, John, Dean of St Paul's, 32, 40

Constable, John (landowner), 99

Constable, Sir Marmaduke (landowner), 74

Coppledyke, Sir John (landowner), 71

Cotham (Markham estate), 49, 96, 98, 106

Coverdale, Miles (translator of Bible), 33, 114, 167, 225, 253 *n* 32

Cox, Richard (theologian, canon lawyer and later Bishop of Ely), 176, 199, 211

Cranmer, Thomas, Archbishop of Canterbury 1533–55, 33, 34, 44, 50, 55, 64, 67, 102, 113, 116, 126, 131, 134–5, 137, 138, 139, 140–3, 145, 170–1, 172, 173, 174, 177, 184, 207, 236, 240, 257 *n* 22 and 24, 260 *n* 7

Cromwell, Richard (relative of Thomas), 75

Cromwell, Thomas, Earl of Essex (Secretary of State 1534–40): rise to power, 36, 37; attitude to Church, 44, 46, 50, 51–2, 53, 55; attack on monasteries, 56, 58 *et seq*; opposition towards, 67, 72, 74, 75, 81, 83; character and policies of, 85–7, 88, 89, 96, 98, 99, 100, 102–3, 104–5, 106, 107–22; *see also* 123, 124, 125, 126, 127, 129, 131, 134, 137, 139, 140, 141, 142, 153, 154, 155, 156, 159, 161, 170, 187, 201, 207, 246 *n* 21, 247 *ns* 23 and 27, 250 *n* 35, 252 *n* 14, 255 *n* 61, 256 *ns* 67 and 12

Crome, Edward, Vicar of St Mary Aldermary (Protestant divine), 130–1, 133, 173, 181, 183, 191, 192, 198–200, 201, 202, 203, 208, 212, 213, 218

Culpepper, Thomas (lover of Catherine Howard), 136–7

Dalyson, Lady Elizabeth (second wife of Sir Francis Ayscough), 239

Dalyson, William, 64, 65, 158

Darcy, Thomas, 1st Baron, 69, 82, 101, 108, 155

Dare, Christopher (examines Anne Ayscough), 188–90, 234

Dawson, Lawrence (serving-man and heretic), 43

Denny, Sir Anthony (courtier), 141, 173, 174, 257 *n* 23, 264 *n* 51

Denny, Lady Joan, 149, 175, 220, 222, 262 *n* 31

Dereham, Francis (lover of Catherine Howard), 133, 135, 136–7

Digby, Sir John (landowner), 90

Dighton, Robert (landowner), 158

Disney family; 253 *n* 31

Disney, Jane, *see* Ayscough, Jane

Disney, Richard, 99, 160–1, 259 *n* 13

Dixon, Patrick (landowner), 24

Dorset, Henry Grey, Marquis of, 237

Dudley, John, *see* Lisle, Viscount

Dycker, Roger (soldier), 96–7

Dymock family, 249 *n* 21, 251 *n* 7

Dymock, Arthur, 80, 82

——, Sir Edward, 71, 73, 75–6, 80, 81, 82, 248 *n* 18, 249 *n* 21
——, Sir Robert, 71–2, 80, 82
——, Sir Thomas, 156, 157, 158

Edward IV, King 1461–83, 8, 9
Edward VI, King 1547–53, 25, 176, 215, 236, 237, 261 *n* 12
Edward, Prince of Wales, 8, 9
Eland, Sir Edward (chaplain), 106
Elizabeth I, Queen 1558–1603, 26, 53, 98, 154, 175, 237, 238, 240, 244 *n* 27, 249 *n* 21, 252 *n* 11, 259 *n* 22, 260 *n* 23
Ellerker, Sir Ralph (soldier), 153
Erasmus, Desiderius (theologian and man of letters), 31, 32, 33, 40
Eton, George (serving-man), 70

Ferdinand, King of Spain, 9, 16
Field of Cloth of Gold, 19, 23, 90
Filmer, Henry (Protestant martyr), 139, 140, 146, 149
Fisher, Robert, Bishop of Rochester 1504–35, 47, 55, 99
Fitzjames, Richard, Bishop of Lincoln 1506–22, 30
Fitzwilliam, Lady Jane, 175, 220
Fitzwilliam, Sir William (alderman of London), 175
Fitzwilliam, Sir William (Lord Privy Seal), *see* Southampton, Earl of
Foster, Anthony (bailiff to Bishop of Lincoln), 49
Foster, Sir Humphrey, 149
Foster, John (priest), 246 *n* 21, 253 *n* 37
Foxe, John (martyrologist), 87, 147, 148, 213, 218, 223, 235, 257 *n* 22, 263 *ns* 40, 41 and 42, 264 *ns*, 46, 50, 51 and 52, 266 *ns* 1 and 1, 267 *ns*, 2, 3 and 6
Francis I, King of France, 18, 19, 20, 178, 184
French, John (heretic), 42
Friskney (Kyme estate), 160, 162–3, 164, 165, 197, 203, 258 *n* 10
Frith, John (Protestant writer and martyr), 31, 33, 41, 94, 225, 269 *n* 10

Gardiner, Germaine (nephew of Stephen), 140, 149
Gardiner, Stephen, Bishop of Winchester 1531–50, 1553–5, 109, 112–13, 117, 120, 121, 122, 124–5, 126,

127–8, 130, 131, 132, 139–40, 142–3, 146, 147, 148–50, 169, 170, 176, 180, 186, 187, 198–9, 200–2, 206, 207, 209–11, 217–18, 225, 227, 236, 237, 248 *n* 12, 255 *n* 61, 261 *n* 10, 266 *n* 2
Garnish, Lady, 210, 211, 212
Garrett, Thomas (Protestant martyr), 32, 33, 53, 126, 127, 247 *n* 27, 256 *n* 6
Gibson, Margaret, *see* Ayscough, Margaret
Gibson, Thomas (landowner), 159
Goodrich, Thomas, Bishop of Ely 1534–54, 67
Grantham, Vincent (merchant), 162
Graves, Walter (friend of Cromwell), 60
Great Bible, 114–15, 138, 144
Greenhaugh, Roger (Justice of Peace), 105
Grove, John (Protestant sacramentary), 234

Hadlam, John (tailor and Protestant martyr), 213, 214, 232
Hales, Sir Christopher, Master of Rolls, 72
Hall, Edward (historian), 193, 264 *n* 49
Hall, John (father of Edward), 264 *n* 49
Hall, Mary (*née* Lascelles), 91, 100, 133, 134, 135, 257 *n* 14
Hanschey (*alias* Smith), Robert (heretic), 158
Hansard, Agnes (*née* Tyrrwhit), 22
Hansard, Bridget, *see* Moigne, Bridget
Hansard, Elizabeth (second wife of Sir William Ayscough), *see* Ayscough, Elizabeth
Hansard, Elizabeth (Mrs Girlington), 22, 34–5
Hansard, Elizabeth (first wife of Sir Francis Ayscough), *see* Ayscough, Elizabeth
Hansard, William, 21, 22
Hansard, Sir William, 19, 20, 21
Hare, Sir Nicholas (Judge), 125
Harman, Edmund (courtier), 139, 147
Harrington, Sir John, 74, 250 *n* 26
Harrison, Nicholas, Parson of Pleasley, 105
Harrison, Robert, Abbot of Kirkstead, 82
Hastings, Sir Thomas (courtier), 239

Heath, Nicholas, Bishop of Worcester 1543–52, 1553–5 (later Archbishop of York), 199, 213
Hemsley, John (Protestant martyr), 228, 232, 267 *n* 5
Heneage family, 64, 152, 250 *ns* 24 and 34
Heneage, George, Dean of Lincoln, 42, 73, 121, 204
——, John, 62, 69, 74, 83, 158, 258 *n* 10
——, Sir Thomas, 64, 66, 83
Henry V, King 1413–22, 170
Henry VI, King 1422–61, 7, 9
Henry VII, King 1485–1509, 9, 15, 22, 128
Henry VIII, King 1509–47: as a child, 15; at war with France 16–18, 171–2, 177, 215; at the Field of Cloth of Gold, 19–20, 23; and Charles V, 19–20, 23, 120–1, 170–1, 176, 215, 180; and Catherine of Aragon, 15 *n*, 18–20 (divorce), 36, 44, 45–8, 246 *n* 14; and Anne Boleyn, 53; and Jane Seymour, 55; and Dissolution of the Monasteries, 56, 58–9, 110, 114; and Lincolnshire Rising, 67, 75, 77–8, 80, 82; and Thomas Cromwell, 37, 85–6, 97–8, 99, 103, 109, 111–12; reform of his household, 115–18; and Anne of Cleves, 109, 119–120, 129; and Catherine Howard, 120–4, 132, 134–7, 256 *n* 1; and Charles Brandon, Duke of Suffolk, 75, 81, 128, 184; and Stephen Gardiner, 127, 130, 139, 146–7, 180, 198–9, 218, 227, 235–6, 261 *n* 10; and Thomas Cranmer, 34, 140–3, 172, 174, 200–202, 260 *n* 7; and Catherine Parr, 149–50, 172–3, 175, 217–19, 224–8; at war with Scotland, 169–170, 184, 215; and Sir Anthony Denny, 141, 173, 257 *n* 23; and Sir William Butts, 172; and Sir George Blagge, 132, 173–4, 201, 228–9, 266 *n* 2; and English Church, (King's Book) 143, (speech to Parliament, 1545), 184–6; and martyrdom of Anne Ayscough 216, 230–1, 235; and *passim*
Herbert, Lady Anne (*née* Parr), 174, 175, 176, 219, 226
Herbert, Sir William (later 1st Earl of Pembroke), 174

Hercy family, 13, 96, 99, 107, 167
Hercy, Lady Elizabeth (*née* Stanley), 91
——, Humphrey, 90, 91, 252 *n* 14
——, Sir John, 90, 91, 104, 105, 106, 107
Herman, Richard (merchant of Antwerp), 245 *n* 13
Hertford, Anne Countess of, 149, 175, 220, 221
Hertford, Edward Seymour, Earl of, 128–9, 134, 137, 149, 169–70, 171, 174, 175, 178, 183, 184, 186, 198, 219, 235, 237, 247 *n* 23, 260 *n* 6, 261 *n* 12, 266 *n* 2
Hey, Allan, 98
Heynes, Simon, Dean of Exeter, 139, 140
Hilsey, John, Bishop of Rochester 1535–40, 67
Hinde, Sergeant, 81
Hoby, Sir Philip (courtier), 139, 140, 147, 174, 258 *n* 30
Holbein, Hans (painter), 119–20
Holden Thomas (chantry priest), 102
Holme, Wilfrid, *quoted*, 27–8
Horsey, Sir John, Sheriff of Dorset and Somerset, 179
Houghton, John (monk), 104
Houre, Thomas (holy water clerk), 39
Howard, Catherine, Queen, 100, 109, 120, 121, 122, 123, 124, 131, 133–7, 187, 256 *n* 1, 257 *ns* 14 and 15
Howard, Henry, *see* Surrey, Earl of
Howard, Thomas, *see* Norfolk, Duke of
Howard, Lord William, 100, 136
Hudswell, George, 65
Huick, Robert (Henry VIII's physician), 131, 172–3, 174, 199, 200, 202, 206
Huntingdon, George Hastings, 1st Earl of, 75
Huntington, John, 191, 192
Hussey, John, Lord, 66, 69, 70, 71, 72–3, 74, 75, 81, 82, 155, 249 *n* 23
Hussey, Margaret, Lady, 75
Hussey, Sir William Sheriff of Lincoln, 19

Ingram, William, 101

Jerome, William (Protestant martyr), 126, 127

Johnson brothers (merchants), 124, 266 n 30

Jordan, Thomas, Vicar of Friskney, 163

Joye, George (Protestant writer), 31, 33, 41, 225, 245 n 8

Kettleby (Tyrrwhit estate), 22, 64, 66

*King's Book, The,* 143–4, 189

Kirby, John (heretic), 203

Knyvett, Sir Anthony, Lieutenant of Tower, 221–3

Knolys, Dr, Vicar of Wakefield, 106

Kyme, family, 258 n 10

Kyme, Guy (merchant and rebel), 6, 8, 74, 82, 83, 160

——, Thomas (husband of Anne Ayscough), 159–60, 163–4, 165, 180–1, 203–4, 205, 207, 208

Lane, Maud, Lady, 175, 219, 226

Lane, Sir Ralph, 175

Lascelles, family, 14, 96, 99, 107, 167, 239–40, 241

Lascelles, Sir Bryan, 238

——, George (landowner), 91, 94, 101, 105, 106, 108, 231, 238, 253 n 24

——, Joan (*née* Topcliffe, wife of Ralph), 91

——, John (sewer of King's Chamber and Protestant martyr), 91, 94–6, 100, 104, 105–6, 107, 118, 124–5, 131, 132 *et seq,* 137, 174, 181, 182, 199, 200, 202, 207, 228, 229, 230, 232, 234, 235, 236–7, 252 n 17, 257 n 14, 260 n 23, 267 n 6 and 10

——, Mary, *see* Hall, Mary

——, Ralph, 90

——, Richard, 91, 252 n 12

Lathbury, Hugh (hermit), 48

Latimer, Hugh, Bishop of Worcester 1535–9, 33, 35, 53, 67, 102, 113, 138, 181, 201–2, 207, 212, 237

Laurence, Robert, Prior of Beauvale, 98–9

Layton, Richard (agent of Cromwell), 51–2, 56

Leach, Nicholas (parson and rebel), 71, 82

Leach, Robert, 80

Leach, William (rebel), 82

Lee, Edward, Archbishop of York 1531–45, 43, 44, 51, 52, 106

Leigh, Thomas (agent of Cromwell), 56

Leke, Margaret, *see* Markham, Margaret

Leo X, Pope, 18

Lincoln, John de la Pole, Earl of, 9

Lincolnshire Rising, 60–84, 86, 102, 151, 154–5, 160

Lisle, John Dudley, Viscount (later Duke of Northumberland), 149, 174, 178, 186, 198, 210, 235, 237, 261 n 12, 266 n 12

Litherland, Henry, Vicar of Newark, 104

Littlebury, Thomas (landowner), 71

Littleton, Edward (courtier), 228

Lollardy, 27–8, 31, 33, 37–9, 94, 101, 167, 245 n 35

London, John, Warden of New College, Oxford, 32, 40, 139, 140, 146, 148

Longland, John, Bishop of Lincoln 1521–47, 32, 37–54, 67, 74, 89, 112, 126, 131, 135, 204, 228, 246 ns 14 and 21, 247 ns 23 and 27, 255 n 66

Loud, Archdeacon John, 232–3, 263 n 43

Lucas, Mr (Commissioner for Six Articles), 213

Lukine, Thomas (servant), 183

Luther, Martin, 28–9, 31, 33, 86, 269 n 10

Lutheranism, 29, 42–3, 44, 94, 111, 119, 126, 132, 173, 261 n 11

Mackerell, Matthew, Abbot of Barlings, 82

Maddison, Sir Edward, 64, 67, 69, 248 n 13

Manox, Henry (lover of Catherine Howard), 133, 135

Marbeck, John (musician), 139, 140, 141

Margaret of Anjou, Queen, 7, 8, 9

Markham family, 12, 96, 99, 107, 167, 241

Markham, Alice (Skipworth), 89

——, Sir John, 49–50, 88–9, 90, 97, 98, 99, 102, 104, 105, 246 n 21

——, Sir John (Chief Justice of England 1460–69), 89

——, Margaret (*née* Leke), 89
Marshall, John (agent of Cromwell), 83–4, 89
Mary I, Queen 1553–8, 45, 47, 55, 172, 207, 237, 238, 246 *n* 14, 259 *n* 22, 260 *n* 23, 264 *n* 43, 266 *n* 16
Mary Tudor, *see* Suffolk, Duchess of
Maximilian I, Emperor, 16, 18
May, William, Dean of St Paul's, 199
Melton, Nicholas, *see* Cobbler, Captain
Meves, Laurence, 240
Merying, Sir William, 246 *n* 21
Miller, Thomas, Lancaster Herald, 79
Missenden, Sir Thomas (landowner), 64, 67
Moigne, Bridget (*née* Hansard), 22, 35, 64, 70
Moigne, Thomas, Recorder of Lincoln, 35, 64, 65–6, 69, 70, 77–8, 81, 82, 155, 162, 248 *n* 15
Molyneux, Edmund (Justice of Peace), 105
Monmouth, Humphrey (cloth merchant), 257 *n* 13
Monson, Sir John (courtier), 162
More, Sir Thomas, Lord Chancellor 1529–32, 31, 38, 47, 55, 94, 99, 201, 252 *n* 20
Morice, Ralph (Cranmer's secretary), 173, 207, 257 *n* 22
Morice, William, 207, 213
Morland, William (monk and rebel), 66–7, 68, 73, 82

*Necessary Doctrine and Erudition for any Christian Man, The, see King's Book*
Neville, Sir Anthony, 106, 254 *n* 43
Norfolk, Agnes, Dowager Duchess of, 100, 133, 136
Norfolk, Thomas Howard, 3rd Duke of, 36, 75, 81, 100, 106, 109, 111–12, 113, 117, 120, 121, 122, 124, 125, 126, 128, 129, 130, 132, 133, 136, 137, 149, 154, 170, 171, 177, 178, 200, 207, 213, 231, 232, 234–5, 237, 256 *n* 2, 262 *n* 25
Nuthall (Tailboys, then Ayscough estate), 15, 16, 24, 25, 34

Ockham, Robert, 146–7

Oldcastle, Sir John (Lollard martyr), 27, 31

Paget, Sir William (King's Secretary), 147, 177, 211, 212
Parker, Matthew, Archbishop of Canterbury 1559–75, 33
Parkhurst, John (later Bishop of Norwich), 167, 175, 256 *n* 8, 259 *n* 22
Parr, Anne, *see* Herbert, Lady Anne
Parr, Catherine, Queen, 149, 171, 172, 173, 174, 175, 180, 181, 182, 217–19, 225–8, 237, 262 *n* 31, 266 *n* 2
Parr, Sir Thomas, 174
Parr, Sir William (Earl of Essex), 75, 81, 210
Parsons, Anthony (Protestant martyr), 139, 140, 146, 147, 149
Partington, Thomas (landowner), 64, 66, 67, 69
Petre, Sir William, Secretary of State, 171, 186, 200
Pilgrimage of Grace, 59, 82, 86, 101, 112, 154, 247 *ns* 2 and 7, 248 *ns* 17 and 18, 256 *n* 6
Playne ('the skinner'), 199, 202
Plumpton, Elizabeth, 253 *n* 22
Plumpton, Robert, 94, 95
Prynn, Dr, Chancellor of Lincoln, 42, 43
Pylley, Thomas (priest), 101

Raynes, Dr, Chancellor of Lincoln, 61, 62, 71, 76, 82
Redmayne, John, Master of Trinity College, Cambridge, 199
Rich, Richard, 1st Baron, Chancellor of Court of Augmentations and later Lord Chancellor, 72, 110, 201, 206, 207, 208, 209, 213, 216, 217, 219, 220, 222–3, 225, 238, 263 *n* 42, 270 *n* 17
Richard III, King 1483–5, 9
Richmond, Duchess of, 201
Ridley, Nicholas, Bishop of Rochester 1547–50 and London 1550–3, 199
Robinson, Thomas (theologian and canon lawyer), 199, 211
Rogers, John (translator of the Bible), 114
Royal Supremacy, 47, 52, 55, 66, 67, 87, 95–6, 145, 149, 159, 215
Russell, Sir Thomas (later 1st Earl of

Bedford), 75, 143, 146, 147, 174, 175, 179, 229, 232, 233, 257 *n* 24
Rutland, Thomas Manners, 1st Earl of 75, 99, 161
Rycord, Thomas, 249 *n* 24

Sadler, Sir Ralph, 256 *n* 11
St Hugh of Lincoln, Shrine of, 79, 121, 255 *n* 16
St Paul family, 83, 167
St Paul, George, 160, 259 *n* 12
Sanderson, Nicholas, 71, 105
Sandford, Sir Brian, 91
Sandon, Sir William, 71
Saunders, Alice, 39
Saunders, Richard (merchant), 39
Sawtry, Joan (wife of London merchant), 183
Senes, William (choirmaster), 101–3, 245 *n* 11
Seton, Alexander (chaplain to Duke of Suffolk), 131–2, 167, 191, 256 *n* 8
Seymour, Anne, *see* Hertford, Countess of
Seymour, Edward, *see* Hertford, Earl of
Seymour, Jane, Queen, 55, 129
Seymour, Thomas (Lord Seymour of Sudeley), 201, 237
Shaxton, Nicholas, Bishop of Salisbury 1535–9, 35–9, 113, 138, 181, 203, 207, 214, 215, 216–17, 233, 266 *n* 16
Shrewsbury, George Talbot, 4th Earl of, Lord High Steward, 69, 75, 79–80, 81, 99, 102, 105, 252 *n* 13
Skipworth family, 83, 152, 250 *n* 34, 251 *n* 6
Skipworth, Alice, *see* Markham, Alice
——, Edward, 64
——, George, 159
——, Margaret (*née* Gibson), *see* Ayscough, Margaret
——, Sir William, 89
Sleaford (Hussey estate), 69, 72, 73, 74, 75, 77, 249 *n* 24
Smith, William, Bishop of Lincoln 1495–1514, 37
Smythwick (courtier), 124–5, 126
Snelland, Vicar of, 78
South Kelsey (Ayscough estate), 21, 22, 23, 24, 25, 34, 35, 36, 63, 64, 66, 70, 75, 152, 155, 156, 159, 162, 165,

197, 204, 205, 239, 244 *ns* 19 and 28, 259 *n* 13
Southampton, Earls of:
Fitzwilliam, William, Earl of, 75, 121, 135
Wriothesley, Thomas, Earl of, *see* Wriothesley Thomas
Southwell, Sir Richard (member of Privy Council), 201, 207, 263 *n* 42
Spilman, Francis (lawyer), 196–7
Staines, Brian (rebel), 82
Staines, George, 76
Stallingborough (Ayscough estate), 7, 8, 15, 20, 21, 24, 25, 157, 162, 240, 243 *n* 5
Standish, John, Chancellor of Lincoln, 190–1, 192, 193, 194, 264 *n* 43
Starkey, Thomas, 252 *n* 15
Stokesley, John, Bishop of Lincoln 1530–40, 94, 131
Strelley, Elizabeth, *see* Ayscough, Elizabeth
Strelley, John, 160
Strelley, Sir Nicholas, 105, 252 *n* 10, 258 *n* 11
Strype, John (ecclesiastical historian), 148
Suffolk, Catherine (*nee* Willoughby), Duchess of, 83, 128, 149, 160, 166–7, 175, 176, 220, 237, 262 *n* 31
Suffolk, Charles Brandon, Duke of, 17, 75, 77, 80, 81, 83, 128, 131, 132, 149–50, 160, 162, 166–7, 171, 178, 183–4, 186, 237, 250 *n* 34, 259 *n* 12
Suffolk, Mary (*née* Tudor), Duchess of, 128
Surrey, Henry Howard, Earl of, 129, 173, 177, 201, 207, 234–5, 261 *n* 11
Sussex, Anne Countess of, 175, 220
Sussex, Henry Ratcliffe, Earl of, 175
Swenson, Ralph (monk), 104–5
Swynnerton, Thomas (*alias* John Roberts; Protestant divine and writer), 52, 54
Symons, William (inquisitor), 148

Tailboys, John, 8
Tailboys, Margaret, *see* Ayscough, Margaret
Tailboys, Sir William, 8
Taverner, John (organist), 41
Taylor, John, Clerk of Parliaments, 243 *n* 13

Taylor John, Vicar of St Brides, 199, 201, 203

Testwood, Robert (heretic), 139, 140, 146, 149

Thirlby, John, Bishop of Westminster, 171, 261 *n* 8

Throckmorton, Nicholas (courtier), 231, 232

Topcliffe family, 252 *n* 11

Topcliffe, Joan, *see* Lascelles, Joan

——, Sir John, 91

Townby, Richard, 108

Trafford, William, Proctor of Beauvale, 99

Tunstall, Cuthbert, Bishop of London 1522–30 (and Durham 1530–59), 29, 30, 94

Tunstall, Eleanor, *see* Ayscough, Eleanor

Tunstall, Sir Richard, 9

Turner, Richard (priest), 122–3

Turner, William, 144, 169, 225, 257 *n* 25

Tyndale, William (translator of Bible and Protestant martyr), 30, 31, 33, 44, 94, 95, 101, 114, 155, 205, 225, 246 *n* 14, 262 *n* 31, 269 *n* 10

Tyrrwhit family, 152, 241, 250 *n* 34, 251 *n* 6, 262 *n* 17

Tyrrwhit, Anne, *see* Hansard, Anne

——, Sir Robert (the elder), 22, 23, 64, 66, 67, 69

——, Sir Robert (the younger), 74, 116, 156, 157, 158

——, Sir William, 83

Uccello, Paolo (Florentine painter), 17

Underhill, Edward (soldier and Protestant), 174, 261 *n* 12

*Valor Ecclesiasticus*, 56

Vanderdelft, Francis, Imperial Ambassador, 176

Vergil, Polydore (historian), 246 *n* 14, 267 *n* 6

Wadloe, Master (clerk and employee of Wriothesley), 187

Warwick, Richard Nevill, Earl of, 9

Weldon, Sir Thomas (courtier), 139, 147

Wendy, Dr (royal physician), 226

Westminster, Bishop of, *see* Thirlby, John

Weston, Dr, Professor of Divinity and Rector of St Botolph's, Bishopsgate, 196

Weston ('lute-player'), 206

White, Christopher (London merchant), 214, 215, 266 *n* 30

Whitehead, Sir William, Curate of St Catherine Coleman, 181, 191, 192

Wilkinson, Robert (landowner), 244 *n* 23

Willoughby, Sir Christopher (landowner), 19

Willoughby d'Eresby, Catherine, *see* Suffolk, Duchess of

Willoughby d'Eresby, Mary (de Salines), Baroness, 261 *n* 14

Willoughby d'Eresby, William, 10th Baron, 26, 83

Wilson, Dr (Catholic controversialist), 131

Wisdom, Robert (Protestant divine), 131, 145, 203, 266 *n* 17

Wolsey, Thomas, Cardinal Archbishop of York 1514–30, 16, 18, 19, 20, 21, 23, 29, 30, 33, 36, 40–1, 45, 46, 112, 119, 246 *n* 14

Wolsey, Thomas (servant), 71

Woodmansay, William, 76

Worley, (page), 199, 202

Wriothesley, Thomas, Lord Chancellor and later Earl of Southampton, 171, 177, 179, 186–7, 201, 206, 208, 209, 213, 216, 217, 219, 220–1, 222–3, 224, 225, 227–8, 229, 230, 232, 233, 238, 256 *n* 11, 270 *n* 17

Wrottesley, Sir William (landowner), 15, 243 *n* 8,

Wycliffe, John (reformer), 225

Zwingli, 29, 269 *n* 10

Zwinglianism, 111